Mastering Python Data Visualization

Generate effective results in a variety of visually appealing charts using the plotting packages in Python

Kirthi Raman

BIRMINGHAM - MUMBAI

Mastering Python Data Visualization

First published: October 2015

Production reference: 1211015

Published by Packt Publishing Ltd.
Livery Place
35 Livery Street
Birmingham B3 2PB, UK.

ISBN 978-1-78398-832-7

www.packtpub.com

Credits

Author
Kirthi Raman

Reviewers
Julian Quick

Hang (Harvey) Yu

Acquisition Editor
Subho Gupta

Content Development Editor
Riddhi Tuljapurkar

Technical Editor
Humera Shaikh

Copy Editors
Relin Hedly

Sonia Mathur

Project Coordinator
Kinjal Bari

Proofreader
Safis Editing

Indexer
Monica Ajmera Mehta

Graphics
Abhinash Sahu

Jason Monteiro

Production Coordinator
Nilesh Mohite

Cover Work
Nilesh Mohite

About the Author

Kirthi Raman is currently working as a lead data engineer with Neustar Inc, based in Mclean, Virginia USA. Kirthi has worked on data visualization, with a focus on JavaScript, Python, R, and Java, and is a distinguished engineer. Previously, he worked as a principle architect, data analyst, and information retrieval specialist at Quotient, Inc. Kirthi has also worked as a technical lead and manager for a start-up.

He has taught discrete mathematics and computer science for several years. Kirthi has a graduate degree in mathematics and computer science from IIT Delhi and an MS in computer science from the University of Maryland. He has written several white papers on data analysis and big data.

I would like to thank my wife, Radhika, my son, Sid, and daughter, Niya, for putting up with my schedule even when I was on vacation. I would also like to thank my dad, Venkatraman, and my sisters, Vijaya and Meena, for their blessings.

About the Reviewers

Julian Quick is pursuing his bachelor's of science degree in environmental resources engineering at Humboldt State University with a specialization in energy resources and energy data analysis. He wrote Python code for the Earth Observing Laboratory, Canary Instruments, home energy monitoring, and the National Wind Technology Center.

I place on record my gratitude towards my family.

Hang (Harvey) Yu graduated from the University of Illinois at Urbana-Champaign with a PhD in computational biophysics and a master's in statistics. He has extensive experience in data mining, machine learning, and statistics. In the past, Harvey has worked on areas such as stochastic simulations and time series in C and Python as part of his academics. He was intrigued by algorithms and mathematical modeling and has been involved in data analytics since then.

Hang (Harvey) Yu is currently working as a data scientist in Silicon Valley. He is passionate about data science and has developed statistical/mathematical models based on techniques such as optimization and predictive modeling in R. Previously, Harvey has also worked as a computational science intern at ExxonMobil.

When Harvey is not coding, he plays soccer, reads fiction books, or listens to classical music. You can reach him at `hangyu1@illinois.edu` or on LinkedIn at `www.linkedin.com/in/hangyu1`.

www.PacktPub.com

Support files, eBooks, discount offers, and more

For support files and downloads related to your book, please visit www.PacktPub.com.

Did you know that Packt offers eBook versions of every book published, with PDF and ePub files available? You can upgrade to the eBook version at www.PacktPub.com and as a print book customer, you are entitled to a discount on the eBook copy. Get in touch with us at service@packtpub.com for more details.

At www.PacktPub.com, you can also read a collection of free technical articles, sign up for a range of free newsletters and receive exclusive discounts and offers on Packt books and eBooks.

https://www2.packtpub.com/books/subscription/packtlib

Do you need instant solutions to your IT questions? PacktLib is Packt's online digital book library. Here, you can search, access, and read Packt's entire library of books.

Why subscribe?

- Fully searchable across every book published by Packt
- Copy and paste, print, and bookmark content
- On demand and accessible via a web browser

Free access for Packt account holders

If you have an account with Packt at www.PacktPub.com, you can use this to access PacktLib today and view 9 entirely free books. Simply use your login credentials for immediate access.

Table of Contents

Preface   **vii**

Chapter 1: A Conceptual Framework for Data Visualization   **1**

Data, information, knowledge, and insight   **2**
Data   2
Information   3
Knowledge   4
Data analysis and insight   5
The transformation of data   **5**
Transforming data into information   6
Data collection   6
Data preprocessing   7
Data processing   8
Organizing data   8
Getting datasets   9
Transforming information into knowledge   9
Transforming knowledge into insight   10
Data visualization history   **11**
Visualization before computers   12
Minard's Russian campaign (1812)   12
The Cholera epidemics in London (1831-1855)   13
Statistical graphics (1850-1915)   13
Later developments in data visualization   14
How does visualization help decision-making?   **15**
Where does visualization fit in?   16
Data visualization today   17
What is a good visualization?   18
Visualization plots   **21**
Bar graphs and pie charts   26
Bar graphs   26
Pie charts   28

Box plots 30
Scatter plots and bubble charts 31
   Scatter plots 31
   Bubble charts 33
KDE plots 36
Summary **39**
Chapter 2: Data Analysis and Visualization **41**
Why does visualization require planning? **42**
The Ebola example **43**
A sports example **49**
Visually representing the results 52
Creating interesting stories with data **62**
Why are stories so important? 62
Reader-driven narratives 62
   Gapminder 63
   The State of the Union address 64
   Mortality rate in the USA 65
   A few other example narratives 69
Author-driven narratives 70
Perception and presentation methods **72**
The Gestalt principles of perception 73
Some best practices for visualization **75**
Comparison and ranking 76
Correlation 76
Distribution 78
Location-specific or geodata 80
Part-to-whole relationships 81
Trends over time 82
Visualization tools in Python **82**
Development tools 83
   Canopy from Enthought 83
   Anaconda from Continuum Analytics 84
Interactive visualization **85**
Event listeners 85
Layouts 86
   Circular layout 87
   Radial layout 88
   Balloon layout 89
Summary **90**
Chapter 3: Getting Started with the Python IDE **91**
The IDE tools in Python **92**
Python 3.x versus Python 2.7 92

Types of interactive tools	92
IPython	93
Plotly	94
Types of Python IDE	95
PyCharm	96
PyDev	97
Interactive Editor for Python (IEP)	98
Canopy from Enthought	100
Anaconda from Continuum Analytics	104
Visualization plots with Anaconda	**109**
The surface-3D plot	110
The square map plot	112
Interactive visualization packages	**116**
Bokeh	117
VisPy	118
Summary	**119**
Chapter 4: Numerical Computing and Interactive Plotting	**121**
NumPy, SciPy, and MKL functions	**122**
NumPy	122
NumPy universal functions	122
Shape and reshape manipulation	124
An example of interpolation	125
Vectorizing functions	126
Summary of NumPy linear algebra	128
SciPy	129
An example of linear equations	133
The vectorized numerical derivative	134
MKL functions	136
The performance of Python	137
Scalar selection	**138**
Slicing	**139**
Slice using flat	140
Array indexing	**140**
Numerical indexing	141
Logical indexing	142
Other data structures	**143**
Stacks	143
Tuples	144
Sets	145
Queues	146
Dictionaries	146
Dictionaries for matrix representation	148
Sparse matrices	149

Dictionaries for memoization 152
Tries 153
Visualization using matplotlib **155**
Word clouds 156
Installing word clouds 156
Input for word clouds 159
Web feeds 159
The Twitter text 161
Plotting the stock price chart 164
Obtaining data 164
The visualization example in sports **173**
Summary **177**

Chapter 5: Financial and Statistical Models **179**
The deterministic model **180**
Gross returns 180
The stochastic model **191**
Monte Carlo simulation 191
What exactly is Monte Carlo simulation? 191
An inventory problem in Monte Carlo simulation 192
Monte Carlo simulation in basketball 196
The volatility plot 202
Implied volatilities 207
The portfolio valuation 211
The simulation model 214
Geometric Brownian simulation 214
The diffusion-based simulation 218
The threshold model **221**
Schelling's Segregation Model 221
An overview of statistical and machine learning **225**
K-nearest neighbors 226
Generalized linear models 228
Bayesian linear regression 228
Creating animated and interactive plots **231**
Summary **236**

Chapter 6: Statistical and Machine Learning **237**
Classification methods 238
Understanding linear regression 239
Linear regression 242
Decision tree 246
An example 246
The Bayes theorem 251
The Naïve Bayes classifier 252

The Naïve Bayes classifier using TextBlob   254
  Installing TextBlob   254
  Downloading corpora   254
  The Naïve Bayes classifier using TextBlob   255
Viewing positive sentiments using word clouds   259
k-nearest neighbors   **261**
Logistic regression   **265**
Support vector machines   **269**
Principal component analysis   **271**
Installing scikit-learn   275
k-means clustering   **276**
Summary   **280**

Chapter 7: Bioinformatics, Genetics, and Network Models   **281**
Directed graphs and multigraphs   **282**
Storing graph data   283
Displaying graphs   284
  igraph   284
  NetworkX   287
  Graph-tool   293
The clustering coefficient of graphs   **294**
Analysis of social networks   **298**
The planar graph test   **300**
The directed acyclic graph test   **302**
Maximum flow and minimum cut   **304**
A genetic programming example   **306**
Stochastic block models   **308**
Summary   **313**

Chapter 8: Advanced Visualization   **315**
Computer simulation   **316**
Python's random package   317
SciPy's random functions   317
Simulation examples   319
Signal processing   322
Animation   326
Visualization methods using HTML5   328
How is Julia different from Python?   332
D3.js for visualization   333
Dashboards   334
Summary   **336**

Appendix: Go Forth and Explore Visualization   337
An overview of conda   338
Packages installed with Anaconda   342
Packages websites   343
About matplotlib   344

Index   345

Preface

Data visualization is intended to provide information clearly and help the viewer understand them qualitatively. The well-known expression that a picture is worth a thousand words may be rephrased as "a picture tells a story as well as a large collection of words". Visualization is, therefore, a very precious tool that helps the viewer understand a concept quickly. However, data visualization is more of an art than a skill because if you try to overdo it, it could have a reverse effect.

We are currently faced with a plethora of data containing many insights that hold the key to success in the modern day. It is important to find the data, clean it, and use the right tool to visualize it. This book explains several different ways to visualize data using Python packages, along with very useful examples in many different areas such as numerical computing, financial models, statistical and machine learning, and genetics and networks.

This book presents an example code developed on Mac OS X 10.10.5 using Python 2.7, IPython 0.13.2, matplotlib 1.4.3, NumPy 1.9.2, SciPy 0.16.0, and conda build version 1.14.1.

What this book covers

Chapter 1, *A Conceptual Framework for Data Visualization*, expounds that data visualization should actually be referred to as "the visualization of information for knowledge inference". This chapter covers the framework, explaining the transition from data/information to knowledge and how meaningful representations (through logarithms, colormaps, scatterplots, correlations, and others) can make knowledge much easier to grasp.

Chapter 2, Data Analysis and Visualization, explains the importance of visualization and shows several steps in the visualization process, including several options of tools to choose from. Visualization methods have existed for a long time, and we are exposed to them very early; for instance, even young children can interpret bar charts. Interactive visualization has many strengths, and this chapter explains them with examples.

Chapter 3, Getting Started with the Python IDE, explains how you can use Anaconda from Continuum Analytics without worrying about installing each Python library individually. Anaconda has simplified packaging and deployment methods that make it easier to run the IPython notebook alongside other libraries.

Chapter 4, Numerical Computing and Interactive Plotting, covers interactive plotting methods with working examples in computational physics and applied mathematics. Some notable examples are interpolation methods, approximation, clustering, sampling, correlation, and convex optimization using SciPy.

Chapter 5, Financial and Statistical Models, explores financial engineering, which has many numerical and graphical methods that make an interesting use case to explore Python. This chapter covers stock quotes, regression analysis, the Monte Carlo algorithm, and simulation methods with examples.

Chapter 6, Statistical and Machine Learning, covers statistical methods such as linear and nonlinear regression and clustering and classification methods using numpy, scipy, matplotlib, and scikit-learn.

Chapter 7, Bioinformatics, Genetics, and Network Models, covers interesting examples such as social network and instances of directed graphs in real life, data structures that are appropriate for these problems, and network analysis. This chapter uses specific libraries such as graph-tool, NetworkX, matplotlib, scipy, and numpy.

Chapter 8, Advanced Visualization, covers simulation methods and examples of signal processing to show several visualization methods. Here, we also have a comparison of other advanced tools out there, such as Julia and D3.js.

Appendix, Go Forth and Explore Visualization, gives an overview of conda and lists out various Python libraries.

What you need for this book

For this book, you need Python 2.7.6 or a later version installed on your operating system. For the examples in this book, Mac OS X 10.10.5's Python default version (2.7.6) has been used. Other software packages used in this book are IPython, which is an interactive Python environment. The new version of IPython is called Jupyter, which now has kernels for 50 different languages.

Install the prepackaged scientific Python distributions, such as Anaconda from Continuum or Enthought Python Distribution if possible. Anaconda typically comes with over 300 Python packages. For the Python packages that are not included in the prepackaged list, you may either use pip or conda to install them. Some examples are provided in *Appendix, Go Forth and Explore Visualization*.

Who this book is for

There are many books on Python and data visualization. However, there are very few that can be recommended to somebody who wants to build on the existing knowledge about Python, and there are even fewer that discuss niche techniques to make your code easier to work with and reusable. If you know a few things about Python programming but have an insatiable drive to learn more, this book will show you ways to obtain analytical results and produce amazing visual displays.

This book covers methods to produce analytical results using real-world problems. It is not written for beginners, but if you need clarification, you can follow the suggested reading hints in the book. If this book is your first exposure to Python or data visualization, you will do well to study some introductory texts. My favorite is *Introduction to Computer Science and Programming* by Professor John Guttag, which is freely available at MIT OpenCourseWare, and *Visualize This* by Nathan Yau from UCLA.

Conventions

In this book, you will find a number of text styles that distinguish between different kinds of information. Here are some examples of these styles and an explanation of their meaning.

Code words in text, database table names, folder names, filenames, file extensions, pathnames, dummy URLs, user input, and Twitter handles are shown as follows: "First we use `norm()` from SciPy to create normal distribution samples and later, use `hstack()` from NumPy to stack them horizontally and apply `gaussian_kde()` from SciPy."

A block of code is set as follows:

```
import numpy as np
import pandas as pd
import seaborn as sns
import matplotlib.pyplot as plt
students = pd.read_csv("/Users/Macbook/python/data/ucdavis.csv")
g = sns.FacetGrid(students, palette="Set1", size=7)
g.map(plt.scatter, "momheight", "height", s=140, linewidth=.7,
edgecolor="#ffad40", color="#ff8000")
g.set_axis_labels("Mothers Height", "Students Height")
```

When we wish to draw your attention to a particular part of a code block, the relevant lines or items are set in bold:

```
import blockspring
import json

print blockspring.runParsed("stock-price-comparison",
    { "tickers": "FB, LNKD, TWTR",
    "start_date": "2014-01-01", "end_date": "2015-01-01" }).params
```

Any command-line input or output is written as follows:

```
conda install jsonschema

Fetching package metadata: ....
Solving package specifications: .
Package plan for installation in environment /Users/MacBook/anaconda:

The following packages will be downloaded:

    package                    |            build
    ---------------------------|-----------------
    jsonschema-2.4.0           |           py27_0         51 KB

The following NEW packages will be INSTALLED:

    jsonschema: 2.4.0-py27_0

Proceed ([y]/n)?
```

New terms and **important words** are shown in bold. Words that you see on the screen, for example, in menus or dialog boxes, appear in the text like this: "Further, you can select the **Copy code** option to copy the contents of the code block into Canopy's copy-and-paste buffer to be used in an editor."

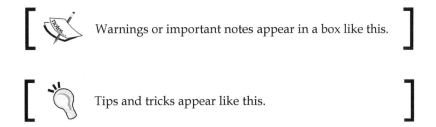

Warnings or important notes appear in a box like this.

Tips and tricks appear like this.

Reader feedback

Feedback from our readers is always welcome. Let us know what you think about this book—what you liked or disliked. Reader feedback is important for us as it helps us develop titles that you will really get the most out of.

To send us general feedback, simply e-mail feedback@packtpub.com, and mention the book's title in the subject of your message.

If there is a topic that you have expertise in and you are interested in either writing or contributing to a book, see our author guide at www.packtpub.com/authors.

Customer support

Now that you are the proud owner of a Packt book, we have a number of things to help you to get the most from your purchase.

Downloading the example code

You can download the example code files from your account at http://www.packtpub.com for all the Packt Publishing books you have purchased. If you purchased this book elsewhere, you can visit http://www.packtpub.com/support and register to have the files e-mailed directly to you.

Downloading the color images of this book

We also provide you with a PDF file that has color images of the screenshots/ diagrams used in this book. The color images will help you better understand the changes in the output. You can download this file from: `https://www.packtpub. com/sites/default/files/downloads/8327OS_Graphics.pdf`.

Errata

Although we have taken every care to ensure the accuracy of our content, mistakes do happen. If you find a mistake in one of our books—maybe a mistake in the text or the code—we would be grateful if you could report this to us. By doing so, you can save other readers from frustration and help us improve subsequent versions of this book. If you find any errata, please report them by visiting `http://www.packtpub. com/submit-errata`, selecting your book, clicking on the **Errata Submission Form** link, and entering the details of your errata. Once your errata are verified, your submission will be accepted and the errata will be uploaded to our website or added to any list of existing errata under the Errata section of that title.

To view the previously submitted errata, go to `https://www.packtpub.com/books/ content/support` and enter the name of the book in the search field. The required information will appear under the **Errata** section.

Piracy

Piracy of copyrighted material on the Internet is an ongoing problem across all media. At Packt, we take the protection of our copyright and licenses very seriously. If you come across any illegal copies of our works in any form on the Internet, please provide us with the location address or website name immediately so that we can pursue a remedy.

Please contact us at `copyright@packtpub.com` with a link to the suspected pirated material.

We appreciate your help in protecting our authors and our ability to bring you valuable content.

Questions

If you have a problem with any aspect of this book, you can contact us at `questions@packtpub.com`, and we will do our best to address the problem.

1
A Conceptual Framework for Data Visualization

The existence of the Internet and social media in modern times has led to an abundance of data, and data sizes are growing beyond imagination. How and when did this begin?

A decade ago, a new way of doing business evolved: of corporations collecting, combining, and crunching large amount of data from sources throughout the enterprise. Their goal was to use a high volume of data to improve the decision-making process. Around that same time, corporations like Amazon, Yahoo, and Google, which handled large amounts of data, made significant headway. Those milestones led to the creation of several technologies supporting *big data*. We will not get into details about big data, but will try exploring why many organizations have changed their ways to use similar ideas for better decision-making.

How exactly are these large amount of data used for making better decisions? We will get to that eventually, but first let us try to understand the difference between data, information, and knowledge, and how they are all related to data visualization. One may wonder, why are we talking about data, information, and knowledge. There is a storyline that connects how we start, what we start with, how all these things benefit the business, and the role of visualization. We will determine the required conceptual framework for data visualization by briefly reviewing the steps involved.

In this chapter, we will cover the following topics:

- The difference between data, information, knowledge, and insight
- The transformation of information into knowledge, and further, to insight
- Collecting, processing, and organizing data
- The history of data visualization
- How does visualizing data help decision-making?
- Visualization plots

Data, information, knowledge, and insight

The terms **data**, **information**, and **knowledge** are used extensively in the context of computer science. There are many definitions of these terms, often conflicting and inconsistent. Before we dive into these definitions, we will understand how these terms are related to visualization. The primary objective of data visualization is to gain insight (hidden truth) into the data or information. The whole discussion about data, knowledge, and insight in this book is within the context of computer science, and not psychology or cognitive science. For the cognitive context, one may refer to https://www.ucsf.edu/news/2014/05/114321/converting-data-knowledge-insight-and-action.

Data

The term **data** implies a premise from which one may draw conclusions. Though data and information appear to be interrelated in a certain context, data actually refers to discrete, objective facts in a digital form. Data are the basic building blocks that, when organized and arranged in different ways, lead to information that is useful in answering some questions about the business.

Data can be something very simple, yet voluminous and unorganized. This discrete data cannot be used to make decisions on its own because it has no meaning and, more importantly, because there is no structure or relationship between them. The process by which data is collected, transmitted, and stored varies widely with the types of data and storage methods. Data comes in many forms; some notable forms are listed as follows:

- CSV files
- Database tables
- Document formats (Excel, PDF, Word, and so on)
- HTML files
- JSON files
- Text files
- XML files

Information

Information is processed data presented as an answer to a business question. Data becomes information when we add a relationship or an association. The association is accomplished by providing a context or background to the data. The background is helpful because it allows us to answer questions about the data.

For example, let us assume that the data given for a basketball player includes height, weight, position, college, date of birth, draft pick, draft round, NBA-debut, and recruiting rank. The answer to the question, "Who is the first draft pick with a height of more than six feet and plays on the point guard position?" is also the information.

Similarly, each player's score is one piece of data. The answer to the question "Who has the highest point per game this year and what is his score" is "LeBron James, 27.47", which is also information.

Knowledge

Knowledge emerges when humans interpret and organize information and use that to drive decision-making. Knowledge is the data, information, and the skills acquired through experience. Knowledge comprises the ability to make the appropriate decision as well as the skills to execute it.

The essential ingredient—connecting the data—allows us to understand the relative importance of each piece of information. By comparing results from the past and by recognizing patterns, we don't have to build a solution to a problem from scratch. The following diagram summarizes the concepts of data, information, and knowledge:

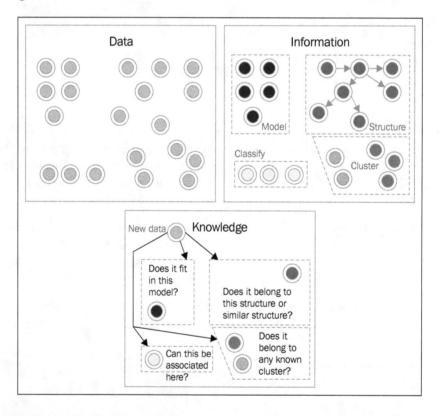

Knowledge changes in an incremental way, particularly when information is rearranged or reorganized or when some computing algorithm changes. Knowledge is like an arrow pointing to the results of an algorithm that is dependent on past information that comes from data. In many instances, knowledge is also gained by visually interacting with the results. Insight on the other hand, opens the way to the future.

Data analysis and insight

Before we dive into the definition of insight and how it relates to business, let us see how the idea of capturing insight ever began. For over a decade, organizations have been struggling to make sense of all the data and information they have, particularly with the exploding data size. They all realized the importance of **data analysis** (also known as **data analytics** or **analytics**) in order to arrive at an optimal or realistic business decision based on existing data and information.

Analytics hinges upon mathematical algorithms to determine the relationships between the data that can yield insight. One simple way to understand insight is by considering an analogy: when data does not have a structure and proper alignment with the business, it gives a clearer and deeper understanding by converting the data to a more structured form and aligning it more closely to the business goals. Insight is that "eureka" moment when there is a breakthrough result that comes out. One should not get confused between the terms Analytics and Business Intelligence. Analytics has predictive capabilities while Business Intelligence provides results based on the analysis of historical data.

Analytics is usually applicable to a broader spectrum of data and, for this reason, it is very common that data collaboration happens internally and/or externally. In some business paradigms, the collaboration only happens internally in an extensive collection of a dataset, but in most other cases, an external connection helps in connecting the dots or completing the puzzle. Two of the most common sources of external data connection are social media and consumer base.

Later in this chapter, we refer to real-life business stories that achieved some remarkable results by applying analytics to gain insight and drive business value, improve decision-making, and understand their customers better.

The transformation of data

By now we know what data is, but now the question is: what is the purpose of collecting data? Data is useful for describing a physical or social phenomenon and to further answer questions about that phenomenon. For this reason, it is important to ensure that the data is not faulty, inaccurate, or incomplete; otherwise, the responses based on that data will also not be accurate or complete.

There are different categories of data, some of which are *past performance data*, *experimental data*, and *benchmark data*. Past performance data and experimental data are pretty self-explanatory. Benchmark data, on the other hand, is data that compares the characteristics of two different items or products to a standard measure. Data gets transformed into information, is processed further, and is then used for answering questions. It is apparent, therefore, that our next step is to achieve that transformation.

Transforming data into information

Data is collected and stored in several different forms depending on the content and its significance. For instance, if the data is about playoff basketball games, then it will be in a text and video format. Another example is the temperature recordings from all the cities of a country, collected and made accessible via different formats. The transformation from data to information involves collection, processing, and organization of data as shown in the following diagram:

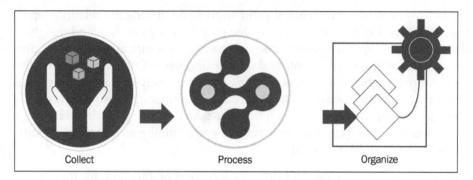

The collected data needs some processing and organizing, which later may or may not have a structure, model, or a pattern. However, this process at least gives us an organized way of finding answers to questions about the data. The process could be a simple sorting based on the total points scored by basketball players or a sorting based on the names of the city and state.

The transformation from data to information could also be a little more than just sorting such as statistical modeling or a computational algorithm. It is this transformation from data to information that is really important and enables the data to be queried, accessed, and manipulated. In some cases, when there is a vast and divergent amount of data, the transformation may involve processing methods such as filtering, aggregating, applying correlation, scaling and normalizing, and classifying.

Data collection

Data collection is a time-consuming process. So, businesses are looking for better ways to automate data capture. However, manual data collection is still prevalent for many processes. Data collection by automatic processes in modern times uses input devices such as sensors. For instance, underwater coral reefs are monitored via sensors; agriculture is another area where sensors are used in monitoring soil properties, controlling irrigation, and fertilization methods.

Another way to collect data automatically is by scanning documents and log files, which is a form of server-side data collection. Manual processes include data collection via web-based methods that get stored in the database, which can then be transformed into information. Nowadays, web-based collaborative environments are benefiting from improved communication and sharing of data.

Traditional visualization and visual analytic tools are typically designed for a single user interacting with a visualization application on a single machine. Extending these tools to include support for collaboration has clearly come a long way towards increasing the scope and applicability of visualizations in the real world.

Data preprocessing

Today, data is highly susceptible to noise and inconsistency due to its size and likely origin from multiple, heterogeneous sources and types. There are several data preprocessing techniques such as *data cleaning*, *data integration*, *data reduction*, and *data transformation*. Data cleaning can be applied to remove noise and correct inconsistencies in the data. Data integration merges and combines the data from multiple sources into a coherent format, mostly known as data warehouse. Data reduction can reduce data size by, for instance, merging, aggregating, and eliminating the redundant features. Data transformations may be applied where data is scaled to fall within a smaller range, thus improving the accuracy and efficiency in processing and visualizing them. The transformation cycle of data is shown in the following diagram:

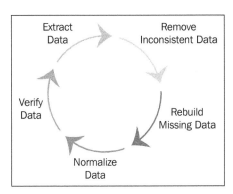

Anomaly detection is the identification of unusual data that might not fall into an expected behavior or pattern in the collected data. Anomalies are also known as outliers or noise; for example in signal data, a particular signal that is unusual is considered noise, and in transaction data, an outlier is a fraudulent transaction. Accurate data collection is essential for maintaining the integrity of data. As much as the down side of anomalies, on the flip side, there is also a significant importance of outliers—specifically in cases where one would want to find fraudulent insurance claims, for instance.

Data processing

Data processing is a significant step in the transformation process. It is imperative that the focus be on data quality. Some processing steps that help in preparing data for analyzing and understanding it better are *dependency modeling* and *clustering*. There are other processing techniques, but we will limit our discussion here with the two most popular processing methods.

Dependency modeling is the fundamental principle of modeling data to determine the nature and structure of the representation. This process searches for relationships between the data elements; for example, a department store might gather data on the purchasing habits of its customers. This process helps the department store deduce the information about frequent purchases.

Clustering is the task of discovering groups in the data that have, in some way or another, a "similar pattern", without using known structures in the data.

Organizing data

Database management systems allow users to store data in a structured format. However, the databases are too large to fit into memory. There are two ways of structuring data:

- Storing large data in disks in a structured format like tables, trees, or graphs
- Storing data in memory using data structure formats for faster access

A data structure comprises a set of different formats for structuring data to be able to store and access it. The general data structure types are arrays, files, tables, trees, lists, maps, and so on. Any data structure is designed to organize the data to suit a specific purpose so that it can be stored, accessed, and manipulated at runtime. A data structure may be selected or designed to store data for the purpose of working on it with various algorithms for faster access.

Data that is collected, processed, and organized to be stored efficiently is much easier to understand, which leads to information that can be better understood.

Getting datasets

For readers who do not have access to organizational data, there are plenty of resources on the Internet with rich datasets from several different sources, such as:

- `http://grouplens.org` (from the University of Minnesota)
- `http://ichart.finance.yahoo.com/table.csv?s=YHOO&c=1962`
- `http://datawrangling.com/some-datasets-available-on-the-web`
- `http://weather-warehouse.com` (weather data)
- `http://www.bjs.gov/developer/ncvs/` (Bureau of Justice Statistics)
- `http://census.ire.org/data/bulkdata.html` (census data)
- `http://ww.pro-football-reference.com` (football reference)
- `http://www.basketball-reference.com` (basketball reference)
- `http://www.baseball-reference.com` (baseball reference)
- `http://archive.ics.uci.edu/ml/datasets.html` (machine learning)
- `http://www.pewresearch.org/data/download-datasets/`
- `http://archive.ics.uci.edu/ml/datasets/Heart+Disease` (heart disease)

Transforming information into knowledge

Information is quantifiable and measurable, it has a shape, and can be accessed, generated, stored, distributed, searched for, compressed and duplicated. It is quantifiable by the volume or amount of information.

Information transforms into knowledge by the application of discrete algorithms, and knowledge is expected to be more qualitative than information. In some problem domains, knowledge continues to go through an evolving cycle. This evolution happens particularly when the data changes in real time.

Knowledge is like the recipe that lets you make bread out of the information, in this case, the ingredients of flour and yeast. Another way to look at knowledge is as the combination of data and information, to which experience and expert opinion is added to aid decision making. Knowledge is not merely a result of filtering or algorithms.

What are the steps involved in this transformation, and how does the change happen? Naturally, it cannot happen by itself. Though the word information is subject to different interpretations based on the definition, we will explore it further within the context of computing.

A simple analogy to illustrate the difference between information and knowledge: course materials for a particular course provide you the necessary information about the concepts, and the teacher later helps the students to understand the concepts through discussions. This helps the students in gaining knowledge about the course. By a similar process, something needs to be done to transform information into knowledge. The following diagram shows the transformation from information to knowledge:

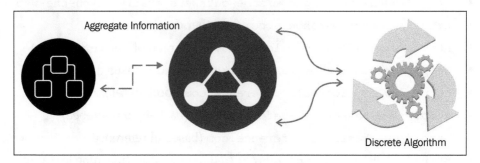

As illustrated in the figure, information when aggregated and run through some discrete algorithms, gets transformed into knowledge. The information needs to be aggregated to get broader knowledge. The knowledge obtained by this transformation helps in answering questions about the data or information such as which quarter did the company have maximum revenue from sales? How much has advertising driven the sales? Or, how many new products have been released this year?

Transforming knowledge into insight

In the traditional system, information is processed, and then analyzed to generate reports. Ever since the Internet came into existence, processed information is already and always available, and social media has emerged as a new way of conducting business.

Organizations have been using external data to gain insights via data analysis. For example, the measure of user sentiments from tweets by consumers via Twitter is used to follow the opinions about product brands. In some cases, there is a higher percentage of users giving a positive message on social media about a new product, say an iPhone or a tablet computer. The analytical tool can provide numerical evidence of that sentiment, and this is where data visualization plays a significant role.

Another example to illustrate this transformation, Netflix announced a competition in 2009 for the best collaborative filtering algorithm to predict user ratings for films, based on previous ratings. The winner of that competition used the pragmatic theory and achieved a 10.05 percent improvement in predicting user ratings, which increased the business value for Netflix.

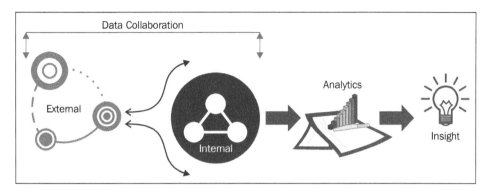

Transforming knowledge into insight is achieved using collaboration and analytics as shown in the preceding diagram. Insight implies seeing the solution and realizing what needs to be done. Achieving data and information is easy and organizations have known methods to achieve that, but getting insight is very hard. Achieving insight requires new and creative thinking and the ability to connect the dots. In addition to applying creative thinking, data analysis and data visualization play a big role in achieving insight. Data visualization is considered both an art and a science.

Data visualization history

Visualization has its roots in a long historical tradition of representing information using primitive paintings and maps on walls, tables of numbers, and paintings on clay. However, they were not known as visualization or data visualization. Data visualization is a new term; it expresses the idea that it involves more than just representing data in a graphical form. The information behind the data should be revealed in an intuitive representation using good display; the graphic should inherently aid viewers in seeing the structure of data.

Visualization before computers

In early Babylonian times, pictures were drawn on clay and in the later periods were rendered on papyrus. The goal of those paintings and maps was to provide the viewer with a qualitative understanding of the information. We also know that understanding pictures are our natural instincts as a visual presentation of information is perceived with greater ease. This section includes only partial details about the history of visualization. For elaborate details and examples, we recommend two interesting resources:

- Data visualization (http://euclid.psych.yorku.ca/datavis/)
- The work of Edward Tufte and Graphics Press (www.edwardtufte.com/tufte)

Minard's Russian campaign (1812)

Charles Minard was a civil engineer working in Paris. He summarized the War of 1812 — Napoleon's march on Moscow — in a figurative map. This map is a simple picture, which is both a visual timeline and a geographic map depicting the size and direction of the army, temperature, and the landmarks and locations. Prof. Edward Tufte famously described this picture as possibly being *the best statistical graphic ever drawn*.

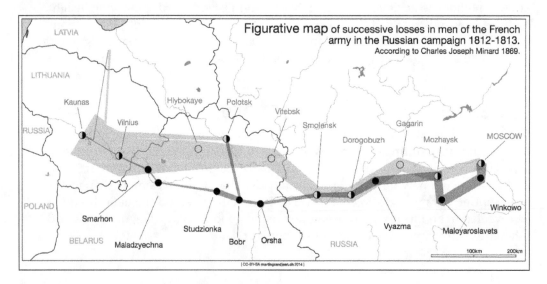

The wedge starts with being thick on the left-hand side, and we see the army begin the campaign at the Polish border with 422,000 men. The wedge becomes narrower as it gets deeper into Russia and the temperature gets lower. This visualization manages to condense a number of different numeric and geographic facts into one image: when the army gets reduced, the reason for the reduction, and subsequently, their retreat.

The Cholera epidemics in London (1831-1855)

In October 1831, the first case of Asiatic cholera occurred in Great Britain, and over 52,000 people died in the epidemic. Subsequently, in 1848-1849 and 1853-1854, more cholera epidemics produced large death tolls.

In 1855, Dr. John Snow produced a map showing the deaths due to cholera clustered around the Broad Street pump in London. This map by Dr. John Snow was a landmark graphic discovery, but unfortunately, it was devised at the end of that period. His map showed the location of each of the deceased, and that provided an insight for his conclusion that the source of outbreak could be localized to contaminated water from a pump on Broad Street. Around that time, the use of graphs became important in economic and state planning.

Statistical graphics (1850-1915)

By the mid 18th century, a rapid growth of visualization had been established throughout Europe. In 1863, one page of Galton's multivariate weather chart of Europe showed barometric pressure, wind direction, rain, and temperature for the month of December 1861 (source: The life, letters and labors of Francis Galton, Cambridge University Press).

During this period, statistical graphics became mainstream and there were many textbooks written on the same. These textbooks contained detailed descriptions of the graphic method, discussing frequencies, and the effects of the choice of scales and baselines on the visual estimation of differences and ratios. They also contained historical diagrams in which two or more time series could be shown on a single chart for comparative views of their histories.

Later developments in data visualization

In the year 1962, John W. Tukey issued a call for the recognition of data analysis as a legitimate branch of statistics; shortly afterwards, he began the invention of a wide variety of new, simple, and effective graphic displays under the rubric **Exploratory Data Analysis (EDA)**, which was followed by **Exploratory Spatial Data Analysis (ESDA)**. Tukey later wrote a book titled *Exploratory Data Analysis* in 1977. There are a number of tools that are useful for EDA with graphical techniques, which are listed as follows:

- Box-and-whisker plot (box plot)
- Histogram
- Multivari chart (from candlestick charts)
- Run-sequence plot
- Pareto chart (named after Vilfredo Pareto)
- Scatter plot
- Multidimensional scaling
- Targeted projection pursuit

Visualization in scientific computing is emerging as an important computer-based field, with the goal to improve the understanding of data and to make quick real-time decisions. Today, the ability of medical doctors to diagnose ailments is dependent upon vision. For example, in hip-replacement surgeries, custom hips can now be fabricated before surgical procedures. Accurate measurements can be made prior to surgery using non-invasive 3D imaging thereby reducing the number of post-operative body rejections from 30 percent to a mere 5 percent (source: `http://bonesmart.org/hip/hip-implants-specialized-and-custom-fitted-options/`).

Visualization of the human brain structure and function in 3D is a research frontier of far-reaching importance. Few advances have transformed the fields of neuroscience and brain-imaging technology, like the ability to see inside and read the brain of a living human. For continued progress in brain research, it will be necessary to integrate structural and functional information at many levels of abstraction.

The rate at which the hardware performance power has been on the rise tells us that we are already able to analyze DNA sequences and visually represent them. The future advances in computing promises a much brighter progress in the fields of medicine and other scientific areas.

How does visualization help decision-making?

There is a variety of ways to represent data visually. However, there are only a few ways in which one can portray the data in a manner that allows one to see something visually and observe new patterns. Data visualization is not as easy as it seems; it is an art and requires a great deal of practice and experience. (Just like painting a picture—one cannot be a master painter from day one, it takes a lot of practice.)

Human perception plays an important role in the field of data visualization. A pair of healthy human eyes has a total field view of approximately 200 degrees horizontally (about 120 degrees of which are shared by both the eyes). About one quarter of the human brain is involved in visual processing, which is more than any other sense. Among the three senses of hearing, seeing, and smelling, human vision has the maximum sense—measured to be sixty per cent (`http://contemplatingmadness.tumblr.com/post/27478393311/10-limits-to-human-perception-and-how-they-shape`).

Effective visualization helps us in analyzing and understanding data. Author Stephen Few described the following eight types of quantitative messages (via visualization) that may help us with understanding or communicating from a set of data (source: `https://www.perceptualedge.com/articles/ie/the_right_graph.pdf`):

- Time-series
- Ranking
- Part-to-whole
- Deviation
- Frequency distribution
- Correlation
- Nominal comparison
- Geographic or geospatial

Scientists have mapped the human genome, and this is one of the reasons why we are faced with the challenges of transforming knowledge into a visual representation for better understanding. In other words, we may have to find new ways to visually present the human genome so that it is not difficult for a common person to understand.

Where does visualization fit in?

It is important to note that data visualization is not scientific visualization. Scientific visualization deals with the data that has an inherent physical structure, such as air molecules flowing over an aircraft wing. Information visualization, on the other hand, deals with abstract data, and helps in solving problems involving large datasets. One of the challenges is to ensure that the data is clean and subsequently, to reduce the dimensions so that unnecessary information is discarded.

Visualization can be used wherever we see increased knowledge or value of data. That can be determined by doing more data analysis and running through algorithms. The data analysis might vary from the simplest form to a more complicated one.

Sometimes, there is value in looking at data beyond the mean, median, or total, because these measurements only measure things that may seem obvious. Sometimes, aggregates or values around a region hide the interesting details that need special focus. One classic example is the "Anscombe's quartet" which comprises of four datasets that have nearly identical simple statistical properties yet appear very different when graphed. For more on this, one can refer to the link, `https://en.wikipedia.org/wiki/Anscombe%27s_quartet`.

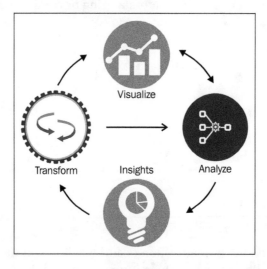

Mostly, datasets that lend themselves well to visualization can take different forms, but some paint a clearer picture to understand than others. In some cases, it is mandatory to analyze them several times to get a much better understanding of the visualization as shown in the preceding diagram.

A good visualization is not just a static picture that one can look at, like an exhibit in a museum. It is something that allows us to drill down and find more about the change in data. For example, view first, zoom and filter, change the values of some scale of display, and view the results in an incremental way, as described in `http://www.mat.ucsb.edu/~g.legrady/academic/courses/11w259/schneiderman.pdf` by Ben Shneiderman. Sometimes, it is much harder to display everything on a single display and on a single scale, and only by experience, one can better understand these visualization methods. Summarizing further, visualization is useful in both organizing and making sense out of data, particularly when it is in abundance.

Interactive visualization is emerging as a new form of communication, which allows users to analyze the information in order to construct their own, new understanding of the data.

Data visualization today

While many areas of computing aim to replace human judgment with automation, visualization systems are unique and are explicitly designed not to replace humans. In fact, they are designed to keep the humans actively involved in the whole process; why is that?

Data Visualization is an art, driven by data and yet created by humans with the help of various computing tools. An artist paints a picture using tools and materials like brushes, and colors. Similarly, another artist tries to create data visualization with the help of computing tools. Visualization can be aesthetically pleasing and helps in making things clear; sometimes, it may lack one or both of those qualities depending on the users who create it.

Today, there are over thirty different visual representations of data, each having a reason to represent data in that specific way. As the visualization methods progress, we have much more than just bar graphs and pie charts. Despite the many benefits of data visualization, they are undermined due to a lack of understanding and, in some cases, due to cluttering together of things on a dashboard that becomes too cumbersome.

There are many ways to present data, but only a handful of those make sense in most cases; this will be explained in detail in later sections of this chapter. Before that discussion, let us take a look at a list of some important things that make a good visualization.

What is a good visualization?

Good visualization helps the users to explore and understand data, providing value and deep insights. It is effective, visually appealing, scalable, and is easy to understand (good visualization does not have to be too complicated). Visualization is a central tool in finding patterns and trends in the data by carrying out research and analysis, using whichever one can answer questions about the data.

The main principle behind an effective visualization is to identify the main point that you want to make, recognize the level and background of your audience, accurately represent the data, and then create a clear presentation that conveys the message to that audience.

Example: The following representations have been created with a small sample data source that shows the percentage of women and men conferred with degrees in ten different disciplines for the years from 1970-2012 (`womens-undergrad-degrees.csv` and `mens-undergrad-degrees.csv` from `http://www.knapdata.com/python/`):

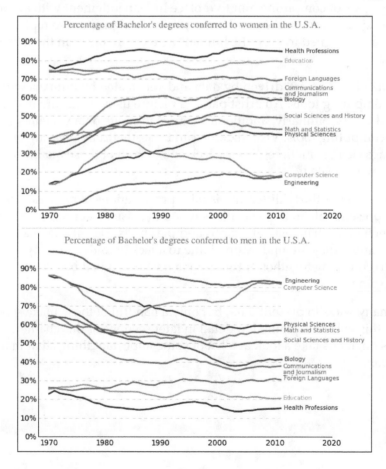

The full data source available at `http://nces.ed.gov/programs/digest/d11/ tables/dt11_290.asp` maintains the complete set of data.

One simple way is to represent them on one scale, although there is no relationship between the numbers between the different disciplines. Let us analyze and see if this representation makes sense, and if it doesn't, then what else do we need? Are there any other representations?

For one thing, all the data about the different disciplines is displayed on one screen, which is an excellent comparison. However, if we need to get the information for the year 2000, there is no straightforward way. Unless there is an interactive mode of display that is similar to a financial stock chart, there is no easy way to determine the information about the degrees conferred in multiple disciplines for the year 2000. Another confusing part of these plots is that the percentage doesn't add up to a sum of 100 percent. On the other hand, the percentage of conferred degrees within one discipline for men and women add up to 100 percent; for instance, the percentage of degrees conferred in the **Health Professions** discipline for men and women are 15.2 percent and 84.8 percent respectively.

Can we represent these through other visualization methods? One can create bubble charts for each year, have an interactive visualization with year selection, and also have a play button that transitions the bubbles for each year.

This visualization better suits the data that we are looking at. We can also use the same slider with the original plot and make it interactive by highlighting the data for the selected year. It is a good habit to visualize the data in several different ways to see if some display makes more sense than the other. We may have to scale the values on a logarithmic scale if there is a very large range of numerical values (for example, from 20 to 200,000).

One can write a program in Python to accomplish this bubble chart. Other alternate languages are JavaScript using D3.js and R using R-Studio. It is left for the reader to explore other visualization options.

Google Motion Chart can be used for visualization to represent this interactive chart at `developers.google.com/chart/interactive/docs/gallery/motionchart?csw=1#Example` where it shows a working example that is similar to this bubble chart. The bubble chart shown here is for only three years, but you can create another one for all the years.

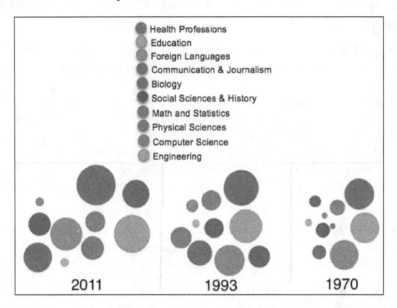

Data visualization is a process that has to be used after data analysis. We also noticed earlier that data transformation, data analysis, and data visualization are done several times; why is that so? We all know the famous quote, *Knowledge is having the right answer, Intelligence is asking the right question*. Data analysis helps us to understand the data better and therefore be in a position to respond to questions about the data. However, when the data is represented visually in several different ways, some new questions emerge, and this is one of the reasons why there is a repeated process of analysis and visualization.

Visualization of data is one of the primary tools for data exploration, and almost always precedes or inspires data analysis. There are many tools to display data visually, but there are fewer tools to do the analysis. Programming languages like Julia, R, and Python have ranked higher for performing data analysis, but for visualization, JavaScript based D3.js has a much greater potential to generate interactive data visualization.

Between R and Python, R is a more difficult language to learn. Python, on the other hand, is much easier. This is also debated on Quora; one may check the validity of this on the internet (`https://www.quora.com/Which-is-better-for-data-analysis-R-or-Python`). Today there are numerous tools in Python for statistical modeling and data analysis, and therefore, it is an attractive choice for data science.

Visualization plots

One of the reasons why we perform visualization is to confirm our knowledge of data. However, if the data is not well understood, you may not frame the right questions about the data.

When creating visualizations, the first step is to be clear on the question to be answered. In other words, how is visualization going to help? There is another challenge that follows this—knowing the right plotting method. Some visualization methods are as follows:

- Bar graph and pie chart
- Box plot
- Bubble chart
- Histogram
- **Kernel Density Estimation (KDE)** plot
- Line and surface plot
- Network graph plot
- Scatter plot
- Tree map
- Violin plot

In the course of identifying the message that the visualization should convey, it makes sense to look at the following questions:

- How many variables are we dealing with, and what are we trying to plot?
- What do the x axis and y axis refer to? (For 3D, z axis as well.)
- Are the data sizes normalized and does the size of data points mean anything?
- Are we using the right choices of colors?
- For time series data, are we trying to identify a trend or a correlation?

If there are too many variables, it makes sense to draw multiple instances of the same plot on different subsets of data. This technique is called **lattice** or **trellis** plotting. It allows a viewer to quickly extract a large amount of information about complex data.

Consider a subset of student data that has an unusual mixture of information about (gender, sleep, tv, exercise, computer, gpa) and (height, momheight, dadheight). The units for computer, tv, sleep, and exercise are hours, height is in inches and gpa is measured on a scale of 4.0.

gender	tv	computer	sleep	height	momheight	dadheight	exercise	gpa
Female	13.0	10.0	3.50	66.0	66.0	71.0	10.0	4.000
Male	20.0	7.0	9.00	72.0	64.0	65.0	2.0	2.300
Male	15.0	15.0	6.00	68.0	62.0	74.0	3.0	2.600
Male	8.0	20.0	6.00	68.0	59.0	70.0	6.0	2.800
Female	2.5	10.0	5.00	64.0	65.0	70.0	6.5	2.620
Male	2.0	14.0	9.00	68.5	60.0	68.0	2.0	2.200
Female	4.0	28.0	8.50	69.0	66.0	76.0	3.0	3.780
Female	8.0	10.0	7.00	66.0	63.0	70.0	4.5	3.200
Male	1.0	15.0	8.00	70.0	68.0	71.0	3.0	3.310
Male	8.0	25.0	4.50	67.0	63.0	66.0	6.0	3.390
Male	3.5	9.0	8.00	68.0	62.0	64.0	8.0	3.000
Female	11.0	20.0	5.00	68.0	64.0	69.0	0.0	2.500
Male	10.0	14.0	8.00	68.0	61.0	72.0	10.0	2.800
Male	1.0	84.0	5.00	61.0	62.0	62.0	3.0	2.340
Female	10.0	11.0	9.00	65.0	62.0	66.0	5.0	2.000

The preceding data is an example that has more variables than usual, and therefore, it makes sense to do a trellis plot to visualize and see the relationship between these variables.

One of the reasons we perform visualization is to confirm our knowledge of data. However, if the data is not well understood, one may not frame the right questions about it.

Since there are only two genders in the data, there are 10 combinations of variables that can be possible (`sleep, tv`), (`sleep, exercise`), (`sleep, computer`), (`sleep, gpa`), (`tv, exercise`), (`tv, computer`), (`tv, gpa`), (`exercise, computer`), (`exercise, gpa`), and (`computer, gpa`) for the first set of variables; another two, (`height, momheight`) and (`height, dadheight`) for the second set. Following are all the combinations except (`sleep, tv`), (`tv, exercise`).

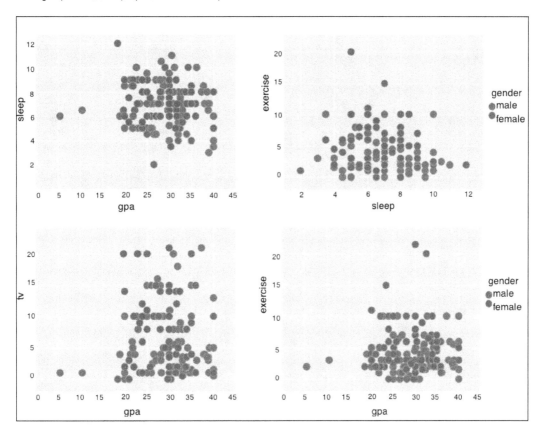

Our goal is to find what combination of variables can be used to make some sense out of this data, or to see if any of these variables have any meaningful impact. Since the data is about students, gpa may be a key variable that drives the relevance of the other variables. The preceding image depicts scatter plots that show that a greater number of female students have a higher gpa than the male students and a greater number of male students spend more time on computer and get a similar gpa range of values. Although all scatter plots are being shown here, the intent is to find out which data plays a more significant role, and what sense can we make out of this data.

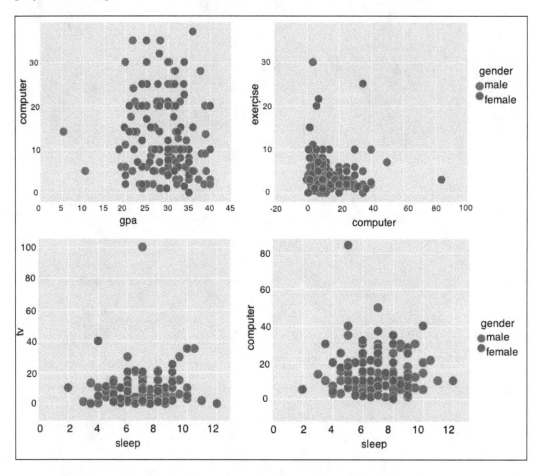

A greater number of blue dots high up (for gpa on the *y* axis) shows that there are more female students with a higher gpa (this data was collected from UCSD).

The data can be downloaded from http://www.knapdata.com/python/ucdavis.csv.

One can use the `seaborn` package and display a scatter plot with very few lines of code, and the following example shows a scatter plot of `gpa` along the x - axis compared with the time spent on computer by students:

```
import pandas as pd
import seaborn as sns
import matplotlib.pyplot as plt

students = pd.read_csv("/Users/kvenkatr/Downloads/ucdavis.csv")

g = sns.FacetGrid(students, hue="gender", palette="Set1", size=6)
g.map(plt.scatter, "gpa", "computer", s=250, linewidth=0.65,
    edgecolor="white")

g.add_legend()
```

Downloading the example code

You can download the example code files for all Packt books you have purchased from your account at http://www.packtpub. com. If you purchased this book elsewhere, you can visit http:// www.packtpub.com/support and register to have the files e-mailed directly to you.

These plots were generated using the `matplotlib`, `pandas`, and `seaborn` library packages. `Seaborn` is a statistical data visualization library based on `matplotlib`, created by Michael Waskom from Stanford University. Further details about these libraries will be discussed in the following chapters.

There are many useful classes in the `Seaborn` library. In particular, the `FacetGrid` class comes in handy when we need to visualize the distribution of a variable or the relationship between multiple variables separately within subsets of data. `FacetGrid` can be drawn with up to three dimensions, that is, row, column and hue. These library packages and their functions will be described in later chapters.

When creating visualizations, the first step is to be clear on the question to be answered. In other words, how is visualization going to help? The other challenge is choosing the right plotting method.

Bar graphs and pie charts

When do we choose bar graphs and pie charts? They are the oldest visualization methods and pie chart is best used to compare the parts of a whole. However, bar graphs can compare things between different groups to show patterns.

Bar graphs, histograms, and pie charts help us compare different data samples, categorize them, and determine the distribution of data values across that sample. Bar graphs come in several different styles varying from single, multiple, and stacked.

Bar graphs

Bar graphs are especially effective when you have numerical data that splits nicely into different categories, so you can quickly see trends within your data.

Bar graphs are useful when comparing data across categories. Some notable examples include the following:

- Volume of jeans in different sizes
- World population change in the past two decades
- Percent of spending by department

In addition to this, consider the following:

- **Add color to bars for more impact**: Showing revenue performance with bars is informative, but adding color to reveal the profits adds visual insight. However, if there are too many bars, colors might make the graph look clumsy.

- **Include multiple bar charts on a dashboard**: This helps the viewer to quickly compare related information instead of flipping through a bunch of spreadsheets or slides to answer a question.

- **Put bars on both sides of an axis**: Plotting both positive and negative data points along a continuous axis is an effective way to spot trends.

- **Use stacked bars or side-by-side bars**: Displaying related data on top of or next to each other gives depth to your analysis and addresses multiple questions at once.

These plots can be achieved with fewer than 12 lines of Python code, and more examples will be discussed in the later chapters.

With bar graphs, each column represents a group defined by a specific category; with histograms, each column represents a group defined by a quantitative variable. With bar graphs, the *x* axis does not have a low-end or a high-end value, because the labels on the *x* axis are categorical and not quantitative. On the other hand, in a histogram, there is going to be a range of values. The following bar graph shows the statistics of Oscar winners and nominees in the US from 2000-2009:

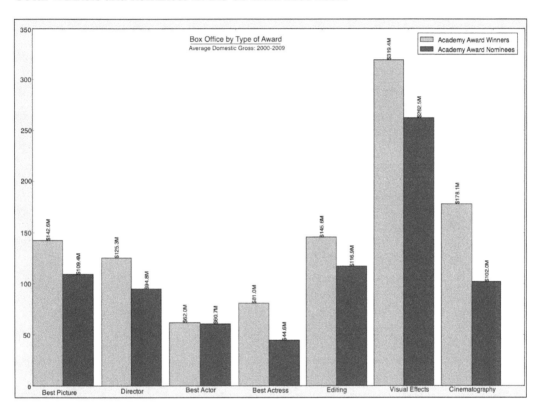

The following Python code uses `matplotlib` to display bar graphs for a small data sample from the movies (This may not necessarily be a real example, but gives an idea of plotting and comparing):

```
[5]: import numpy as np
     import matplotlib.pyplot as plt

     N = 7
     winnersplot = (142.6, 125.3, 62.0, 81.0, 145.6, 319.4, 178.1)

     ind = np.arange(N)  # the x locations for the groups
```

```
width = 0.35          # the width of the bars

fig, ax = plt.subplots()
winners = ax.bar(ind, winnersplot, width, color='#ffad00')

nomineesplot = (109.4, 94.8, 60.7, 44.6, 116.9, 262.5, 102.0)
nominees = ax.bar(ind+width, nomineesplot, width,
  color='#9b3c38')

# add some text for labels, title and axes ticks
ax.set_xticks(ind+width)
ax.set_xticklabels( ('Best Picture', 'Director', 'Best
Actor',
  'Best Actress','Editing', 'Visual Effects',
  'Cinematography'))

ax.legend( (winners[0], nominees[0]), ('Academy Award
Winners',
  'Academy Award Nominees') )

def autolabel(rects):
  # attach some text labels
  for rect in rects:
    height = rect.get_height()
    hcap = "$"+str(height)+"M"
    ax.text(rect.get_x()+rect.get_width()/2., height, hcap,
      ha='center', va='bottom', rotation="vertical")

autolabel(winners)
autolabel(nominees)

plt.show()
```

Pie charts

When it comes to pie charts, one should really consider answering the questions, "Do the parts make up a meaningful whole?" and "Do you have sufficient real-estate to represent them using a circular view?". There are critics who come crashing down on pie charts, and one of the main reasons, for that is that when there are numerous categories, it becomes very hard to get the proportions and compare those categories to gain any insight. (Source: https://www.quora.com/How-and-why-are-pie-charts-considered-evil-by-data-visualization-experts).

Pie charts are useful for showing proportions on a single space or across a map. Some notable examples include the following:

- Response categories from a survey
- Top five company market shares in a specific technology (in this case, one can quickly know which companies have a major share in the market)

In addition to this, consider the following:

- **Limit pie wedges to eight**: If there are more than eight proportions to represent, consider a bar graph. Due to limited real - estate, it is difficult to meaningfully represent and interpret the pieces.
- **Overlay pie charts on maps**: Pie charts can be much easier to spread across a map and highlight geographical trends. (The wedges should be limited here too.)

Consider the following code for a simple pie-chart to compare how the intake of admissions among several disciplines are distributed:

```
[6]: import matplotlib.pyplot as plt

     labels = 'Computer Science', 'Foreign Languages',
        'Analytical Chemistry', 'Education', 'Humanities',
        'Physics', 'Biology', 'Math and Statistics', 'Engineering'

     sizes = [21, 4, 7, 7, 8, 9, 10, 15, 19]
     colors = ['yellowgreen', 'gold', 'lightskyblue',
     'lightcoral',
        'red', 'purple', '#f280de', 'orange', 'green']
     explode = (0,0,0,0,0,0,0,0,0.1)
     plt.pie(sizes, explode=explode, labels=labels,
        autopct='%1.1f%%', colors=colors)
     plt.axis('equal')
     plt.show()
```

The following pie chart example shows the university admission intake in some chosen top-study areas:

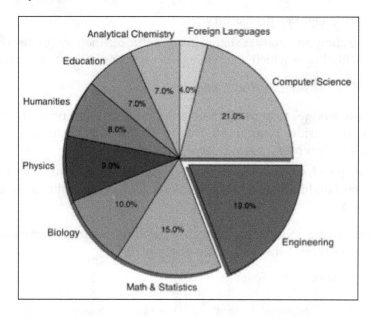

Box plots

Box plots are also known as box-and-whisker plots. This is a standardized way of displaying the distribution of data based on the five number summaries: minimum, first quartile, median, third quartile, and maximum. The following diagram shows how a box plot can be read:

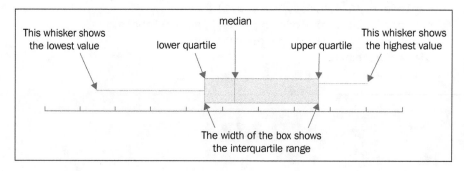

A box plot is a quick way of examining one or more sets of data graphically, and they take up less space to define five summaries at a time. One example that we can think of for this usage is: if the same exam is given to two or more classes, then a box plot can tell when the most students in one class did better than most students in the other class. Another example is that if there are more people who eat burgers, the median is going to be higher or the top whisker could be longer than the bottom one. In such a case, it gives one a good overview of the data distribution.

Before we try to understand when to use box plots, here is a definition that one needs to understand. An outlier in a collection of data values is an observation that lies at an abnormal distance from other values.

Box plots are most useful in showing the distribution of a set of data. Some notable examples are as follows:

- Identifying outliers in the data
- Determining how the data is skewed towards either end

In addition to this, consider the following:

- **Hide the points within the box**: focus on the outliers
- **Compare across distributions**: Box plots are good for comparing quickly with distributions between data set

Scatter plots and bubble charts

A scatter plot is a type of visualization method for displaying two variables. The pattern of their intersecting points can graphically show the relationship patterns. A scatter plot is a visualization of the relationship between two variables measured on the same set of individuals. On the other hand, a Bubble chart displays three dimensions of data. Each entity with its triplet *(a,b,c)* of associated data is plotted as a disk that expresses two of those three variables through the *xy* location and the third shows the quantity measured for significance.

Scatter plots

The data is usually displayed as a collection of points, and is often used to plot various kinds of correlations. For instance, a positive correlation is noticed when the increase in the value of one set of data increases the other value as well. The student record data shown earlier has various scatter plots that show the correlations among them.

In the following example, we compare the heights of students with the height of their mother to determine if there is any positive correlation. The data can be downloaded from `http://www.knapdata.com/python/ucdavis.csv`.

```
import numpy as np
import pandas as pd
import seaborn as sns
import matplotlib.pyplot as plt
students = pd.read_csv("/Users/Macbook/python/data/ucdavis.csv")
g = sns.FacetGrid(students, palette="Set1", size=7)
g.map(plt.scatter, "momheight", "height", s=140, linewidth=.7,
edgecolor="#ffad40", color="#ff8000")
g.set_axis_labels("Mothers Height", "Students Height")
```

We demonstrate this example using the `seaborn` package, but one can also accomplish this using only `matplotlib`, which will be shown in the following section. The scatterplot map for the preceding code is depicted as follows:

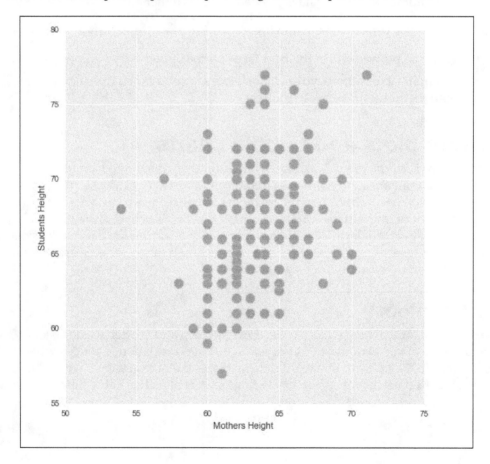

Scatter plots are most useful for investigating the relationship between two different variables. Some notable examples are as follows:

- The likelihood of having skin cancer at different ages in males versus females
- The correlation between the IQ test score and GPA

In addition to this, consider the following:

- **Add a trend line or line of best-fit (if the relation is linear)**: Adding a trend line can show the correlation among the data values
- **Use informative mark types**: Informative mark types should be used if the story to be revealed is about data that can be visually enhanced with relevant shapes and colors

Bubble charts

The following example shows how one can use color map as a third dimension that may indicate the volume of sales or any appropriate indicator that drives the profit:

```
[7]: import numpy as np
     import pandas as pd
     import seaborn as sns
     import matplotlib.pyplot as plt

     sns.set(style="whitegrid")
     mov =
     pd.read_csv("/Users/MacBook/python/data/2014_gross.csv")

     x=mov.ProductionCost
     y=mov.WorldGross
     z=mov.WorldGross

     cm = plt.cm.get_cmap('RdYlBu')
     fig, ax = plt.subplots(figsize=(12,10))

     sc = ax.scatter(x,y,s=z*3, c=z,cmap=cm, linewidth=0.2,
     alpha=0.5)
     ax.grid()
     fig.colorbar(sc)

     ax.set_xlabel('Production Cost', fontsize=14)
     ax.set_ylabel('Gross Profits', fontsize=14)

     plt.show()
...
```

The following scatter plot is the result of the example using color map:

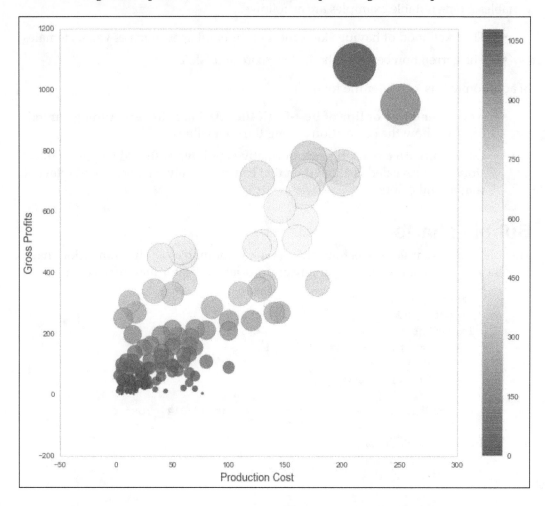

Bubble charts are extremely useful for comparing relationships between data in three numeric-data dimensions: the x axis data, the y axis data, and the data represented by the bubble size. Bubble charts are like XY scatter plots, except that each point on the scatter plot has an additional data value associated with it that is represented by the size of the circle or "bubble" centered on the XY point. Another example of a bubble chart is shown here (without the python code, to demonstrate a different style):

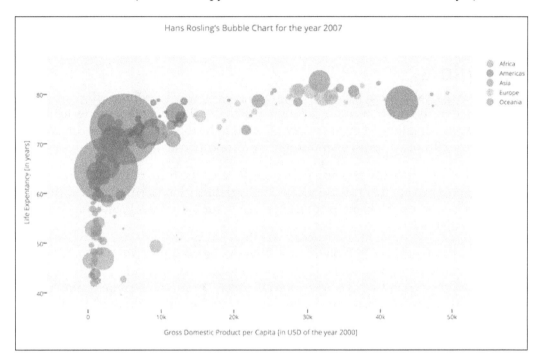

In the preceding display, the bubble chart shows the **Life Expectancy** versus **Gross Domestic Product per Capita** around different continents.

Bubble charts are most useful for showing the concentration of data along two axes with a third data element being the significance value measured. Some notable examples are as follows:

- The production cost of movies and gross profit made, and the significance measured along a heated scale as shown in the example

In addition to this, consider the following:

- **Adding color and shape significance**: By varying the size and color, the data points can be transformed into a visualization that clearly answers some questions

- **Make it interactive**: If there are too many data points, bubble charts could get cluttered, so group them on the time axis or categories, and visualize them interactively

KDE plots

Kernel Density Estimation (KDE) is a non-parametric way to estimate the probability density function and its average across the observed data points to create a smooth approximation. They are closely related to histograms, but sometimes can be endowed with smoothness or continuity by a concept called kernel.

The kernel of a **Probability Density Function (PDF)** is the form of the PDF in which any factors that are not functions of any of the variables in the domain are omitted. We will focus only on the visualization aspect of it; for more theory, one may refer to books on statistics.

There are several different Python libraries that can be used to accomplish a KDE plot at various depths and levels including `matplotlib`, `Scipy`, `scikit-learn`, and `seaborn`. Following are two examples of KDE Plots. There will be more examples in later chapters, wherever necessary to demonstrate various other ways of displaying KDE plots.

In the following example, we use a random dataset of size 250 and the `seaborn` package to show the distribution plot in a few simple lines:

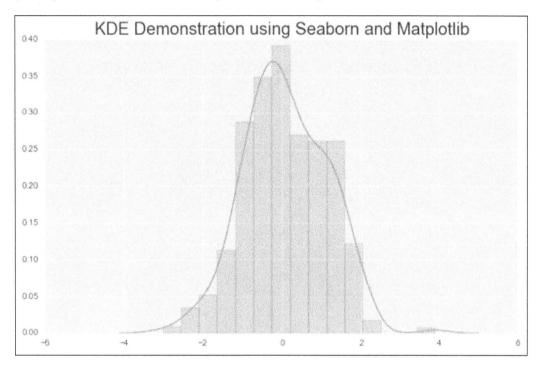

One can display simple distribution of a data plot using `seaborn`, which is demonstrated here using a random sample generated using `numpy.random`:

```
from numpy.random import randn
import matplotlib as mpl
import seaborn as sns
import matplotlib.pyplot as plt

sns.set_palette("hls")
mpl.rc("figure", figsize=(10,6))
data = randn(250)
plt.title("KDE Demonstration using Seaborn and Matplotlib",
fontsize=20)
sns.distplot(data, color='#ff8000')
```

In the second example, we are demonstrating the probability density function using SciPy and NumPy. First we use `norm()` from SciPy to create normal distribution samples and later, use `hstack()` from NumPy to stack them horizontally and apply `gaussian_kde()` from SciPy.

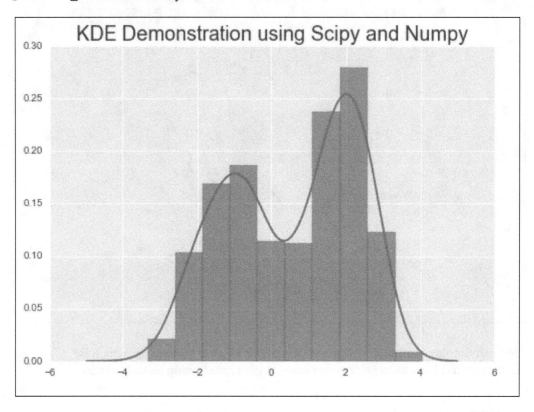

The preceding plot is the result of a KDE plot using SciPy and NumPy, which is shown as follows:

```
from scipy.stats.kde import gaussian_kde
from scipy.stats import norm
from numpy import linspace, hstack
from pylab import plot, show, hist

sample1 = norm.rvs(loc=-1.0, scale=1, size=320)
sample2 = norm.rvs(loc=2.0, scale=0.6, size=320)
sample = hstack([sample1, sample2])
probDensityFun = gaussian_kde(sample)
plt.title("KDE Demonstration using Scipy and Numpy", fontsize=20)
x = linspace(-5,5,200)
plot(x, probDensityFun(x), 'r')
hist(sample, normed=1, alpha=0.45, color='purple')
show()
```

The other visualization methods such as the line and surface plot, network graph plot, tree maps, heat maps, radar or spider chart, and the violin plot will be discussed in the next few chapters.

Summary

The examples shown so far are just to give you an idea of how one should think and plan before making a presentation. The most important stage is the data familiarization and preparation process for visualization. Whether one can get the data first or shape the desired story is mainly influenced by exactly what outcome is attempted. It is like the "chicken and the egg" situation—does data come first or the focus? Initially, it may not be clear what data one may need, but in most cases, after a few iterations, things will be clear as long as there are no errors in the data.

Transform the quality of data by doing some cleanup or reducing the dimensions (if required), and fill gaps if any. Unless the data is good, the efforts that one may put into presenting it visually will be wasted. After a reasonable understanding of the data is achieved, it makes sense to determine what kind of visualization may be appropriate. In some cases, it would be better to display it in several different ways to see the story clearly.

2
Data Analysis and Visualization

Most visualization stories begin with some question that is oriented towards a topic where the data is being either explored or collected. The question contains the premise to the story and leads us to the point at which the data takes an expedition over the storyline. Such data expeditions that start with a question, for example, *How many Ebola deaths were reported in the year 2014?* are implemented by a group of people by collaborating with each other. The role of data communicators should be to create an information experience that transforms how their audiences think about their story.

The key parts of the story relate to the process of placing the visualization in a meaningful context. The context provides knowledge that answers questions such as the following:

- Is there sufficient data?
- Is there a time frame within which this data exists?
- Which associable events around the globe will influence this data?

To reiterate, it is important to understand the data, and identify the context of the question to which an answer is being attempted. Sometimes, one may start digging into the data before even finalizing the question, and in such a case, on gaining a refined understanding of the data, you may have an improved or clearer version of the question.

The process starts with the input data, assuming that one has ways to acquire, parse, and gather the required information from some source. There are some situations where it is better to visualize this collected information to eliminate noise, while in some other cases, one may filter and analyze the data before applying the visualization methods. In this chapter, we will learn the different ways of data exploration to further use them for visualization methods. We will also go through some interesting data stories and the related concepts in the following sequence:

- Acquiring, parsing, and filtering data to detect outliers and abnormalities, data mining and refining, visual representation, and interaction

- Creating interesting stories with data

- Perception, presentation methods, and best practice for visualization

- Interactive visualization—exploring event listeners and layouts

Why does visualization require planning?

The whole process of visualization involves people with different skill sets and domain expertise. Data wranglers diligently collect data and analyze it. Mathematicians and statisticians understand the visual design principles and communicate their data using those principles. Designers or artists (in some cases, frontend developers) have the skills necessary for visualization, while business analysts look out for things like customer behavioral patterns, outliers, or a sudden unusual trend. However, it always starts with either acquiring or gathering data, and with the following steps:

- **Acquire or gather data** from an external source, a website, or from a file on a disk

- **Parse and filter data** using programming methods to parse, clean, and reduce the data

- **Analyze and refine** to remove noise and unnecessary dimensions and find patterns

- **Represent and interact** to present the data in ways that are more accessible and understandable

How much of this process is followed varies with different problems, and in some cases, there is more analysis done than filtering of data. As discussed in the previous chapter, in some instances, the analysis and visualization is done iteratively. In other words, the distribution of these steps is not always predictable and consistent.

The Ebola example

To illustrate the steps mentioned in the previous section and how they lead to an understandable visualization, let us consider the question we had earlier, that is, *How many Ebola deaths were reported in the year 2014?* This particular question leads to very specific data, which is usually maintained by the World Health Organization (http://www.who.int/en/) or Humanitarian Data Exchange (https://hdx.rwlabs.org). The original source of this data is the **World Health Organization (WHO)**, but the **Humanitarian Data Exchange (HDX)** is the contributor. Please note, however, that we shall have all the data, along with the Python source code examples for this book, available at a single place.

The data contains information about the spread of the Ebola disease in Guinea, Liberia, Mali, Nigeria, Senegal, Sierra Leone, Spain, United Kingdom, and the United States of America.

The contributor URL for this information is https://data.hdx.rwlabs.org/dataset/ebola-cases-2014/.

The contents of the data file in the **Comma Separated Value (CSV)** format include the indicator, country name, date, and the number of deaths or the number of infections depending upon what the indicator says. There are 36 different indicators, and the top 10 are listed as follows (others can be viewed in *Appendix, Go Forth and Explore Visualization*):

- Number of probable Ebola cases in the last 7 days
- Number of probable Ebola deaths in the last 21 days
- Number of suspected Ebola cases in the last 21 days
- Number of suspected Ebola cases in the last 7 days
- Number of suspected Ebola deaths in the last 21 days
- Proportion of confirmed Ebola cases that are from the last 21 days
- Proportion of confirmed Ebola cases that are from the last 7 days
- Proportion of confirmed Ebola deaths that are from the last 21 days
- Proportion of suspected Ebola cases that are from the last 7 days
- Proportion of suspected Ebola deaths that are from the last 21 days

At this point, after looking at the list of indicators, the single question that we had initially, that is, *How many Ebola deaths were reported in the year 2014?* could be changed to multiple sets of questions. For simplicity, we stay focused on that single question and see how we can further analyze the data and come up with a visualization method. First, let us take a look at the ways to read the data file.

In any programming language, there is more than one way to read a file, and one of the options is to use the **pandas** library for Python, which has high performance and uses data structures and data analysis tools. The other option is to use the **csv** library to read the data file in the CSV format. What is the difference between them? They both can do the job. In the older version of pandas there were issues with memory maps for large data (that is, if the data file in the CSV format was very large), but now that has been optimized. So let's start with the following code:

```
[1]:  with open('("/Users/kvenkatr/python/ebola.csv ', 'rt') as f:
          filtereddata = [row for row in csv.reader(f) if row[3] !=
      "0.0" and
          row[3] != "0" and "deaths" in row[0]]


[2]:     len(filtereddata)
Out[2]: 1194
```

The preceding filter can also be performed using pandas, as follows:

```
import pandas as pd
eboladata = pd.read_csv("/Users/kvenkatr/python/ebola.csv")
filtered = eboladata[eboladata["value"]>0]
filtered = filtered[filtered["Indicator"].str.contains("deaths")]
len(filtered)
```

The data can be downloaded from `http://www.knapdata.com/python/ebola.csv`. The next step is to open the data file with the **read text (rt)** format. It reads each row and further filters the rows with zero number of deaths as the indicator string has the word `deaths` in it. This is a very straightforward filter applied to ignore the data with no reported cases or deaths. Printing only the top five rows of the filtered data shows the following:

```
[3]:  filtereddata[:5]
Out[3]:
[['Cumulative number of confirmed Ebola deaths',
'Guinea','2014-08-29', '287.0'],
  ['Cumulative number of probable Ebola deaths','Guinea','2014-08-29',
    '141.0'],
  ['Cumulative number of suspected Ebola deaths','Guinea','2014-08-29',
    '2.0'],
  ['Cumulative number of confirmed, probable and suspected Ebola
deaths',
    'Guinea','2014-08-29','430.0'],
  ['Cumulative number of confirmed Ebola deaths',
    'Liberia','2014-08-29','225.0']]
```

If all the data about the reported cases of Ebola in each country are to be separated, how do we further filter this? We can sort them on the country column. There are four columns in this data file, `indicator`, `country`, `date`, and `number value`, as shown in the following code:

```
[4]:  import operator
      sorteddata = sort(filtereddata, key=operator.itemgetter(1))
[5]:  sorteddata[:5]
Out[5]:
[['Cumulative number of confirmed Ebola deaths',
'Guinea','2014-08-29', '287.0'],
 ['Cumulative number of probable Ebola deaths','Guinea','2014-08-29',
  '141.0'],
 ['Cumulative number of suspected Ebola deaths','Guinea','2014-08-29',
  '2.0'],
 ['Cumulative number of confirmed, probable and suspected Ebola
deaths',
  'Guinea','2014-08-29','430.0'],
 ['Number of confirmed Ebola deaths in the last 21 days', 'Guinea',
  '2014-08-29','8.0']]
```

After looking at the data so far, there are two indicators that appear to be of interest in the context in which we started this data expedition:

- Cumulative number of confirmed Ebola deaths
- Cumulative number of confirmed, probable, and suspected Ebola deaths

By applying visualization several times, we also notice that among the several countries, Guinea, Liberia, and Sierra Leone had more confirmed deaths than the others. We will now see how the reported deaths in these three countries could be plotted:

```
import matplotlib.pyplot as plt
import csv
import operator
import datetime as dt

with open('/Users/kvenkatr/python/ebola.csv', 'rt') as f:
  filtereddata = [row for row in csv.reader(f) if row[3] != "0.0" and
  row[3] != "0" and "deaths" in row[0]]

sorteddata = sorted(filtereddata, key=operator.itemgetter(1))
guineadata  = [row for row in sorteddata if row[1] == "Guinea" and
```

```
    row[0] == "Cumulative number of confirmed Ebola deaths"]
sierradata  = [row for row in sorteddata if row[1] == "Sierra Leone"
and
    row[0] == "Cumulative number of confirmed Ebola deaths"]
liberiadata = [row for row in sorteddata if row[1] == "Liberia" and
    row[0] == "Cumulative number of confirmed Ebola deaths"]

g_x = [dt.datetime.strptime(row[2], '%Y-%m-%d').date() for
    row in guineadata]
g_y = [row[3] for row in guineadata]

s_x = [dt.datetime.strptime(row[2], '%Y-%m-%d').date() for
    row in sierradata]
s_y = [row[3] for row in sierradata]

l_x = [dt.datetime.strptime(row[2], '%Y-%m-%d').date() for
    row in liberiadata]
l_y = [row[3] for row in liberiadata]

plt.figure(figsize=(10,10))
plt.plot(g_x,g_y, color='red', linewidth=2, label="Guinea")
plt.plot(s_x,s_y, color='orange', linewidth=2, label="Sierra Leone")

plt.plot(l_x,l_y, color='blue', linewidth=2, label="Liberia")
plt.xlabel('Date', fontsize=18)

plt.ylabel('Number of Ebola Deaths', fontsize=18)

plt.title("Confirmed Ebola Deaths", fontsize=20)

plt.legend(loc=2)


plt.show()
```

The result would look like the following image:

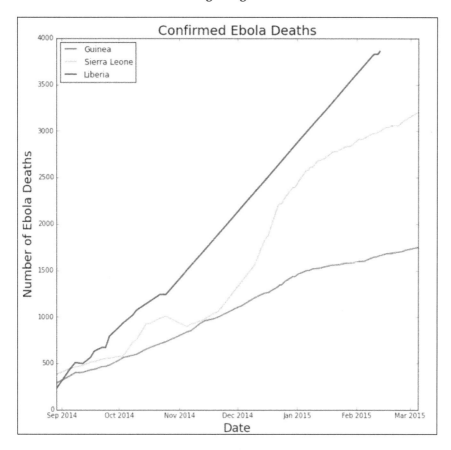

We can construct a similar plot for the other indicator, that is, *cumulative number of confirmed, probable, and suspected Ebola deaths*. (This may not be the best way to do so, but we could include the data from more countries and plot a similar result.)

```
import matplotlib.pyplot as plt
import csv
import operator
import datetime as dt

with open('/Users/kvenkatr/python/ebola.csv', 'rt') as f:
   filtereddata = [row for row in csv.reader(f) if row[3] != "0.0" and
   row[3] != "0" and "deaths" in row[0]]

sorteddata = sorted(filtereddata, key=operator.itemgetter(1))

guineadata  = [row for row in sorteddata if row[1] == "Guinea" and
```

```
    row[0] == "Cumulative number of confirmed, probable and suspected
Ebola deaths"]
sierradata  = [row for row in sorteddata if row[1] == "Sierra Leone"
and
   row[0] == " Cumulative number of confirmed, probable and suspected
Ebola deaths "]
liberiadata = [row for row in sorteddata if row[1] == "Liberia" and
   row[0] == " Cumulative number of confirmed, probable and suspected
Ebola deaths "]

g_x = [dt.datetime.strptime(row[2], '%Y-%m-%d').date() for
   row in guineadata]
g_y = [row[3] for row in guineadata]

s_x = [dt.datetime.strptime(row[2], '%Y-%m-%d').date() for
   row in sierradata]
s_y = [row[3] for row in sierradata]

l_x = [dt.datetime.strptime(row[2], '%Y-%m-%d').date() for
   row in liberiadata]
l_y = [row[3] for row in liberiadata]

plt.figure(figsize=(10,10))
plt.plot(g_x,g_y, color='red', linewidth=2, label="Guinea")
plt.plot(s_x,s_y, color='orange', linewidth=2, label="Sierra Leone")

plt.plot(l_x,l_y, color='blue', linewidth=2, label="Liberia")
plt.xlabel('Date', fontsize=18)

plt.ylabel('Number of Ebola Deaths', fontsize=18)

plt.title("Probable and Suspected Ebola Deaths", fontsize=20)

plt.legend(loc=2)


plt.show()
```

The plot should look like this:

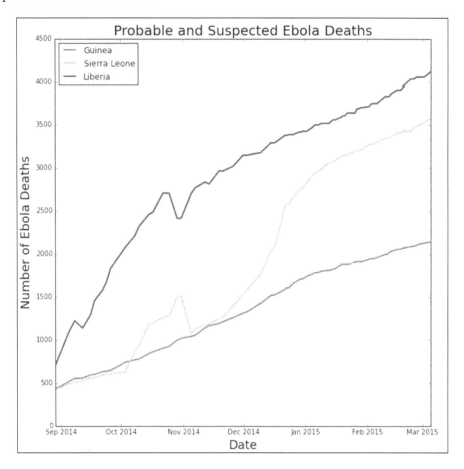

A sports example

To illustrate another example, and how a specific visualization method works better than another, let us consider a different question: *What are the top five record touchdowns by quarterbacks in American Football as of Feb 2015?* The original source of data for this are the Len Dawson NFL and AFL Statistics. (Data source: http://www.pro-football-reference.com/players/D/DawsLe00.htm.)

The data contains information about the top 22 quarterbacks: Peyton Manning, Brett Favre, Dan Marino, Drew Brees, Tom Brady, Frank Tarkenton, John Elway, Warren Moon, John Unitas, Vinny Testaverda, Joe Montana, Dave Krieg, Eli Manning, Sonny Jurgensen, Dan Fouts, Philip Rivers, Ben Roethlisberger, Drew Bledsoe, Boomer Esiason, John Hadle, Tittle, and Tony Romo:

Name	Year	Age	Cmp	Att	Yds	TD	Teams
Peyton Manning	1998	22	326	575	3739	26	Multi
Peyton Manning	1999	23	331	533	4135	26	Multi
Peyton Manning	2000	24	357	571	4413	33	Multi
Peyton Manning	2001	25	343	547	4131	26	Multi
Peyton Manning	2002	26	392	591	4200	27	Multi
Peyton Manning	2003	27	379	566	4267	29	Multi
Peyton Manning	2004	28	336	497	4557	49	Multi
Peyton Manning	2005	29	305	453	3747	28	Multi
Peyton Manning	2006	30	362	557	4397	31	Multi
Peyton Manning	2007	31	337	515	4040	31	Multi
Peyton Manning	2008	32	371	555	4002	27	Multi
Peyton Manning	2009	33	393	571	4500	33	Multi
Peyton Manning	2010	34	450	679	4700	33	Multi
Peyton Manning	2011	35	0	0	0	0	Multi
Peyton Manning	2012	36	400	583	4659	37	Multi
Peyton Manning	2013	37	450	659	5477	55	Multi

Before we think of a visualization method, a little bit of analysis needs to be done. These quarterbacks had played in different time periods. For example, Brett Favre played from 1991 to 2010, and Dan Marino played from 1983 to 1999. The challenge is that if we use a bar graph or a bubble chart, they will show the results in only one dimension.

The first step is to parse the CSV file, and we have several options here. We can either use the pandas `read_csv` function or the `csv` module, which has some convenient functions such as `DictReader`:

```
import csv
import matplotlib.pyplot as plt

# csv has Name, Year, Age, Cmp, Att, Yds, TD, Teams
```

```
with open('/Users/MacBook/java/qb_data.csv') as csvfile:
    reader = csv.DictReader(csvfile)
    for row in reader:
        name = row['Name']
        tds = row['TD']
```

The quarterback data was downloaded from the source listed previously in this section; the filtered data is also available at http://www.knapdata.com/python/qb_data.csv. The csv module includes classes for working with rows as dictionaries so that the fields can be named. The DictReader and DictWriter classes translate the rows to dictionaries instead of lists. Keys for the dictionary can be passed in or inferred from the first row in the input (where the row contains headers). Reading the contents of the CSV file is achieved via DictReader, where the column input values are treated as strings:

```
#ways to call DictReader

# if fieldnames are Name, Year, Age, Cmp, Att, Yds, TD, Teams
fieldnames = ['Name', 'Year', 'Age', 'Cmp', 'Att', 'Yds', 'TD',
'Teams']

reader = csv.DictReader(csvfile, fieldNames=fieldnames)
# If csv file has first row as Name, Year, Cmp, Att, Yds, TD, Teams
#   we don't need to define fieldnames, the reader automatically
recognizes
#   them.
```

In order to convert some of the values to a number, we may need a function that converts and returns a numeric value. We have also added functions like getcolors() and num() in prepare.py, which can be used in future examples:

```
# num(s) and getcolors() functions
def num(s):
    try:
        return int(s)
    except ValueError:
        return 0

def getcolors():
    colors = [(31, 119, 180), (255,0,0), (0,255,0), (148, 103, 189),
    (140, 86, 75), (218, 73, 174), (127, 127, 127), (140,140,26), (23,
    190, 207), (65,200,100), (200, 65,100), (125,255,32), (32,32,198),
    (255,191,201), (172,191,201), (0,128,0), (244,130,150), (255,
    127, 14), (128,128,0), (10,10,10), (44, 160, 44), (214, 39, 40),
    (206,206,216)]
```

```
for i in range(len(colors)):
  r, g, b = colors[i]
  colors[i] = (r / 255. , g / 255. , b / 255.)
return colors
```

Visually representing the results

Based on the field names in the input data, for every quarterback, their touchdown statistics or passing-yards statistics can be plotted on a timeline. Now that we know what to plot, the next step is to figure out how to plot it.

Simple *X-Y* plots with the fields (year, touchdown) or (touchdown, year) should be a good start. However, there are 252 quarterbacks so far in this input data file, and a majority of them are not relevant. Therefore, showing them all with different colors would not make sense. (Why? Do we have 252 different colors?) We can attempt to plot the top 7 or top 10 results, as seen in the following image:

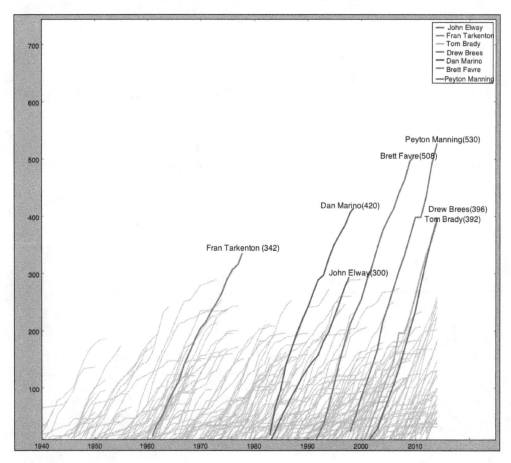

The following Python program demonstrates how one can use `matplotlib` to display the top 10 quarterbacks in terms of the number of touchdowns and the plot produced by this program is shown in the preceding image:

```python
import csv
import matplotlib.pyplot as plt

# The following functions can be in separate file
#   (If it does, you need to import)
def num(s):
  try:
    return int(s)
  except ValueError:
    return 0

def getcolors():
  colors = [(31, 119, 180), (255,0,0), (0,255,0), (148, 103, 189),
(140, 86, 75), (218, 73, 174), (127, 127, 127), (140,140,26), (23,
190, 207), (65,200,100), (200, 65,100), (125,255,32), (32,32,198),
(255,191,201), (172,191,201), (0,128,0), (244,130,150), (255,
127, 14), (128,128,0), (10,10,10), (44, 160, 44), (214, 39, 40),
(206,206,216)]

  for i in range(len(colors)):
    r, g, b = colors[i]
    colors[i] = (r / 255. , g / 255. , b / 255.)
  return colors

def getQbNames():
  qbnames = ['Peyton Manning']
  name=''
  i=0
  with open('/Users/MacBook/java/qb_data.csv') as csvfile:
    reader = csv.DictReader(csvfile)
    for row in reader:
      if ( row['Name'] != name and qbnames[i] != row['Name']):
        qbnames.append(row['Name'])
        i = i+1
  return qbnames

def readQbdata():
  resultdata = []
  with open('/Users/MacBook/java/qb_data.csv') as csvfile:
    reader = csv.DictReader(csvfile)
    resultdata = [row for row in reader]
```

```
        return resultdata

fdata=[]
prevysum=0

#      -- functions End --

qbnames = getQbNames()
fdata = readQbdata()

i=0
rank=0
prevysum=0
lastyr=0
highrank=244
colorsdata = getcolors()

fig = plt.figure(figsize=(15,13))
ax=fig.add_subplot(111,axisbg='white')

# limits for TD
plt.ylim(10, 744)
plt.xlim(1940, 2021)

colindex=0
lastage=20

for qbn in qbnames:
  x=[]
  y=[]
  prevysum=0
  for row in fdata:
    if ( row['Name'] == qbn and row['Year'] != 'Career'):
      yrval = num(row['Year'])
      lastage = num(row['Age'])
      prevysum += num(row['TD'])
      lastyr = yrval
      x += [yrval]
      y += [prevysum]

  if ( rank > highrank):
    plt.plot(x,y, color=colorsdata[colindex], label=qbn,
linewidth=2.5)
    plt.legend(loc=0, prop={'size':10})
```

```
    colindex = (colindex+1)%22
    plt.text(lastyr-1, prevsum+2, qbn+"("+str(prevsum)+"):"
+str(lastage), fontsize=9)

  else:
    plt.plot(x,y, color=colorsdata[22], linewidth=1.5)
    rank = rank +1
plt.xlabel('Year', fontsize=18)

plt.ylabel('Cumulative Touch Downs', fontsize=18)

plt.title("Cumulative Touch Downs by Quarter Backs", fontsize=20)
plt.show()
```

When the plot (X, Y) is switched to (Y, X), there is enough room to display the quarterback names. In the preceding code snippet, we might have to make the following change:

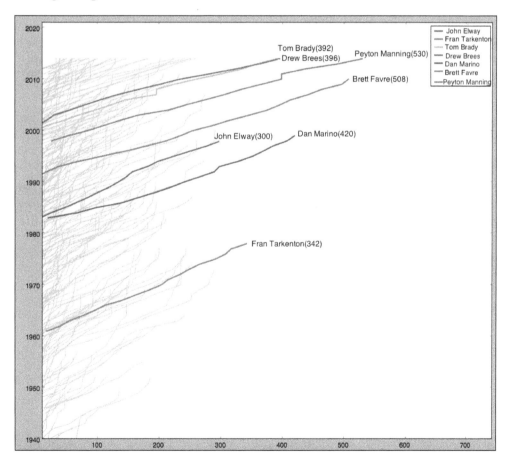

If we flip the x and y axes, then there is more room to display the name of the quarterback and the total touchdown score, as shown in the preceding plot. In order to accomplish this, one may have to switch x and y, and have the label text properly positioned according to the new x and y axes.

```
plt.xlim(10, 744)
plt.ylim(1940, 2021)

# remaining code all un-changed except

y += [num(row['Year'])]
x += [prevysum]

# Don't forget to switch the x,y co-ordinates of text display

plt.text(prevysum+2, lastyr-1, qbn+"("+str(prevysum)+"):"
str(lastage), fontsize=9)
```

At first glance, we can only make out the quarterbacks who are leading in the number of touchdown scores in their career (as of the 2014-2015 football season). Based on this visualization, you can further try to analyze and understand what else can we infer from this data. The answer to this is based on the answers of the following questions:

- Which quarterback has played the longest in their career?
- Are there any quarterbacks today who can surpass Peyton Manning's touchdown records?

Among the fields that we read from the input file, Age happens to be one of the field values that we have. There are many ways to experiment with the starting value of Age that can be used to plot the Age versus Touchdown statistics. To answer the first question, we have to keep track of Age instead of Year. The following snippet can be either used in a separate function (if one has to use it often), or included in the main script:

```
maxage = 30

with open('/Users/MacBook/java/qb_data.csv') as csvfile:
  reader = csv.DictReader(csvfile)
    for row in reader:
      if ( num(row['Age']) > maxage ):
        maxage = num(row['Age'])

print maxage
```

Running the preceding block of code shows 44 as the maximum age of a quarterback (when actively played in the league, and there were three such quarterbacks: Warren Moon, Vinny Testaverde, and Steve DeBerg. Technically, George Blanda played until he was 48 (which is the maximum age as a player), but he started as quarterback and was also a kicker for some years).

In order to answer the other question, we plot the touchdown statistics against the quarterback age, as follows:

```python
import csv
import matplotlib.pyplot as plt

# The following functions can be in a separate file
#      -- functions Begin --
def num(s):
  try:
    return int(s)
  except ValueError:
    return 0

def getcolors():
  colors = [(31, 119, 180), (255,0,0), (0,255,0), (148, 103, 189),
(140, 86, 75), (218, 73, 174), (127, 127, 127), (140,140,26), (23,
190, 207), (65,200,100), (200, 65,100), (125,255,32), (32,32,198),
(255,191,201), (172,191,201), (0,128,0), (244,130,150), (255,
127, 14), (128,128,0), (10,10,10), (44, 160, 44), (214, 39, 40),
(206,206,216)]

  for i in range(len(colors)):
    r, g, b = colors[i]
    colors[i] = (r / 255. , g / 255. , b / 255.)
  return colors

def getQbNames():
  qbnames = ['Peyton Manning']
  name=''
  i=0
  with open('/Users/MacBook/java/qb_data.csv') as csvfile:
    reader = csv.DictReader(csvfile)
    for row in reader:
      if ( row['Name'] != name and qbnames[i] != row['Name']):
        qbnames.append(row['Name'])
```

```
        i = i+1
   return qbnames

def readQbdata():
   resultdata = []
   with open('/Users/MacBook/java/qb_data.csv') as csvfile:
     reader = csv.DictReader(csvfile)
     resultdata = [row for row in reader]
   return resultdata

fdata=[]
prevysum=0

#     -- functions End --

qbnames = getQbNames()
fdata = readQbdata()

i=0
rank=0
prevysum=0
lastyr=0
highrank=244
colorsdata = getcolors()

fig = plt.figure(figsize=(15,13))
ax=fig.add_subplot(111,axisbg='white')

# limits for TD
plt.ylim(10, 744)
#change xlimit to have age ranges
plt.xlim(20, 50)

colindex=0
lastage=20

for qbn in qbnames:
   x=[]
   y=[]
   prevysum=0
   for row in fdata:
     if ( row['Name'] == qbn and row['Year'] != 'Career'):
```

```
        yrval = num(row['Year'])
        lastage = num(row['Age'])
        prevysum += num(row['TD'])
        lastyr = yrval
        x += [lastage]
        y += [prevysum]

    if ( rank > highrank):
      if ( lastage == 44):
        plt.plot(x,y, color='red', label=qbn, linewidth=3.5)
      else:
        plt.plot(x,y, color=colorsdata[colindex], label=qbn,
linewidth=2.5)
        plt.legend(loc=0, prop={'size':10})

      colindex = (colindex+1)%22
      plt.text(lastage-1, prevysum+2, qbn+"("+str(prevysum)+"):"
+str(lastage), fontsize=9)

    else:
      if ( lastage == 44):
        plt.plot(x,y, color='red', label=qbn, linewidth=3.5)
        plt.text(lastage-1, prevysum+2, qbn+"("+str(prevysum)+"):"
+str(lastage), fontsize=9)
      else:
        plt.plot(x,y, color=colorsdata[22], linewidth=1.5)
      rank = rank +1

plt.xlabel('Age', fontsize=18)

plt.ylabel('Number of Touch Downs', fontsize=18)

plt.title("Touch Downs by Quarter Backs by Age", fontsize=20)
plt.show()
```

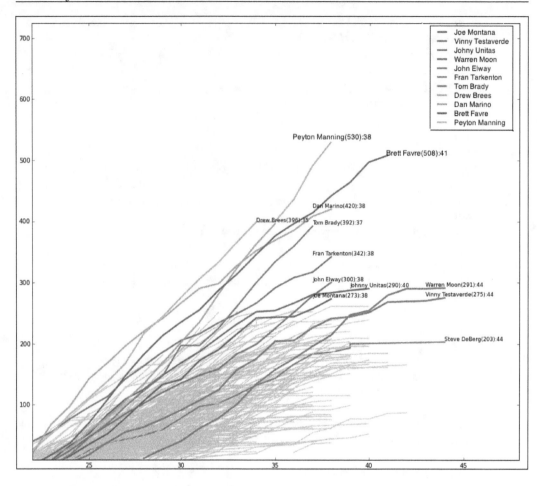

When you take a look at the plotting results, only two quarterback results are comparable to Peyton Manning at the age of 35, which are Drew Brees and Tom Brady. However, given the current age of Tom Brady and his accomplishments so far, it appears that only Drew Brees has a better probability of surpassing Peyton Manning's touchdown records.

This conclusion is shown in the following image with a simpler plot for data based on the age of 35. Comparing the top four quarterback results—Peyton Manning, Tom Brady, Drew Brees, and Brett Favre—we see that Drew Brees's achievement at the age of 35 is comparable to that of Peyton at the same age. Although the write-up by *NY Times* with the title *Why Peyton Manning's record will be hard to beat* concludes differently, the following plot, at least, is inclined towards the possibility that Drew Brees might beat the record:

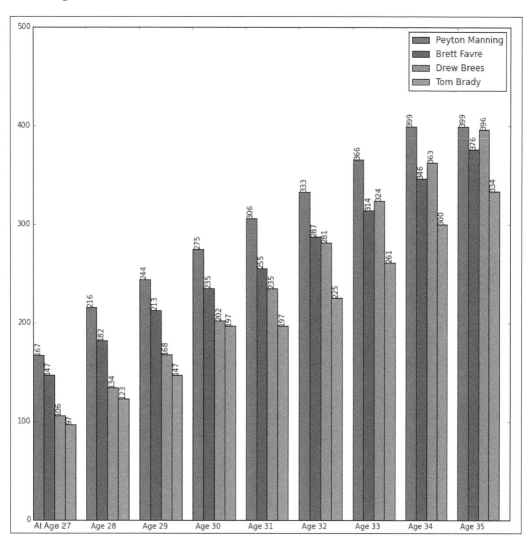

Creating interesting stories with data

Data visualization regularly promotes its ability to reveal stories with data, and in some cases, reveal the not so trivial stories visually. In the recent past, journalists have been integrating visualizations more into their narratives, often helping us better understand their stories. In the commercial world, there are few that grasp the ways in which data can be associated with a meaningful story that appeals both emotionally and intelligently to the audience. As Rudyard Kipling wrote, *If history were taught in the form of stories, it would never be forgotten*; a similar thought applies to data. We should, therefore, understand that data would be understood and remembered better if presented in the right way.

Why are stories so important?

There are many tools and methods of visualization that we have today: bar and pie charts, tables, line graphs, bubble charts, scatter plots, and so on—the list is long. However, with these tools, the focus is on data exploration, and not on aiding a narrative. While there are examples of visualizations that do help tell stories, they are rare. This is mainly because finding the story is significantly harder than crunching the numbers. There are **reader-driven narratives** and **author-driven narratives** as well.

An author-driven narrative has data and visualization that are chosen by the author and presented to the public reader. A reader-driven narrative, on the other hand, provides tools and methods for the reader to play with the data, which gives the reader more flexibility and choices to analyze and understand the visualization.

Reader-driven narratives

In 2010, researchers at Stanford University studied and reviewed the emerging importance of storytelling and suggested some design strategies for narrative visualization. According to their study, a purely author-driven approach has a strict linear path through the visualization, relies on messaging, and has no interactivity, whereas a reader-driven approach has no prescribed ordering of images, no messaging, and has a high degree of interactivity. An example of the author-driven approach is a slideshow presentation. The seven narratives of visualization listed by that study include magazine style, annotated chart, partitioned poster, flow chart, comic strip, slideshow, and a film/video/animation.

Gapminder

A classic example of a reader-driven narrative combined with a data-driven one is Gapminder World (`http://gapminder.org/world`). It has a collection of over 600 data indicators in international economy, environment, health, technology, and much more. It provides tools that students can use to study real-world issues and discover patterns, trends, and correlations. This was developed by the Trendalyzer software that was originally developed by Hans Rosling's foundation in Sweden, and later acquired by Google in March 2007.

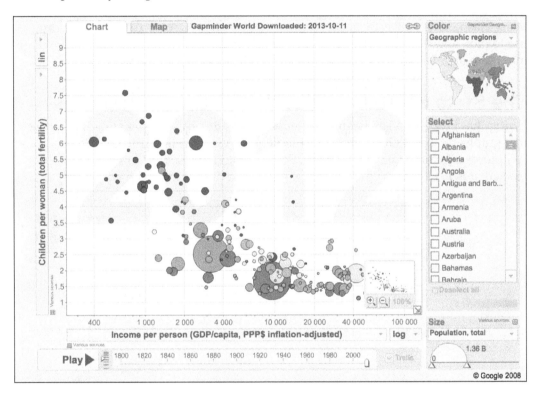

The information visualization technique used by Gapminder is an interactive bubble chart with the default set to five variables: X, Y, bubble size, color, and a time variable that is controlled by a slider. This sliding control and the selection of what goes along the X and Y axes makes it interactive. However, creating a story, even with a tool like this, is not necessarily easy. Storytelling is a craft and can be an effective knowledge-sharing technique, because it conveys the context and emotional content more effectively than most other modes of communication.

The most attractive storytellers grasp the importance of understanding the audience. They might tell the same story to a child and an adult, but the articulation would be different. Similarly, a data-driven or reader-driven story should be adjusted based on who is listening or studying it. For example, to an executive, statistics are likely the key, but a business intelligence manager would most likely be interested in methods and techniques.

There are many JavaScript frameworks that are available today for creating interactive visualization, and the most popular one is D3.js. Using Python, there are only a few ways today in which one can create an interactive visualization (without using Flash). One way is by generating the data in the JSON format that D3.js can use to plot, and the second option is to use Plotly (http://www.plot.ly). We will go into more detail about Plotly in the concluding section of this chapter.

The State of the Union address

Twitter has created a visualization from the tweets during President Obama's speech that graphs the tweets by location and topic. This visualization is interesting because it captures a lot of details in one place. Scroll through the speech to see how Twitter reacted; it is posted at http://twitter.github.io/interactive/sotu2015/#p1.

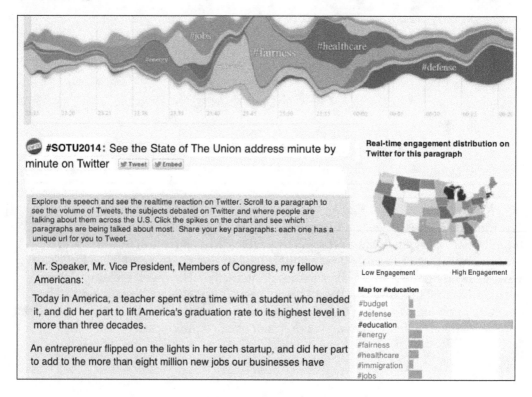

Mortality rate in the USA

The mortality rate in the USA fell by about 17 percent from 1968 to 2010, years for which we have detailed data (from `http://www.who.int/healthinfo/mortality_data/en/`). Almost all of this improvement can be attributed to improved survival prospects for men. It looks like progress stopped in the mid 1990s, but one of the reasons may be that the population has aged a lot since then. One may read a complete description of this from Bloomberg, but here we attempt to display two visualizations:

- Mortality rate during the period 1968-2010 among men, women, and combined
- Mortality rate for seven age groups to show some interesting results

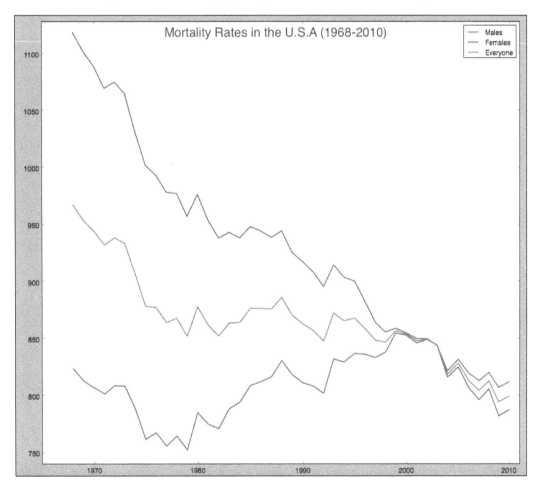

The code for this example is as follows:

```
import csv
import matplotlib.pyplot as plt

fig = plt.figure(figsize=(15,13))
plt.ylim(740,1128)
plt.xlim(1965,2011)
# Data from http://www.who.int/healthinfo/mortality_data/en/
with open('/Users/MacBook/Downloads/mortality1.csv') as csvfile:
  mortdata = [row for row in csv.DictReader(csvfile)]

x=[]
males_y=[]
females_y=[]
every_y=[]
yrval=1968
for row in mortdata:
  x += [yrval]
  males_y += [row['Males']]
  females_y += [row['Females']]
  every_y += [row['Everyone']]
  yrval = yrval + 1

plt.plot(x, males_y, color='#1a61c3', label='Males', linewidth=1.8)
plt.plot(x, females_y, color='#bc108d', label='Females',
linewidth=1.8)
plt.plot(x, every_y, color='#747e8a', label='Everyone', linewidth=1.8)
plt.legend(loc=0, prop={'size':10})
plt.show()
```

The mortality rates were measured per 100,000 people. By dividing the population into separate age cohorts, the improvements in life expectancy are shown to have been ongoing, particularly showing most progress for the age group below 25. What exactly happened to the population falling under the age group of 25-44 (shown in red)? The narrative on Bloomberg lays out the reason very well by connecting another fact that the number of deaths caused by AIDS had an effect on that age group during that time.

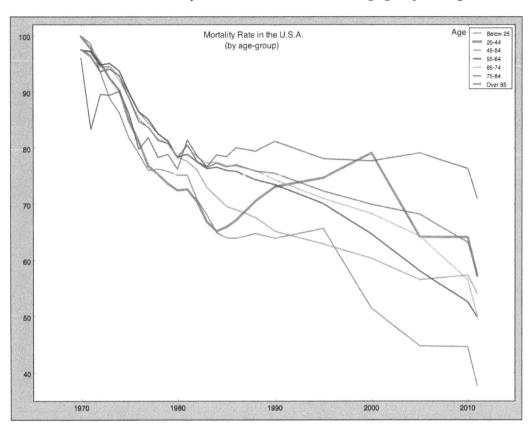

AIDS killed more than 40,000 Americans a year and 75 percent of them were in the age group of 25-44. Therefore, the unusual results are seen during that window of time.

```
import csv
import matplotlib.pyplot as plt

fig = plt.figure(figsize=(15,13))
plt.ylim(35,102)
```

```
plt.xlim(1965,2015)

colorsdata = ['#168cf8', '#ff0000', '#009f00', '#1d437c', '#eb912b',
'#8663ec', '#38762b']
labeldata = ['Below 25', '25-44', '45-54', '55-64', '65-74', '75-84',
'Over 85']

# using reader() instead of DictReader() so that we could loop to
# build y-values in list
with open('/Users/MacBook/Downloads/mortality2.csv') as csvfile:
  mortdata = [row for row in csv.reader(csvfile)]

x=[]
for row in mortdata:
  yrval = int(row[0])
  if ( yrval == 1969 ):
    y = [[row[1]],[row[2]],[row[3]],[row[4]],[row[5]],[row[6]],[r
ow[7]]]
  else:
   for col in range(0,7):
     y[col] += [row[col+1]]
  x += [yrval]

for col in range(0,7):
  if ( col == 1 ):
    plt.plot(x, y[col], color=colorsdata[col], label=labeldata[col],
linewidth=3.8)
   else:
     plt.plot(x, y[col], color=colorsdata[col], label=labeldata[col],
linewidth=2)

plt.legend(loc=0, prop={'size':10})
plt.show()
```

The difference between csv.reader() and csv.DictReader() is that when the input CSV file has fieldnames (or column names), DictReader() uses the fieldnames as keys and the actual value in that column as the data value. In the preceding example, we have used reader(), because it is convenient when there is looping involved (y[col] = [row[col+1]]). Moreover, with reader(), if the column names exist in the CSV file, that first row should be ignored.

We have also made filtered data for both these examples available as mortality1. csv and mortality2.csv at http://www.knapdata.com/python.

For `mortdata[:4]`, the result would be different in each of these methods of reading. In other words, the result of `mortdata[:4]` when we use `reader()` will be as follows:

```
[['1969', '100', '99.92', '97.51', '97.47', '97.54', '97.65',
'96.04'], ['1970', '98.63', '97.78', '97.16', '97.32', '96.2',
'96.51', '83.4'], ['1971', '93.53', '95.26', '94.52', '94.89',
'93.53', '93.73', '89.63'], ['1972', '88.86', '92.45', '94.58',
'95.14', '94.55', '94.1', '89.51']]
```

With `DictReader()`, assuming that the CSV file has fieldnames, the four rows will be displayed as follows:

```
[{'25-44': '99.92', '45-54': '97.51', '55-64': '97.47', '65-74':
'97.54', '75-84': '97.65', 'Below 25': '100', 'Over 85': '96.04',
'Year': '1969'},
 {'25-44': '97.78', '45-54': '97.16', '55-64': '97.32', '65-74':
'96.2', '75-84': '96.51', 'Below 25': '98.63', 'Over 85': '83.4',
'Year': '1970'},
 {'25-44': '95.26', '45-54': '94.52', '55-64': '94.89', '65-74':
'93.53', '75-84': '93.73', 'Below 25': '93.53', 'Over 85': '89.63',
'Year': '1971'},
 {'25-44': '92.45', '45-54': '94.58', '55-64': '95.14', '65-74':
'94.55', '75-84': '94.1', 'Below 25': '88.86', 'Over 85': '89.51',
'Year': '1972'}]
```

A few other example narratives

There are numerous examples that one can explore, visualize, interact and play with. Some notable ones are as follows:

- **How the recession reshaped the economy in 255 charts (NY Times)**: This narrative shows how, in five years since the end of the Great Recession, the economy regained the lost nine million jobs, highlighting which industries recovered faster than others. (Source: `http://tinyurl.com/nwdp3pp`.)

- **Washington Wizards shooting stars of 2013 (Washington Post)**: This interactive graphic was created a few years ago based on the performance of the Washington Wizards in 2013, trying to analyze and see how the signing of Paul Pierce could bring much improved shooting from the mid-range. (Source: `http://www.washingtonpost.com/wp-srv/special/sports/wizards-shooting-stars/`.)

Author-driven narratives

The New York Times produces some of the world's best data visualization, multimedia, and interactive stories. Their ambition for these projects has always been to meet the journalistic standards at a very prestigious level and to create genuinely new kinds of experiences for the readers. The storytelling culture among them is one of the sources of energy behind this work.

For example, there is a combination of data and author-driven narrative titled *The Geography of Chaos in Yemen*. On March 26, 2015, Saudi Arabian jets struck targets in Yemen in a drive against the Houthi rebel group. Yemen plays an important role for the key players such as Saudi Arabia, Iran, and the United States. The Houthis' influence has grown over the past years, which was captured visually by the authors at the NY Times.

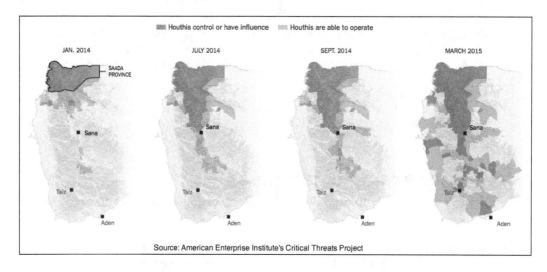

Yemen is home to one of Al Qaeda's most active branches in the Arabian Peninsula. Since 2009, the United States has carried out at least 100 airstrikes in Yemen. In addition to Al Qaeda's occupation, the Islamic State also has activities in that region, and recently, they claimed responsibility for the bombings at two Shiite mosques in Sana that killed more than 135 people. The following visualization comes from The Bureau of Investigative Journalism, American Enterprise Institute's Critical Threat Project:

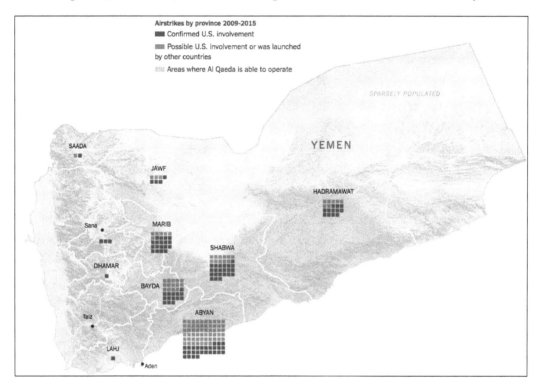

Another good example is the visualization of the Atlantic's past by David McCandless, which shows what the oceans were like before over-fishing. It is hard to imagine the damage that over-fishing is wreaking on the oceans. The effects are invisible, hidden in the ocean. The following image shows the biomass of the popularly-eaten fish in the North Atlantic Ocean in 1900 and 2000. The popularly-eaten fish include tuna, cod, haddock, hake, halibut, herring, mackerel, pollock, salmon, sea trout, striped bass, sturgeon, and turbot, many of which are now vulnerable or endangered.

Dr. Villy Christensen and his colleagues at the University of British Columbia used ecosystem models, underwater terrain maps, fish-catch records, and statistical analysis to render the biomass of the Atlantic fish at various points in this century.

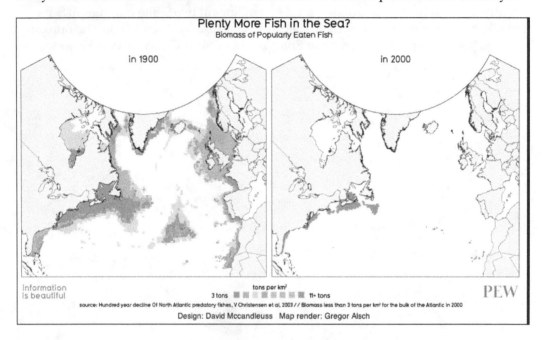

Perception and presentation methods

In the past, data size and variety did not impose much of a challenge; therefore, perceiving and analyzing data was straightforward. Today there are large quantities of data in innumerable fields, and visualization can provide valuable assistance to humans for perceiving and interacting with visualization of the data. Human factors contribute significantly to the whole visualization process in order to better understand data and aid in decision-making tasks.

Visualization techniques can be categorized into two areas:

- **Scientific visualization**: This involves scientific data with an inherent physical entity
- **Information visualization**: This involves abstract data (spatial or non-spatial)

Most visualization systems are designed so that humans and computers can cooperate, each performing the following tasks:

- Visually representing data to enhance data analysis
- Visually displaying models, interpretations of data, ideas, hypotheses, and insight
- Helping users to improve their models by finding either supporting or contradictory evidence for their hypotheses
- Helping users to organize and share their ideas

New insights into visual perception are arising from work in various disciplines besides information visualization, such as human factors and human-computer interaction. One of the great strengths of data visualization is our ability to process visual information much more rapidly than verbal information. Psychologists studied perceptual organization during the 1920s in Germany, and the first group of them was the Gestalt Theorists.

The Gestalt principles of perception

The word Gestalt means "organized whole" or, in other words, when parts identified individually have different characteristics to the whole. For example, for describing a tree, you can say that it has different parts such as the trunk, leaves, branches, fruit (in some cases). However, when we look at an entire tree, we are not conscious of the parts, but aware of the whole object—in this case, the tree.

The principles of Gestalt perception are as follows:

- **Proximity**: Objects that are close together or connected to each other are perceived as a group, reducing the need to process smaller objects separately.

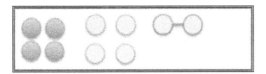

- **Similarity**: Objects that share similar attributes, color, or shape are perceived as a group.

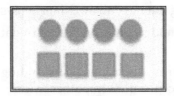

- **Common fate**: When both the principles of proximity and similarity are in place, a movement takes place. Then they appear to change grouping.

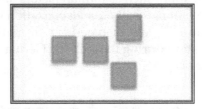

- **Good continuation**: Some things are important as a whole, which means if there are interruptions, then it changes the perceptive reading. In the following image, we perceive the two crossed lines instead of four lines meeting at the center:

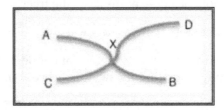

- **Closure**: Even if a part of the border of a shape is missing, we still tend to see the shape as completely enclosed by the border and ignore the gaps.

It is very useful to know these principles for creating any visualization method.

Let's elaborate this further with an example. Proximity refers to the visual approach of grouping shapes together if they appear similar to each other. Such a group is usually perceived as a single unit. For instance, the following image shows how one can distinguish proximity:

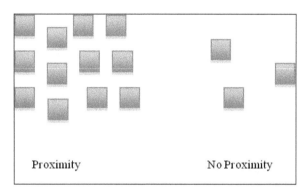

Proximity   No Proximity

Some best practices for visualization

The first important step one can take to make a great visualization is to know what is the goal behind the effort. How does one know if the visualization has a purpose? It is also very important to know who the audience is and how this will help them.

Once the answers to these questions are known, and the purpose of visualization is well understood, the next challenge is to choose the right method to present it. The most commonly-used types of visualization could further be categorized according to the following:

- Comparison and ranking
- Correlation
- Distribution
- Location-specific or geodata
- Part-to-whole relationships
- Trends over time

Comparison and ranking

Comparing and ranking can be done in more than one way, but the traditional way is by using bar charts. A bar chart is believed to encode quantitative values as length on the same baseline. However, it is not always the best way to display comparison and rankings. For instance, to display the top 12 countries in Africa by GDP, the following presentation is a creative way to visualize (courtesy: *Stats Legend, Andrew Gelman and Antony Unwin*):

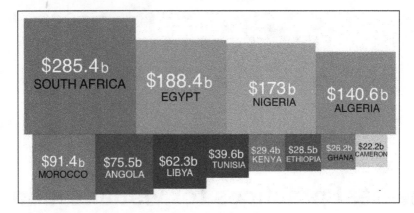

Correlation

A simple correlation analysis is a great place to start for identifying the relationships between measures, although correlation doesn't guarantee a relationship. To confirm that the relationship truly exists, a statistical methodology is often required. The following is an example to build a simple scatter plot to detect the correlations between two factors, say `gpa` and `tv` or `gpa` and `exercise` among the students from a university:

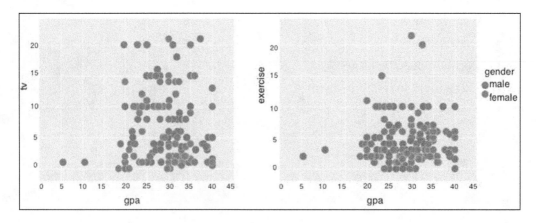

However, we can use other ways in order to display the correlation matrix. For instance, one can use scatter plots, heat maps, or some specific example to show the influence network amongst stocks in the S&P 100. (The following two plots are taken from *Statistical Tools for High Throughput Analysis* at http://www.sthda.com.) To emphasize further, a correlation matrix involves data in a matrix form. The data is correlated by using a scaled color map, as shown in the following examples. For more details, we suggest you to refer to the site, http://www.sthda.com.

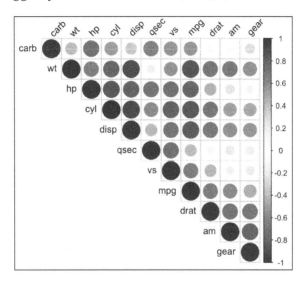

A correlation matrix is used to investigate the dependence between multiple variables at the same time. The result is a table containing the **correlation coefficients** between each variable and the others. Heat maps originated in 2D display of the values in a data matrix. There are many different color schemes that can be used to illustrate the heat map, with perceptual advantages and disadvantages for each.

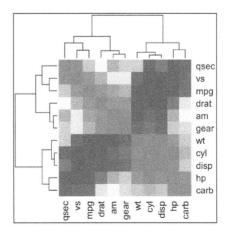

Distribution

A distribution analysis shows how the quantitative values are distributed across their range, and is therefore, extremely useful in data analysis. For example, compare the grade distribution of homework the midterm, the final exam, and the total course grade of a class of students. In this example, we will discuss two of the most commonly used chart types for this purpose. One is a **histogram** (as shown in the following image), and the other is a **box plot** or **box-and-whisker** plot.

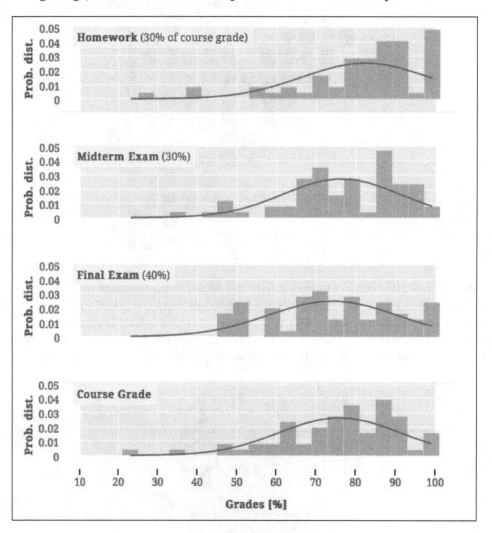

The shape of a histogram depends strongly on the specified bin size and locations. The box-and-whisker plots are excellent for displaying multiple distributions. They pack all the data points—in this case, grades per student—into a box-and-whisker display. Now you can easily identify the low values, the 25th-percentile values, the medians, the 75th-percentiles, and the maximum values across all categories—all at the same time.

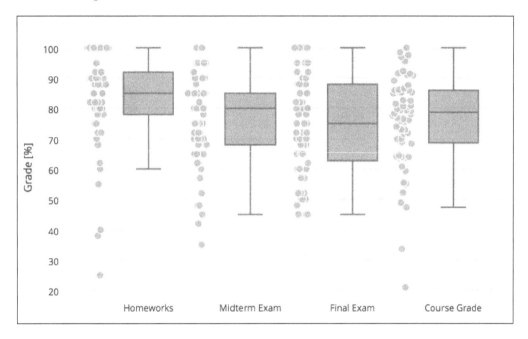

One of the many ways to conveniently plot these in Python is by using Plotly, which is an online analytics and visualization tool. Plotly provides online graphing, analytics, and statistics tools as well as scientific plotting libraries for Python, R, Julia, and JavaScript. For examples of histograms and box-and-whisker plots, refer to `https://plot.ly/python/histograms-and-box-plots-tutorial`.

Location-specific or geodata

Maps are the best way to display data that is location-specific. Maps are best used when paired with another chart that details what the map is displaying (such as a bar chart sorted from greatest to least, line chart showing the trends, and so on). For example, the following map shows the intensity of an earthquake compared across continents:

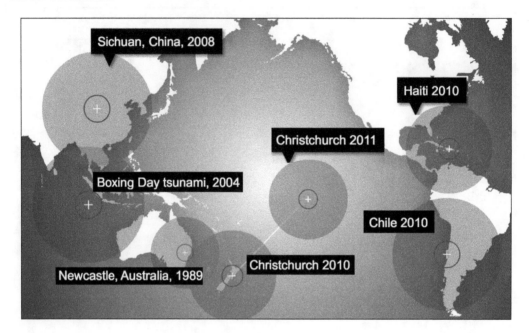

Part-to-whole relationships

Pie charts are known to be common for displaying part-to-whole relationships, but there are other ways to do it. Grouped bar charts are good for comparing each element in the categories with the others, and for comparing elements across categories. However, grouping makes it harder to tell the difference between the total of each group. This is where the stacked column charts come in.

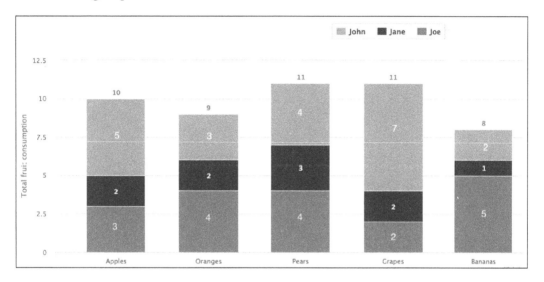

The stacked column charts are great for showing the total because they visually aggregate all the categories in a group. The downside is that it becomes harder to compare the sizes of the individual categories. Stacking also indicates a part-to-whole relationship.

Trends over time

One of the most frequently used visualization methods to analyze data is to display a trend over a period of time. In the following example, the investment in wearables startups from 2009-2015 has been plotted. It shows that the investment in wearables has been on the rise for a few years; activity shot through the roof in 2014, with 61 completed deals totaling $427 million, when compared to 43 deals worth only $166 million in 2013 (just a year earlier).

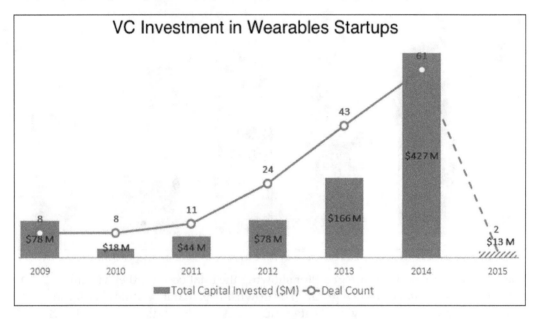

With this observation, it will be interesting to see how the marketplace evolves over the coming years.

Visualization tools in Python

Analyzing and visualizing data requires several software tools: a text editor to write the code (preferably syntax highlighted), Python and additional libraries to run and test the code, and perhaps a tool to present the results. There are two categories of software tools: general-purpose software tools and specific software components.

Development tools

The general-purpose software tool is an **integrated development environment (IDE)**, which is an application that has all the productivity tools within one package. These IDEs are usually very convenient from the standpoint of handling the Python libraries. More details about these IDE tools will be discussed in the following chapter. In this chapter, we'll limit our discussion to a brief introduction to *Canopy from Enthought* and *Anaconda from Continuum Analytics*.

The specific software component are Python plotting libraries such as `Bokeh`, `IPython`, `matplotlib`, `NetworkX`, `SciPy` and `NumPy`, `Scikit-learn`, and `Seaborn`. Both the IDEs have a very convenient way to handle the adding, removing, and updating to later versions of these plotting libraries.

Canopy from Enthought

Enthought Canopy has a free version that is released under the BSD-style license, and comes with **GraphCanvas**, **SciMath**, and **Chaco** as plotting tools, among several other libraries. It has an advanced text editor, integrated IPython console, graphics package manager, and online documentation links. The Canopy analysis environment streamlines data analysis, visualization, algorithm design, and application development for scientists, engineers, and analysts.

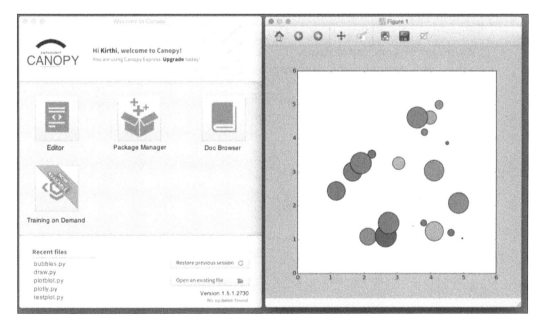

Anaconda from Continuum Analytics

Anaconda IDE is based on the conda application. Conda is an application for finding and installing software packages. A conda package is a binary tarball containing system-level libraries, Python modules, executable programs, or other components. Conda keeps track of the dependencies between packages and platform specifics, making it simple to create working environments from different sets of packages.

Anaconda has **sypder-app**, a scientific Python development environment, which has an IPython viewer as well. In addition to this, IPython can be launched as a GUI or a web-based notebook. The most convenient thing is that you can install Python in the home directory without touching the system-installed Python. Not all packages are ready to work with Python 3 as yet; therefore, it is better to use Python 2 with these IDEs.

IPython (`http://ipython.scipy.org/`) provides an enhanced, interactive Python shell, and is highly recommended mostly because data analysis and visualization is interactive in nature. IPython is supported on most platforms. Some additional features that come with IPython are as follows:

- **Tab completion**: This involves completion of variables, functions, methods, attributes, and filenames. Tab completion is achieved with the GNU Readline library (`http://tiswww.case.edu/php/chet/readline/rltop.html`) and is highly addictive. It is very hard to go back to a regular command-line interface after you are exposed to GNU Readline.

- **Command history capabilities**: This issues the command history for a full account of the previously used commands.

Interactive visualization

For a visualization to be considered interactive, it must satisfy two criteria:

- **Human input**: The control of some aspect of the visual representation of information must be available to humans
- **Response time**: The changes made by humans must be incorporated into the visualization in a timely manner

When large amounts of data must be processed to create a visualization, this becomes very hard, sometimes impossible, even with the current technology; therefore, "interactive visualization" is usually applied to systems that provide feedback to the users within several seconds of input. Many interactive visualization systems support a metaphor of navigation, analogous to navigation through the physical world.

The benefit of interaction is that people can explore a larger information space in a shorter time, which can be understood through one platform. However, a disadvantage to this interaction is that it requires a lot of time to exhaustively check every possibility to test the visualization system. Moreover, designing systems to guarantee immediate response to user actions can require significant algorithmic attention.

Any visualization method needs a good plan of layout. Some layout methods automatically lead to symmetrical drawings; alternatively, some drawing methods start by finding symmetries in the data. Interactive visualization is implemented using event listeners, and to some, this is well understood as common knowledge, but in any case, the following section describes what it is all about.

Event listeners

An event listener is a process that is used when a mouse is either moved or clicked. Technically, there are many kinds of events, but purely for interactive visualization, you need to only know what happens when the user navigates through the visualization with the mouse. The latency of interaction, that is, the time it takes for the system to respond to the mouse action, matters immensely.

The most obvious principle is that the user should indeed have some sort of confirmation that the action has completed, rather than being left dangling wondering whether the action is still in progress. Thus, feedback such as highlighting a selected item is a good way to confirm that the desired operation has completed successfully. Visual feedback should typically take place within the immediate response latency class of around one second. The following is an example of a JavaScript event listener in Google Charts:

```
chart = new google.visualization.PieChart(document.getElementById(
'chart_div'));
google.visualization.events.addListener(chart, 'select',
selectHandler);
chart.draw(data, options);

function selectHandler() {
  var selectedItem = chart.getSelection()[0];
  var value = data.getValue(selectedItem.row, 0);
  alert('The user selected ' + value);
}
```

Another principle is that if an action takes significantly longer than a user would naturally expect, some kind of progress indicator should be shown to the user. It is much easier to write event listeners in JavaScript, but in order to create an interactive visualization using plotting methods written in Python, one should use Plotly.

There is another module, **graph-tool** (https://graph-tool.skewed.de), that can be harnessed to perform animations in a straightforward manner. It uses GTK+ to display animations in an interactive window as well as off-screen to a file. The idea is to easily generate visualizations, which can be used in presentations and embedded in websites.

Layouts

In order to display data visually and efficiently, it is very important to know the layout methods. Aesthetics is one of the criteria that measures the strength and weakness of the layout algorithm. In order to make the layout results more readable, the structure needs to have either an hierarchy or a symmetry, if possible; one critical factor is the utilization of space.

A good layout is essential for untangling and understanding any graphic. Generally, each layout is uniquely suited to different kinds of data visualization in order to be best understood. A few notable layout methods are as follows:

- Circular layout
- Radial layout
- Balloon layout

Circular layout

Tables are natural containers for data. Whenever information is presented, chances are very high that it is presented by means of a table. In many cases, however, when this information is complex (and the table, therefore, is large), a tabular presentation is difficult to parse visually and the patterns in the tabulated data remain opaque.

In other words, a useful container is not always a useful way to present data. The table presents individual data very well, but their inter-relationship and the patterns that they compose are hardly visible. A circular layout can use several different combinations (qualitative and quantitative) to be displayed in a single visualization as shown in the following image:

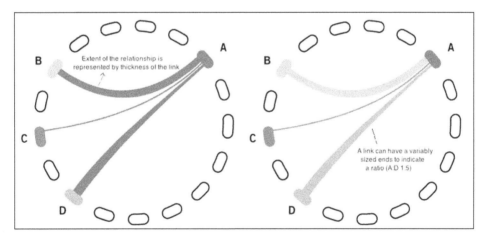

For instance, it is intuitive to display a complex relationship within a limited space as shown in the preceding image.

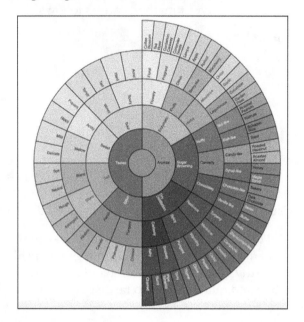

The preceding image shows an example of a complex hierarchical relationship displayed in a circular layout.

Radial layout

Sunburst visualization is a radial space-filling visualization technique for displaying tree-like structures (as shown in the preceding image). There are other space-filling visualization methods that use other visual encodings for describing hierarchies. For example, the treemap is a space-filling visualization that uses "containment" to show "parent-child" relationships. There are a couple of subtle changes that can improve the way the information is communicated by this visualization.

Since the length of each orbit increases with the radius, there tends to be more room for the nodes. A radial tree will spread the larger number of nodes over a larger area as the levels increase.

Balloon layout

There are different variations to a balloon layout, and one may even view these as bubbles. However, if we use different colors and sizes of the balloons (or circles/bubbles), a lot more can be displayed in this visualization, as shown in the following image:

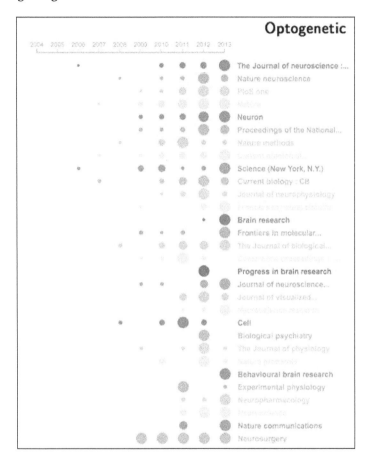

Summary

The principles of visualization methods are useful to follow for creating an effective story. The narratives explained in this chapter give an idea of aesthetics and the vast variation of approaches.

The goal of data visualization is to communicate information clearly and efficiently to the users, via the visual display method selected. Effective visualization helps in analyzing and reasoning about data and evidence. It makes complex data more accessible, understandable, and usable. Users may have particular analytical tasks, such as making comparisons or understanding causality, and the design principle of the graphic follows the task.

Tables are generally used where users will look up a specific measure of a variable, while charts of various types are used to show patterns or relationships in the data for one or more variables.

Data visualization is both an art and a science and it is like solving a mathematical problem. There is no one right way to solve it. Similarly, there is no one right way to create a visualization method. There are many tools out there for visualization, and we know a few tools that support Python. In the following chapter, more details about these tools will be discussed.

3
Getting Started with the Python IDE

Python is a widely used programming language that has been around for over 20 years. Among many other things, this language is quite popular for its simplicity and dynamic typing. *Type(datum)* dynamically determines the type of the data object. It has a syntax that allows programmers to write a very few lines of code. Python supports multiple programming paradigms that include functional, object-oriented, and procedural styles.

Python interpreters are available on almost every operating system that is in use. Its built-in data structures combined with dynamic binding make it very attractive to use as a high performance language to connect the existing manipulative components quickly. Even in distributed applications, Python is used as a glue in conjunction with Hive (NoSQL) to accomplish something very quick and efficient. Python, which is powerful and popular in the software development community, needs an interactive environment to create, edit, test, debug, and run programs.

An **integrated development environment** (**IDE**) is a software application that provides a comprehensive and powerful set of tools to build applications for target systems that run Windows, Linux, or Mac OS operating systems. These tools provide a single and consistent integrated environment and are designed to maximize productivity. There are many choices of IDE for Python programming. The details will be discussed in the following section of this chapter. In addition, we will discuss the following topics:

- The IDE tools in Python
- The installation guide — instructions to download and install tools
- The conda **command-line interface** (**CLI**) and Spyder

- The data visualization tools in the IDE tools that are specific to libraries that are useful for visualization
- Interactive visualization packages
- Some plotting examples using the IDE tools

The IDE tools in Python

Analyzing and visualizing data requires several software tools: a text editor to write code (preferably the syntax highlight), additional tools and libraries to run and test the code, and perhaps another set of tools to present the results. There are many advantages of an IDE. Some notable ones are as follows:

- The syntax highlight (showing errors or warnings right away)
- Stepping through code in the debug mode
- The interactive console
- Integration with the interactive graphic notebook (such as IPython)

Python 3.x versus Python 2.7

Python 3.x is not backward compatible with the 2.x version. This is why Python 2.7 is still being used. In this book, we will use Python 2.7 and try not to focus on Python 3.x. This issue is beyond the scope of this book, and we recommend that you search for information about how to write code that works with different versions. Some IDE tools have specific instructions to use both these versions. In some cases, the code may have to be written a little differently.

Types of interactive tools

Before discussing further about the Python IDEs, it is important to consider the different ways available to display interactive data visualization. There are many options to create interactive data visualization, but here, we will consider only two popular tools to accomplish this:

- IPython
- Plotly

IPython

In the year 2001, Fernando Perez began working on IPython, an enhanced interactive Python shell with improvements, such as history caching, profiles, object information, and session logging. Originally focused on the interactive computing in Python, it later included Julia, R, Ruby, and so on. Some features—such as automatic parenthesizing and tab completion—are small timesavers and very productive in terms of usability. In standard Python, to do tab completion, you have to import a few modules, whereas IPython offers tab completion by default.

IPython provides the following rich set of tools for Python scripting:

- Terminal commands and Qt-based tools that are convenient
- An interactive environment that is purely a web-based notebook with the same core features as the standalone notebook; it also supports code, text, mathematical expressions, and inline plots
- A convenient interactive data visualization; this capability has been the reason for many IDEs having integrated support for IPython
- Easy-to-use and high-performance tools for multiprocess computing

The four most helpful commands for IPython with a brief description:

Command	Description
?	This specifies the introduction and overview of IPython's features
%quickref	This denotes quick reference
--help-all	This specifies Python's help
%who/%whos	This gives information about identifiers

The IPython notebook is a web-based interactive computational environment. Here, you can merge code, mathematics, and plotting into a single document.

IPython (http://ipython.scipy.org/) provides an enhanced interactive Python shell and is highly recommended mostly because data analysis and visualization are interactive in nature. IPython is supported on most platforms. Some added features that come with IPython are:

- **Tab completion**: This involves the completion of variables, functions, methods, attributes, and filenames. Tab completion is achieved using the GNU Readline library (http://tiswww.case.edu/php/chet/readline/rltop.html). It is very hard to go back to a regular command-line interface after you have been exposed to GNU Readline.

- **Command history capabilities**: This issues the command history for a full account of the previously used commands.

An example that was run on IPython is shown in the following screenshot. To learn more about IPython and the IPython notebook, refer to http://nbviewer.ipython.org.

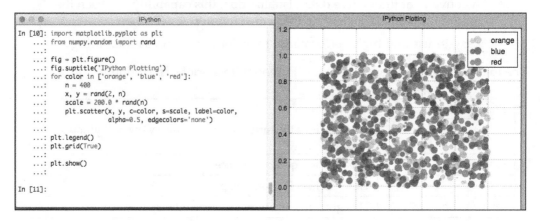

Plotly

Plotly is an online analytics and data visualization tool that provides online graphing, analytics, and statistical tools for better collaboration. This tool was built using Python with a user interface that uses JavaScript and a visualization library that uses D3.js, HTML, and CSS. Plotly includes the scientific graphic libraries for many languages, such as Arduino, Julia, MATLAB, Perl, Python, and R. For an example source of Plotly, refer to https://plot.ly/~etpinard/84/fig-31a-hans-roslings-bubble-chart-for-the-year-2007/.

The following is the infamous example of bubble chart that shows GDP per capita around the globe.

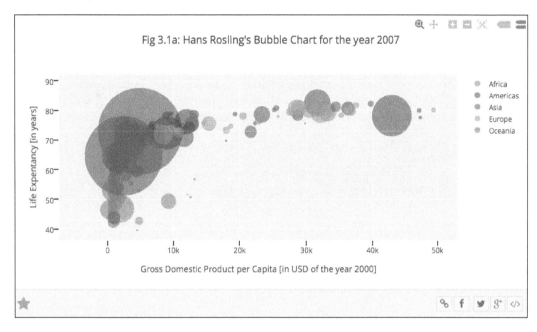

Plotly provides a convenient way to convert plots from `matplotlib` to Plotly, as shown in the following code (assuming that you have a Plotly account and signed in with your credentials):

```
import plotly.plotly as py
import matplotlib.pyplot as plt
#auto sign-in with credentials or use py.sign_in()
mpl_fig_obj = plt.figure()
#code for creating matplotlib plot
py.plot_mpl(mpl_fig_obj)
```

Types of Python IDE

The following are some of the popular Python IDEs that are available today:

- **PyCharm**: This specifies the user interface based on Java Swing
- **PyDev**: This denotes the user interface based on SWT (works on Eclipse)
- **Interactive Editor for Python (IEP)**
- **Canopy from Enthought**: This is based on PyQt
- **The Anaconda distribution of Spyder from Continuum Analytics**: This is also based on PyQt

PyCharm

PyCharm is one of the few popular IDEs that has great features, and the community version is free. The PyCharm 4.0.6 community edition is the current version that is available for free download at https://www.jetbrains.com/pycharm/download. They have shortcuts reference cards available for Mac, Linux, and Windows.

Dr. Pedro Kroger had written an elaborate description on PyCharm at http://pedrokroger.net/getting-started-pycharm-python-ide/. You can refer to this link for more details. Among many interesting features, the code wizard and the NumPy array viewer are shown in the following screenshot:

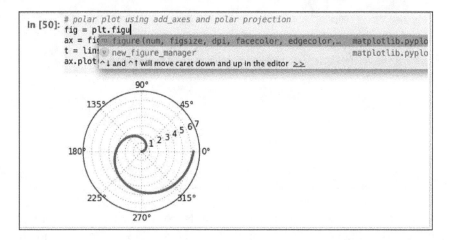

Polar projection can be done quickly, as shown in the preceding screenshot, and the creation of an array of random samples is shown in the following screenshot:

```
rand_4 = 5 * np.random.random_sample((10, 10, 10, 10)) - 1

rand_5 = 5 * np.random.random_sample((10, 10, 10, 30, 30)) - 1

rand_l = 5 * np.random.random_sample((1000, 1000)) - 1
```

Array View: rand_5[0][0][0][0:30, 0:30]

	0	1	2	3	4	5	6
0	3.30686	0.76201	2.59465	1.95064	2.13588	-0.47945	0.25524
1	0.69049	2.40274	0.16976	1.61471	3.01351	-0.02497	-0.5104
2	2.16509	3.30983	2.89093	2.91995	-0.89928	3.41354	-0.9305
3	-0.56654	0.32871	-0.25487	2.91167	3.68438	-0.26844	3.22064
4	2.47725	0.71579	-0.92717	0.44241	3.21497	3.64521	0.34920
5	2.51846	-0.69581	-0.67700	3.45241	-0.87558	2.04674	1.62063
6	2.43312	-0.00153	3.68738	0.20117	2.82539	-0.71048	3.16096
7	-0.37831	-0.31096	0.29403	1.40866	1.23149	-0.69872	0.40280
8	3.89901	2.48931	0.48815	1.94214	1.04629	1.25740	2.94104
9	2.86190	2.72455	2.11487	3.43960	1.39577	-0.79483	2.23903

A similar random sample is created in a different IDE (such as Spyder); here is an example:

```
rand_4 = np.random.random_sample((2,2,2,2))-1
array([[[[-0.6565232 , -0.2920045 ],
[-0.45976502, -0.70469325]],
[[-0.80218558, -0.77538009],
[-0.34687551, -0.42498698]]],
[[[-0.60869175, -0.9553122 ],
[-0.05888953, -0.70585856]],
[[-0.69856656, -0.21664848],
[-0.29017137, -0.61972867]]]])
```

PyDev

PyDev is a plugin for the Eclipse IDE. In other words, rather than creating a new IDE, a plugin for Eclipse was sufficient to make use of other default functionalities that a regular IDE may have. PyDev supports code refactoring, graphical debugging, interactive console, code analysis, and code folding.

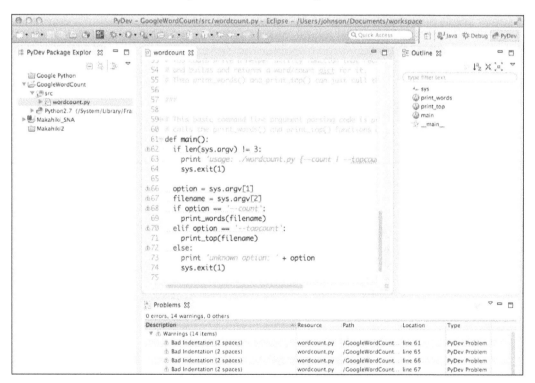

You can install PyDev as a plugin for Eclipse or install LiClipse, an advanced Eclipse distribution. LiClipse adds support not only for Python, but also for languages such as CoffeeScript, JavaScript, Django templates, and so on.

PyDev comes preinstalled in LiClipse, but it requires Java 7 to be installed first. For the complete installation steps, you can refer to `http://pydev.org/manual_101_install.html`.

Interactive Editor for Python (IEP)

IEP is another Python IDE that has similar tools available in other IDEs, but appears similar to any tool that you may have used on Microsoft Windows.

IEP is a cross-platform Python IDE aimed at interactivity and introspection, which makes it very suitable for scientific computing. Its practical design is aimed at simplicity and efficiency.

IEP consists of two main components, the editor and the shell, and uses a set of pluggable tools to help the programmer in various ways. Some example tools are source structure, project manager, interactive help, and workspace. Some key features are as follows:

- Code introspection like in any modern IDE
- Either run the Python script from the command line or interactively via a file or the IPython interface
- Shells run as a background process
- Multiple shells can use different Python versions (from v2.4 to 3.x)

The following screenshot shows how you can use two different versions of Python in the same IDE:

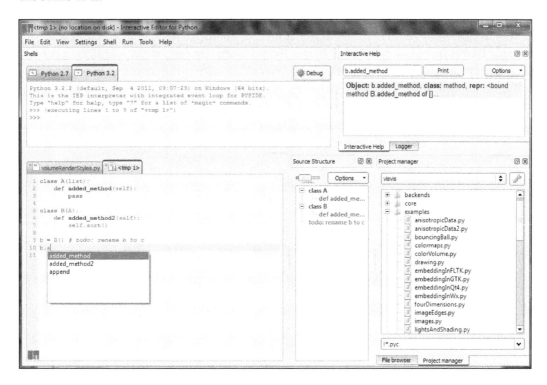

Some people do not consider IEP as an IDE tool, but it serves the purpose of developing the programs of Python, editing them, and running them. It supports multiple Python shells simultaneously. Therefore, it is a very productive tool for someone who wants to program using more than one GUI toolkit, such as PySide, PyQt4, GTK, and Tk interactively.

IEP is written in (pure) Python 3 and uses the Qt GUI toolkit, but it can be used to execute code on any Python version available. You can download IEP from `http://www.iep-project.org/downloads.html`.

Canopy from Enthought

Enthought Canopy has a free version that is released under the BSD-style license, which comes with **GraphCanvas**, **SciMath**, and **Chaco** as plotting tools, among several other libraries. Like all the IDEs, it has a text editor. It also has the IPython console that is quite useful to be able to run and visualize results. In addition, it comes with a graphics package manager as well. When Canopy is launched, it gives an option with an **Editor**, **Package Manager**, and **Doc Browser** to choose from. One may also attempt to use their training materials, as shown in the following screenshot:

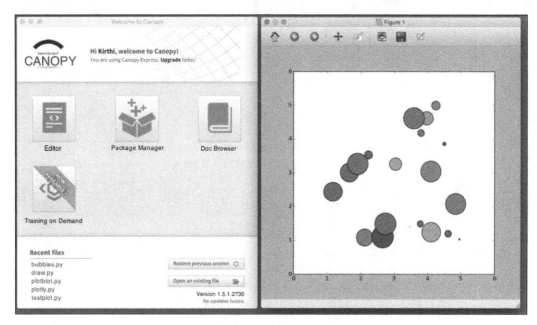

Besides other development code, Canopy has the IPython notebook integrated and convenient functions that you can use to create data visualization. Like most IDEs, this has an editor, a file browser, and the IPython console. In addition, there is a status display that shows the current editing status. These components of Canopy IDE mainly perform the following:

- **The file browser**: With this, you can read or write Python programs from the hard drive

- **The Python code editor**: This specifies a syntax-highlighted code editor with additional features specifically meant for Python code

- **The Python pane**: This is an integrated IPython (interactive Python) prompt that can be used to run the Python program interactively, rather than from a file

- **The editor status bar**: This can be used to display the line number, the column number, the file type, and the file path

The following screenshot shows the number highlighted. This represents the components of IDEs described before this. The file browser and Python panes can be dragged and dropped onto the different positions in a code editor window or outside the borders. When a pane is dragged, the location where it could dock is highlighted in blue, as shown in the following screenshot:

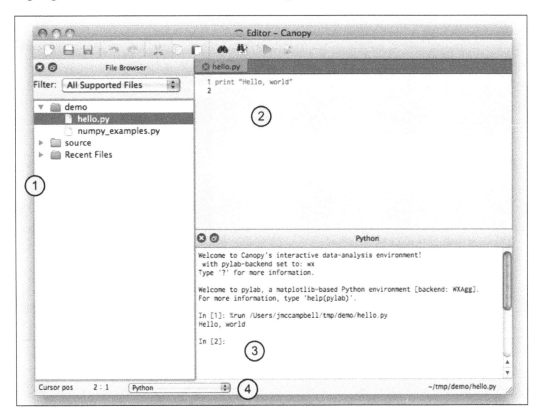

The documentation is organized via a browser called *Canopy Documentation Browser*, which is accessible from the **Help** menu. This includes the links to documentation for some commonly used Python packages.

One significant feature of *Documentation Browser* is that it provides easy access to the sample code presented in the documentation. When a user right-clicks on a sample code box, a display to the context menu is shown. Further, you can select the **Copy code** option to copy the contents of the code block into Canopy's copy-and-paste buffer to be used in an editor.

Canopy comes in several different products for individuals, and the free version is called **Canopy Express** with approximately 100 core packages. This free version is a useful tool for easy Python development for scientific and analytic computing. You can download this at `https://store.enthought.com/downloads/` after selecting the target operating system as one of Windows, Linux, or Mac OS.

One of the challenges in the Python development environment is that managing the packages of many different libraries and tools can be a very time-consuming and daunting task. This is how their **Documentation Browser** looks like.

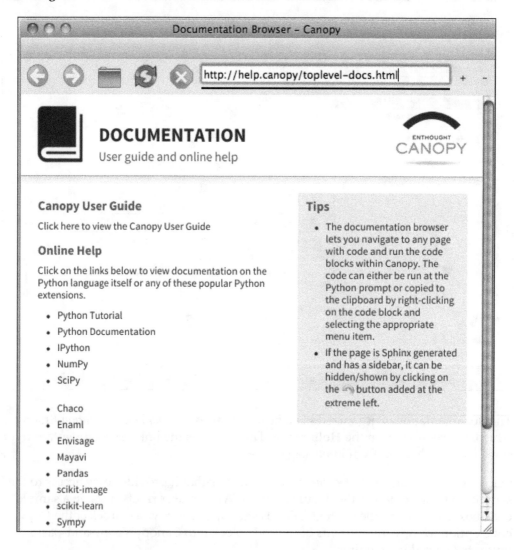

Canopy has a package manager that can be used to discover the Python packages available with Canopy and decide which additional ones to install and which ones to remove. There is a convenient search interface to find and install any available packages and to revert to the previous states of packages.

Canopy uses a Python capability to determine the Python packages that are available. When Canopy starts, it looks for packages first in the virtual environment and displays them, as shown in the following screenshot:

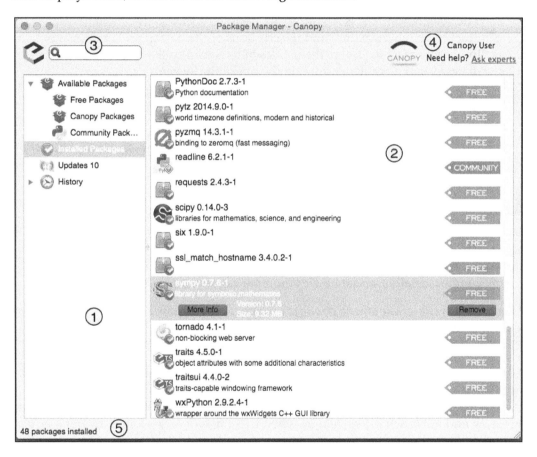

The numbered highlighted areas of the IDE are:

1. **The navigation panel**: This is similar to any IDE; the navigation has a tree-list kind of structure to select the components of the package manager.

2. **The main view area**: Once the selection on the left-hand side changes, the right-hand side panel will display the item selected, along with the associated package listings (as shown in the preceding screenshot), the specific package information with a button titled **More Info**, and so on.

3. **The search bar**: This is similar to any search functionality and helps to quickly search the names and descriptions of the packages. For example, the typing machine filters the list down to eleven packages (the number of matches may vary depending on the operating system).

4. **The subscription status and help**: This is where the link to subscription and the name of the account currently in use will be displayed.

5. **The status bar**: For every navigation that the user makes, the status bar will show the details about the current state of results based on the navigational changes.

Anaconda from Continuum Analytics

Anaconda is one of the most popular IDEs that is being used by the community. It comes with a compiled long list of packages that are already integrated. This IDE is based on the core component called conda (which is explained in detail later), and you may either install or update the Python packages using `conda` or `pip`.

Anaconda is a free collection of powerful packages for Python that enables large-scale data management, analysis, and visualization for business intelligence, scientific analysis, engineering, machine learning, and more.

Anaconda has a **Scientific PYthon Development EnviRonment (Spyder)**, which has an IPython viewer as well. In addition, IPython can be launched as a GUI or a web-based notebook. The most convenient aspect is that you can install Python in a home directory and not touch the system installed Python. Not all packages are yet ready to work with Python 3; therefore, it is better to use Python 2 with these IDEs. The Anaconda IDE has two important components and is based on the `conda` package manager. The two components are `conda` and `spyder`.

The following screenshot appears when Anaconda is launched. This gives users several options that include the IPython console, the IPython notebook, the Spyder IDE, and glueviz:

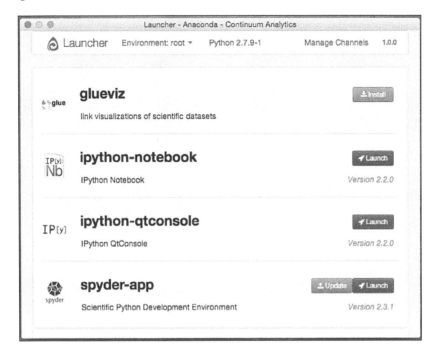

An overview of Spyder

Spyder is a Python development environment that comes with the following components:

- **The Python code editor**: This comes with a separate browser for functions, and the class editor comes with a support for Pylint code analysis. Code completion has become a norm today and is convenient on all the IDEs, so it supports this too.

- **The interactive console**: The Python language is most suited for interactive work; therefore, it is imperative that consoles have all the necessary tools that support instant evaluation of the code written in the editor.

- **Exploring variables**: Exploring variables during any interactive execution helps in the overall productivity. Editing the variables is also possible, such as a dictionary and sometimes arrays.

The code editor and the IPython console are shown in the following screenshot:

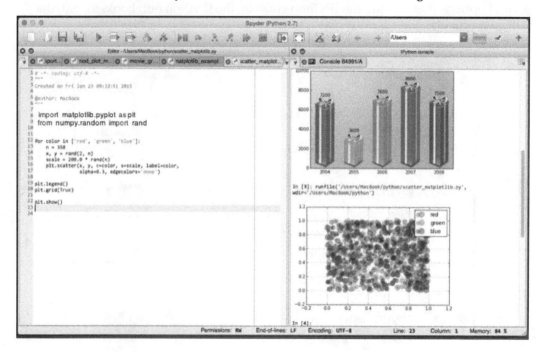

An overview of conda

Conda is a command-line tool used for managing environments and the packages of Python, rather than using `pip`. There are ways to query and search the packages, create new environments if necessary, and install and update the Python packages in the existing conda environments. This command-line tool also keeps track of dependencies between packages and platform specifics, helping you to create working environments from the different combination of packages. To check which version of conda is running, you can enter the following code (in my environment, it shows the 3.10.1 version):

```
Conda -v
3.10.1
```

A **conda environment** is a filesystem directory that contains a specific collection of conda packages. As a concrete example, you may want to have one environment that provides NumPy 1.7 and another environment that provides NumPy 1.6 for legacy testing; conda makes this kind of mixing and matching easy. To begin using an environment, simply set the PATH variable to point to its bin directory.

Let's take a look at an example of how to install a package called SciPy with conda. Assuming that you have installed Anaconda correctly and conda is available in the running path, you may have to enter the following code to install SciPy:

```
$ conda install scipy

Fetching package metadata: ....
Solving package specifications: .
Package plan for installation in environment /Users/MacBook/anaconda:

The following packages will be downloaded:

    package                    |            build
    ---------------------------|-----------------
    flask-0.10.1               |           py27_1        129 KB
    itsdangerous-0.23          |           py27_0         16 KB
    jinja2-2.7.1               |           py27_0        307 KB
    markupsafe-0.18            |           py27_0         19 KB
    werkzeug-0.9.3             |           py27_0        385 KB

The following packages will be linked:

    package                    |            build
    ---------------------------|-----------------
    flask-0.10.1               |           py27_1
    itsdangerous-0.23          |           py27_0
    jinja2-2.7.1               |           py27_0
    markupsafe-0.18            |           py27_0
    python-2.7.5               |               2
    readline-6.2               |               1
    sqlite-3.7.13              |               1
    tk-8.5.13                  |               1
    werkzeug-0.9.3             |           py27_0
    zlib-1.2.7                 |               1

Proceed ([y]/n)?
```

You should note that any dependencies on the package that is being tried to install would be recognized, downloaded, and linked automatically. If any Python package needs to be installed or updated, you will have to use the following code:

```
conda install <package name>  or conda update <package name>
```

Here is an example of package update from the command line using conda (to update matplotlib):

```
conda update matplotlib


Fetching package metadata: ....
Solving package specifications: .
Package plan for installation in environment /Users/MacBook/anaconda:


The following packages will be downloaded:

    package                    |                build
    ---------------------------|-----------------
    freetype-2.5.2             |                    0         691 KB
    conda-env-2.1.4            |             py27_0          15 KB
    numpy-1.9.2                |             py27_0         2.9 MB
    pyparsing-2.0.3            |             py27_0          63 KB
    pytz-2015.2                |             py27_0         175 KB
    setuptools-15.0            |             py27_0         436 KB
    conda-3.10.1               |             py27_0         164 KB
    python-dateutil-2.4.2      |             py27_0         219 KB
    matplotlib-1.4.3           |         np19py27_1        40.9 MB
    ------------------------------------------------------------
                                           Total:        45.5 MB

The following NEW packages will be INSTALLED:

    python-dateutil: 2.4.2-py27_0

The following packages will be UPDATED:

    conda:          3.10.0-py27_0      --> 3.10.1-py27_0
```

```
conda-env:      2.1.3-py27_0      --> 2.1.4-py27_0
freetype:       2.4.10-1          --> 2.5.2-0
matplotlib:     1.4.2-np19py27_0  --> 1.4.3-np19py27_1
numpy:          1.9.1-py27_0      --> 1.9.2-py27_0
pyparsing:      2.0.1-py27_0      --> 2.0.3-py27_0
pytz:           2014.9-py27_0     --> 2015.2-py27_0
setuptools:     14.3-py27_0       --> 15.0-py27_0
```

```
Proceed ([y]/n)?
```

In order to check the packages that are installed using Anaconda, navigate to the command line and enter the following command to quickly display the list of all the packages installed in the default environment:

```
conda list
```

In addition, you can always install a package with the usual means, for example, `pip install`, or from the source using a `setup.py` file. Although conda is the preferred packaging tool, there is nothing special about Anaconda that prevents the usage of a standard Python packaging tool (such as `pip`).

IPython is not required, but it is highly recommended. IPython should be installed after Python, GNU Readline, and PyReadline are installed. Anaconda and Canopy do these things by default. There are Python packages that are used in all the examples in this book for a good reason. In the following section, we have updated this list.

Visualization plots with Anaconda

From getting data, manipulating and processing data to visualizing and communicating the research results, Python and Anaconda support a variety of processes in the scientific data workflow. Python can be used in a wide variety of applications (even beyond scientific computing); users can adopt this language quickly and don't need to learn new software or programming languages. Python's open source availability enhances the research results and enables users to connect with a large community of scientists and engineers around the world.

The following are some of the common plotting libraries that you can use with Anaconda:

- **matplotlib**: This is one of the most popular plotting libraries for Python. Coupled with NumPy and SciPy, this is one of the major driving forces in the scientific Python community. IPython has a pylab mode, which was specifically designed to perform interactive plotting using matplotlib.

- **Plotly**: This is a collaborative plotting and analytics platform that works on a browser. It supports interactive graphs using IPython notebooks. Graphs are interactive and can be styled by modifying the code and viewing the results interactively. Any plotting code that is generated using matplotlib can be easily exported to a Plotly version.

- **Veusz**: This is a GPL-scientific plotting package written in Python and PyQt. Veusz can also be embedded in other Python programs.

- **Mayavi**: This is a three-dimensional plotting package that is fully scriptable from Python and is similar to a simple pylab and MATLAB-like interface for plotting arrays.

- **NetworkX**: This is a Python language software package for the creation, manipulation, and study of the structure, dynamics, and functions of complex networks.

- **pygooglechart**: This is a powerful package that enables you to create visualization methods and allows you to interface with the Google Chart API.

The surface-3D plot

Three-dimensional plots are generated from the data defined as Z as a function of (X, Y). This is mathematically denoted as $Z=f(X,Y)$. In our example here, we will plot $Z=sin(sqrt(X2+Y2))$, and this is essentially similar to a two-dimensional parabola. The following steps need to be followed for our plot:

1. First, generate the X and Y grid with the following code:

```
import numpy as np

X = np.arange(-4, 4, 0.25)
Y = np.arange(-4, 4, 0.25)
X, Y = np.meshgrid(X, Y)
Generate the Z data:
R = np.sqrt(X**2 + Y**2)
Z = np.sin(R)
```

Plotting a simple three-dimensional surface *sin(sqrt(X**2+Y**2))* using the
`mpl_toolkits` package is shown here; the blow and the plot diagram is
represented using a color bar:

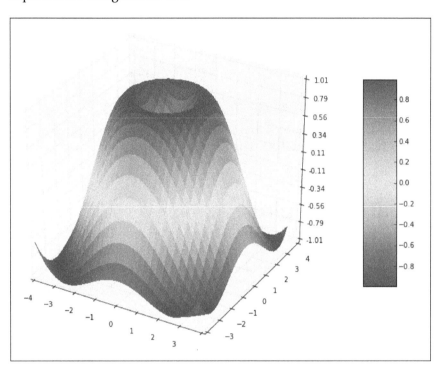

2. Then, plot the surface, as shown in the following code:

```
from mpl_toolkits.mplot3d import Axes3d
from matplotlib import cm
from matplotlib.ticker import LinearLocator, FormatStrFormatter
import matplotlib.pyplot as plt
import numpy as np

fig = plt.figure(figsize=(12,9))
ax = fig.gca(projection='3d')
X = np.arange(-4, 4, 0.25)
Y = np.arange(-4, 4, 0.25)
X, Y = np.meshgrid(X, Y)
R = np.sqrt(X**2 + Y**2)
Z = np.sin(R)
```

```
    surf = ax.plot_surface(X, Y, Z, rstride=1, cstride=1, cmap=cm.
    coolwarm, linewidth=0, antialiased=False)

    ax.set_zlim(-1.01, 1.01)
    ax.zaxis.set_major_locator(LinearLocator(10))
    ax.zaxis.set_major_formatter(FormatStrFormatter('%.02f'))

    fig.colorbar(surf, shrink=0.6, aspect=6)

    plt.show()
```

In order to make this three-dimensional plot work, you have to make sure that matplotlib and NumPy are installed. The default package in Anaconda comes with these installed.

The square map plot

With the comparison and ranking example that we discussed in the previous chapter to display the top 12 countries in Africa by GDP using the squarify algorithm (with matplotlib), you can obtain a plot that looks similar to a tree map, as shown in the following code:

```
# Squarified Treemap Layout : source file (squarify.py)
# Implements algorithm from Bruls, Huizing, van Wijk, "Squarified
Treemaps"
# squarify was created by Uri Laserson
# primarily intended to support d3.js

def normalize_sizes(sizes, dx, dy):
  total_size = sum(sizes)
  total_area = dx * dy
  sizes = map(float, sizes)
  sizes = map(lambda size: size * total_area / total_size, sizes)
  return sizes

def pad_rectangle(rect):
  if rect['dx'] > 2:
    rect['x'] += 1
    rect['dx'] -= 2
  if rect['dy'] > 2:
    rect ['y'] += 1
    rect['dy'] -= 2

def layoutrow(sizes, x, y, dx, dy):
  covered_area = sum(sizes)
```

```
    width = covered_area / dy
    rects = []
    for size in sizes:
      rects.append({'x': x, 'y': y, 'dx': width, 'dy': size / width})
      y += size / width
    return rects


def layoutcol(sizes, x, y, dx, dy):
  covered_area = sum(sizes)
  height = covered_area / dx
  rects = []
  for size in sizes:
    rects.append({'x': x, 'y': y, 'dx': size / height, 'dy': height})
    x += size / height
  return rects

def layout(sizes, x, y, dx, dy):
  return layoutrow(sizes, x, y, dx, dy) if dx >= dy else
layoutcol(sizes, x, y, dx, dy)

def leftoverrow(sizes, x, y, dx, dy):
  covered_area = sum(sizes)
  width = covered_area / dy
  leftover_x = x + width
  leftover_y = y
  leftover_dx = dx - width
  leftover_dy = dy
  return (leftover_x, leftover_y, leftover_dx, leftover_dy)

def leftovercol(sizes, x, y, dx, dy):
  covered_area = sum(sizes)
  height = covered_area / dx
  leftover_x = x
  leftover_y = y + height
  leftover_dx = dx
  leftover_dy = dy - height
  return (leftover_x, leftover_y, leftover_dx, leftover_dy)

def leftover(sizes, x, y, dx, dy):
  return leftoverrow(sizes, x, y, dx, dy) if dx >= dy else
leftovercol(sizes, x, y, dx, dy)

def worst_ratio(sizes, x, y, dx, dy):
```

```
    return max([max(rect['dx'] / rect['dy'], rect['dy'] / rect['dx'])
for rect in layout(sizes, x, y, dx, dy)])

def squarify(sizes, x, y, dx, dy):
  sizes = map(float, sizes)
  if len(sizes) == 0:
    return []
  if len(sizes) == 1:
    return layout(sizes, x, y, dx, dy)
  # figure out where 'split' should be
  i = 1
  while i < len(sizes) and worst_ratio(sizes[:i], x, y, dx, dy) >=
worst_ratio(sizes[:(i+1)], x, y, dx, dy):
    i += 1
  current = sizes[:i]
  remaining = sizes[i:]
  (leftover_x, leftover_y, leftover_dx, leftover_dy) =
leftover(current, x, y, dx, dy)
  return layout(current, x, y, dx, dy) + \
squarify(remaining, leftover_x, leftover_y, leftover_dx, leftover_dy)

def padded_squarify(sizes, x, y, dx, dy):
  rects = squarify(sizes, x, y, dx, dy)
  for rect in rects:
    pad_rectangle(rect)
  return rects
```

The squarify function displayed in the preceding code can be used to display the top 12 countries by GDP in Africa, as shown in the following code:

```
import matplotlib.pyplot as plt
import matplotlib.cm
import random
import squarify

x = 0.
y = 0.
width = 950.
height = 733.
norm_x=1000
norm_y=1000

fig = plt.figure(figsize=(15,13))
```

```
ax=fig.add_subplot(111,axisbg='white')

initvalues = [285.4,188.4,173,140.6,91.4,75.5,62.3,39.6,29.4,28.5,
26.2, 22.2]
values = initvalues
labels = ["South Africa", "Egypt", "Nigeria", "Algeria", "Morocco",
"Angola", "Libya", "Tunisia", "Kenya", "Ethiopia", "Ghana", "Cameron"]

colors = [(214,27,31),(229,109,0),(109,178,2),(50,155,18),
(41,127,214),(27,70,163),(72,17,121),(209,0,89),
(148,0,26),(223,44,13), (195,215,0)]
# Scale the RGB values to the [0, 1] range, which is the format
matplotlib accepts.
for i in range(len(colors)):
  r, g, b = colors[i]
  colors[i] = (r / 255., g / 255., b / 255.)

# values must be sorted descending (and positive, obviously)
values.sort(reverse=True)

# the sum of the values must equal the total area to be laid out
# i.e., sum(values) == width * height
values = squarify.normalize_sizes(values, width, height)

# padded rectangles will probably visualize better for certain cases
rects = squarify.padded_squarify(values, x, y, width, height)

cmap = matplotlib.cm.get_cmap()

color = [cmap(random.random()) for i in range(len(values))]
x = [rect['x'] for rect in rects]
y = [rect['y'] for rect in rects]
dx = [rect['dx'] for rect in rects]
dy = [rect['dy'] for rect in rects]

ax.bar(x, dy, width=dx, bottom=y, color=colors, label=labels)

va = 'center'
idx=1

for l, r, v in zip(labels, rects, initvalues):
  x, y, dx, dy = r['x'], r['y'], r['dx'], r['dy']
  ax.text(x + dx / 2, y + dy / 2+10, str(idx)+"--> "+l, va=va,
      ha='center', color='white', fontsize=14)
```

```
    ax.text(x + dx / 2, y + dy / 2-12, "($"+str(v)+"b)", va=va,
        ha='center', color='white', fontsize=12)
    idx = idx+1
ax.set_xlim(0, norm_x)
ax.set_ylim(0, norm_y)
plt.show()
```

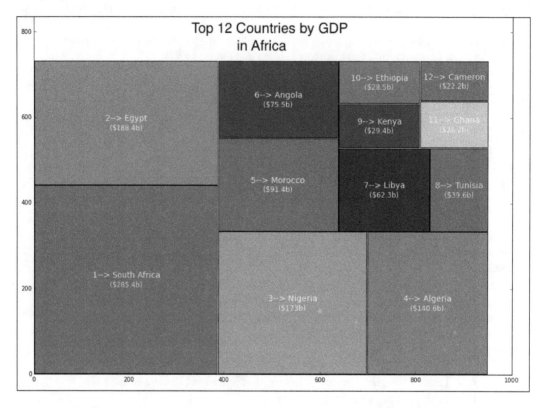

Interactive visualization packages

A few years ago, there were not many interactive tools besides IPython. In order to understand how you can make any visualization interactive, it makes sense to compare it with an existing tool (such as D3.js). One of the reasons why D3.js is very powerful is that a JavaScript-based plotting framework can make the plots to be presented on the Web. Moreover, it comes with all the event-driven functions that can be configured easily.

There are two visualization libraries called **Bokeh** and **VisPy** that are popular among a few that are available today. There is another tool called **Wakari**. This is mainly used for data analytics with a resemblance to IPython in terms of how you can create a browser-based visualization. The **Ashiba** project was another tool that was developed by Clayton Davis at Continuum, but since the focus of Continuum shifted to Bokeh and Wakari, there is very little work that has been done on Ashiba in the past few years.

Bokeh

Bokeh is an interactive visual library that is developed in Python and is targeted to work via web browsers. Where does the name Bokeh come from? This is a Japanese word that describes the blurring or the parts of an image that are out of focus. The goal was to develop a library that closely resembles the aesthetics of D3.js; the choice of the name Bokeh seemed to match. Bokeh writes to the HTML5 Canvas library and therefore guarantees to work on browsers that support HTML5. This is useful because you would want to compare the JavaScript-based plots with Python.

We will not elaborate much about this tool. You can read and explore more about this at `http://bokeh.pydata.org`. However, what is important is to know the dependencies of the Bokeh library. Before installing the Bokeh library, it is required that `jsonschema` be installed, as follows:

```
conda install jsonschema


Fetching package metadata: ....
Solving package specifications: .
Package plan for installation in environment /Users/MacBook/anaconda:


The following packages will be downloaded:

    package                    |                build
    ---------------------------|------------------
    jsonschema-2.4.0           |             py27_0         51 KB

The following NEW packages will be INSTALLED:

    jsonschema: 2.4.0-py27_0


Proceed ([y]/n)?
```

The examples of interactive visualization using Bokeh, pandas, SciPy, matplotlib, and ggplot can be found at `http://nbviewer.ipython.org/gist/fonnesbeck/ad091b81bffda28fd657`.

VisPy

VisPy is a visualization library for 2D or 3D plotting that is interactive and has high performance. You can take advantage of the OpenGL knowledge to create visualization quickly. It also has methods that do not necessarily require a deep understanding of OpenGL. For more information, you can read the documentation at `vispy.org`.

In order to install the VisPy library, one may attempt the `conda install vispy` command, but it most likely responds with the binstar search `-t` `conda vispy` suggestion. The following code is one of those in the list:

```
conda install --channel https://conda.binstar.org/asmeurer vispy
```

With this command, you will obtain the following the response:

```
Fetching package metadata: ......
Solving package specifications: .
Package plan for installation in environment /Users/MacBook/anaconda:

The following packages will be downloaded:

    package                    |            build
    ---------------------------|-----------------
    numpy-1.8.2                 |          py27_0         2.9 MB
    vispy-0.3.0                 |      np18py27_0         679 KB
    ------------------------------------------------------------
                                           Total:         3.6 MB

The following NEW packages will be INSTALLED:

    vispy: 0.3.0-np18py27_0

The following packages will be DOWNGRADED:

    numpy: 1.9.2-py27_0 --> 1.8.2-py27_0

Proceed ([y]/n)?
```

There are many examples in the gallery collection of VisPy. One particular example of the display of points that uses the `vispy.gloo` command and GLSL shading code can be viewed at `http://vispy.org/gloo.html?highlight=gloo#module-vispy.gloo`.

Summary

There is a good set of tools and packages for Python developers that are available today. Python has a large standard library. This is commonly cited as one of Python's greatest strengths. It has modules to create the graphical user interfaces, connecting to relational databases, pseudorandom number generators, arithmetic with arbitrary precision decimals, manipulating regular expressions. In addition, there are high-performance packages to plot 2D and 3D graphics, machine learning and statistical algorithms, and so on.

We have seen that the IDE tools (such as Canopy and Anaconda) have leveraged the efficient development work from a computation and visualization standpoint, among many other areas. There are many effective ways to produce visualization methods using these tools. In the following few chapters, interesting examples will be shown with these tools and packages.

4

Numerical Computing and Interactive Plotting

The field of high-performance numerical computing lies at the crossroads of a number of disciplines and skill sets. In order to be successful at using high-performance computing today, it requires knowledge and skills of programming, data science, and applied mathematics. In addition to these, efficient implementation of the computational problems requires some understanding of processing and storage devices.

The role of computing in science has evolved to a different level in recent years. Programming languages (such as R and MATLAB) were common in academic research and scientific computing. Today, Python plays a big role in scientific computing for a good reason. The Python community has put together many efficient tools and packages that is being used not only by the research community, but also successful commercial organizations such as Yahoo, Google, Facebook, and Amazon.

There are two popular packages that are widely used in scientific computing. They are **Numerical Python Package (NumPy)** and **Scientific Python Package (SciPy)**. NumPy is popular for efficient arrays and in particular the ease of indexing. In the following sections, we will discuss the following topics:

- NumPy, SciPy, and MKL functions
- Numerical indexing and logical indexing
- Data structures—stacks, queues, tuples, sets, tries, and dictionaries
- Visualizing plots using matplotlib, and so on
- Optimization and interpolation using NumPy and SciPy with examples
- Integrating Cython with NumPy and advantages of Cython

NumPy, SciPy, and MKL functions

Almost all scientific and numerical computing requires the representation of data in the form of vectors and matrices, and NumPy handles all these in terms of arrays.

NumPy and SciPy are computational modules of Python that provide convenient mathematical and numerical methods in precompiled, fast functions. The NumPy package provides basic routines to manipulate large arrays and matrices of numeric data. The SciPy package extends NumPy with a collection of useful algorithms with applied mathematical techniques. In NumPy, *ndarray* is an array object that represents a multidimensional, homogeneous array of items that have a known size.

NumPy

NumPy not only uses array objects, but also linear algebraic functions that can be conveniently used for computations. It provides a fast implementation of arrays and associated array functionalities. Using an array object, one can perform operations that include matrix multiplication, transposition of vectors and matrices, solve systems of equations, perform vector multiplication and normalization, and so on.

NumPy universal functions

A universal function (*ufunc*) is a function that operates on ndarrays by each element, supporting type casting and several other standard features. In other words, ufunc is a vectorized wrapper for a function that takes scalar inputs and produces scalar outputs. Many built-in functions are implemented in the compiled C code, which makes it faster.

NumPy universal functions are faster than Python functions because looping is performed in compiled code. Also, since arrays are typed, their type is known before any sort of computation occurs.

A simple example of ufunc operating on each element is shown here:

```
import numpy as np
x = np.random.random(5)
print x
print x + 1    # add 1 to each element of x

[ 0.62229809  0.18010463  0.28126201  0.30701477  0.39013144]
[ 1.62229809  1.18010463  1.28126201  1.30701477  1.39013144]
```

Other examples are np.add and np.subtract.

NumPy's `ndarray` is similar to the lists in Python, but it is rather strict in storing only a homogeneous type of object. In other words, with a Python list, one can mix the element types, such as the first element as a number, the second element as a list, and the next element as another list (or dictionary). The performance in terms of operating the elements of `ndarray` is significantly faster for a large size array, which will be demonstrated here. The example here demonstrates that it is faster because we will measure the running time. However, for readers who are curious about NumPy implementations in C, there is a documentation on the same available at `http://docs.scipy.org/doc/numpy/reference/internals.code-explanations.html`.

```
import numpy as np

arr = np.arange(10000000)
listarr = arr.tolist()

def scalar_multiple(alist, scalar):
    for i, val in enumerate(alist):
        alist[i] = val * scalar
    return alist

# Using IPython's magic timeit command
timeit arr * 2.4
10 loops, best of 3: 31.7 ms per loop
# above result shows 31.7 ms (not seconds)

timeit scalar_multiple(listarr, 2.4)
1 loops, best of 3: 1.39 s per loop
# above result shows 1.39 seconds (not ms)
```

In the preceding code, each array element occupies 4 bytes. Therefore, a million integer arrays occupy approximately 44 MB of memory, and the list uses 711 MB of memory. However, arrays are slower for small collection sizes, but for large collection sizes, they use less memory space and are significantly faster than lists.

NumPy comes with many useful functions that are broadly categorized as trigonometric functions, arithmetic functions, exponent and logarithmic functions, and miscellaneous functions. Among many miscellaneous functions, `convolve()` for linear convolution and `interp()` for linear interpolation are popular. In addition, for most experimental work that involve equally spaced data, the `linspace()` and `random.rand()` functions are among a few that are used widely.

Shape and reshape manipulation

Changing the shape of an existing array can be more efficient than creating a new array from the old data with a new shape. In the first example, reshape happens in memory (the array is not stored in a variable), whereas in the following code, the array is first stored in a variable a and then a is reshaped:

```
import numpy as np

np.dandom.rand(2,4)
array([[ 0.96432148,   0.63192759,   0.12976726,   0.56131001],
       [   0.27086909,   0.92865208,   0.27762891,   0.40429701]])

np.random.rand(8).reshape(2,4)
array([[ 0.39698544,   0.88843637,   0.66260474,   0.61106802],
       [ 0.97622822,   0.47652548,   0.56163488,   0.43602828]])
```

In the preceding example, after creating 8 values, they are reshaped into a valid dimension of choice, as shown in the following code:

```
#another example
a = np.array([[11,12,13,14,15,16],[17,18,19,20,21,22]])

print a
[[11, 12, 13, 14, 15, 16], [17, 18, 19, 20, 21, 22]]

# the following shows shape is used to know the dimensions
a.shape
(2,6)

#Now change the shape of the array
a.shape=(3,4)
print a
[[11 12 13]  [14 15 16]  [17 18 19]  [20 21 22]]
```

xrange is used instead of range because it is faster for loops and avoids the storage of the list of integers; it just generates them one by one. The opposite of shape and reshape is ravel(), as shown in the following code:

```
#ravel example
a = np.array([[11,12,13,14,15,16],[17,18,19,20,21,22]])

a.ravel()
array([11, 12, 13, 14, 15, 16, 17, 18, 19, 20, 21, 22])
```

An example of interpolation

Here is an example of interpolation using `interp()`:

```
n=30

# create n values of x from 0 to 2*pi
x = np.linspace(0,2*np.pi,n)

y = np.zeros(n)

#for range of x values, evaluate y values
for i in xrange(n):
    y[i] = np.sin(x[i])
```

The image displayed in the following picture is the result of a simple sine curve interpolation:

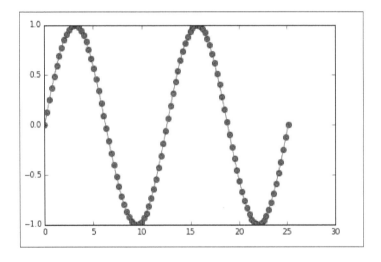

The following code shows the plotting curves with and without interpolation:

```
import numpy as np
import matplotlib.pyplot as plt

# create n values of x from 0 to 2*pi
x = np.linspace(0, 8*np.pi, 100)

y = np.sin(x/2)

#interpolate new y-values
yinterp = np.interp(x, x, y)
```

```
#plot x,y values using circle marker (line style)
plt.plot(x, y, 'o')

#plot interpolated curve using dash x marker
plt.plot(xvals, yinterp, '-x')

plt.show()
```

Vectorizing functions

Vectorizing functions via `vectorize()` in NumPy and SciPy can be very efficient. Vectorize has the capability to convert a function that takes scalars as arguments to a function that takes arrays as arguments by applying the same rule element-wise. We will demonstrate this here with two examples.

The first example uses a function that takes three scalar arguments to produce a vectorized function that takes three array arguments, as shown in the following code:

```
import numpy as np

def addition(x, y, z):
    return x + y + z

def addpoly():
    i = np.random.randint(25)
    poly1 = np.arange(i, i+10)
    i = np.random.randint(25)
    poly2 = np.arange(i, i+10)
    poly3 = np.arange(10, 18)
    print poly1
    print poly2
    print poly3
    print '-' * 32
    vecf = np.vectorize(addition)
    print vecf(poly1,poly2,poly3)

addpoly()

[ 4  5  6  7  8  9 10 11 12 13]
[13 14 15 16 17 18 19 20 21 22]
[10 11 12 13 14 15 16 17 18 19]
--------------------------------
[27 30 33 36 39 42 45 48 51 54]
```

Note that `arrange` is an array-valued version of the built-in Python `range` function.

The second example uses a function that takes one scalar argument to produce a **vectorized** function that takes an array argument, as shown in the following code:

```
import numpy as np

def posquare(x):
   if x >= 0: return x**2
   else: return -x

i = np.random.randint(25)
poly1 = np.arange(i,i+10)

print poly1
vecfunc = vectorize(posquare, otypes=[float])
vecfunc(poly1)

[14 15 16 17 18 19 20 21 22 23]
array([ 196., 225., 256., 289., 324., 361., 400., 441., 484., 529.])
```

There is yet another example that is interesting to study with the help of an example code. This example shows three ways to increment the array elements by a constant and measure the running time to determine which method is faster:

```
import numpy as np
from time import time

def incrembyone(x):
    return x + 1

dataarray=np.linspace(1,5,1000000)

t1=time()
lendata = len(dataarray)
print "Len = "+str(lendata)
print dataarray[1:7]
for i in range(lendata):
    dataarray[i]+=1
print " time for loop (No vectorization)->" + str(time() - t1)

t2=time()

vecincr = np.vectorize(incrembyone) #1
vecincr(dataarray) #2
print " time for vectorized version-1:" + str(time() - t2)
t3 = time()
```

```
# This way to increment array elements with one line
# is pretty powerful, accomplishes same thing as #1 and #2
dataarray+=1  # how does this achieve the results
print dataarray[1:7]
print " time for vectorized version-2:" + str(time() - t3)

Len = 1000000
 [ 1.000004 1.000008 1.000012 1.000016 1.00002 1.000024]
time for loop (No vectorization)->0.473765850067
time for vectorized version-1:0.221153974533 # half the time

 [ 3.000004 3.000008 3.000012 3.000016 3.00002 3.000024]
time for vectorized version-2:0.00192213058472 # in fraction time
```

Besides the vectorizing techniques, there is another simple coding practice that could make programs more efficient. If there are prefix notations that are being used in loops, it is best practice to create a local alias and use this alias in the loop. One such example is shown here:

```
fastsin = math.sin

x = range(1000000)
for i in x:
    x[i] = fastsin(x[i])
```

Summary of NumPy linear algebra

The following is a list of some well-known functions that NumPy offers in linear algebra:

Name	Description
dot(a,b)	This is a dot product of two arrays
linalg.norm(x)	This is a matrix or vector norm
linalg.cond(x)	This specifies the condition number
linalg.solve(A,b)	This solves linear system Ax=b
linalg.inv(A)	This represents an inverse of A
linalg.pinv(A)	This specifies a pseudo-inverse of A
linalg.eig(A)	These are eigenvalues/vectors of square A
linalg.eigvals(A)	These are eigenvalues of general A
linalg.svd(A)	This is a singular value decomposition

SciPy

NumPy has already many convenient functions that can be used in computation. Then, why do we need SciPy? SciPy is an extension of NumPy for mathematics, science, and engineering that has many packages available for linear algebra, integration, interpolation, fast Fourier transforms, large matrix manipulation, statistical computation, and so on. The following table shows a brief description of these packages:

Subpackage	Brief description of functionalities
`scipy.cluster`	This specifies the functions for clustering, including vector quantization and k-means.
`scipy.fftpack`	This denotes the functions of fast Fourier transform.
`scipy.integrate`	This specifies the functions for performing numerical integration using trapezoidal, Simpson's, Romberg, and other methods. It also specifies methods for integration of ordinary differential equations. One can perform single, double, and triple integrations on a function object with the functions `quad`, `dblquad`, and `tplquad`.
`scipy.interpolate`	This denotes the functions and classes for interpolation objects with discrete numeric data and linear and spline interpolation.
`scipy.linalg`	This is a wrapper for the package `linalg` in NumPy. All the functionalities from NumPy is part of `scipy.linalg`, along with several other functions.
`scipy.optimize`	This denotes the maximization and minimization functions that include Neider-Mead Simplex, Powell's, conjugate gradient BFGS, least squares, constrained optimizers, simulated annealing, Newton's method, bisection method, Broyden Anderson, and line search.
`scipy.sparse`	This specifies the functions that can work with large sparse matrices.
`scipy.special`	This has special functions for computational physics, such as elliptic, bessel, gamma, beta, hypergeometric, parabolic, cylinder, mathieu, and spheroidal wave.

In addition to the preceding listed subpackages, SciPy also has a `scipy.io` package that has functions to load a matrix called `spio.loadmat()`, save a matrix called `spio.savemat()`, and read images via `scio.imread()`. When there is a need to develop computational programs in Python, it is good practice to check the SciPy documentation to see whether it contains the functions that already accomplish the intended task.

Let's take a look at an example using `scipy.polyId()`:

```
import scipy as sp

# function that multiplies two polynomials
```

```
def multiplyPoly():
    #cubic1 has coefficients 3, 4, 5 and 5
    cubic1 = sp.poly1d([3, 4, 5, 5])

    #cubic2 has coefficients 4, 1, -3 and 3
    cubic2 = sp.poly1d([4, 1, -3, 3])

    print cubic1
    print cubic2

    print '-' * 36

    #print results of polynomial multiplication
    print cubic1 * cubic2

multiplyPoly()   # produces the following result

   3     2
3 x + 4 x + 5 x + 5
   3     2
4 x + 1 x - 3 x + 3
------------------------------------
    6      5      4      3      2
12 x + 19 x + 15 x + 22 x + 2 x + 15
```

The result matches with the multiplication done in the traditional term-by-term method, as follows:

$$(3x^3 + 4x^2 + 5x + 5)(4x^3 + x^2 - 3x + 3)$$
$$= (12x^6 + 9x^5 + 15x^4 + 22x^3 + 2x^2 + 15)$$

As such, polynomial representation can be used for integration, differentiation, and other computational physics. These capabilities along with many more functions in NumPy, SciPy, and other package extensions clearly indicate that Python is another alternative to MATLAB and is therefore used in some academic environments.

There are many different kinds of interpolation that SciPy offers. The following example uses interpolate.splev, which uses B-spline and its derivatives and interpolate.splprep for the B-spline representation of two-dimensional curves (N-dimensional in general):

```
import numpy as np
import matplotlib.pyplot as plt
import scipy as sp
```

```
t = np.arange(0, 2.5, .1)
x = np.sin(2*np.pi*t)
y = np.cos(2*np.pi*t)

tcktuples,uarray = sp.interpolate.splprep([x,y], s=0)
unew = np.arange(0, 1.01, 0.01)

splinevalues = sp.interpolate.splev(unew, tcktuples)

plt.figure(figsize=(10,10))
plt.plot(x, y, 'x', splinevalues[0], splinevalues[1],
np.sin(2*np.pi*unew), np.cos(2*np.pi*unew), x, y, 'b')

plt.legend(['Linear', 'Cubic Spline', 'True'])
plt.axis([-1.25, 1.25, -1.25, 1.25])
plt.title('Parametric Spline Interpolation Curve')

plt.show()
```

The following diagram is the result of this spline interpolation using SciPy and NumPy:

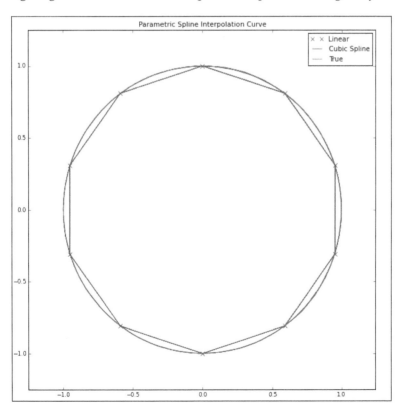

Let's take a look at an example in numerical integration and solve linear equations using some of the SciPy functions (such as Simpson's and Romberg) and compare these with the NumPy function trapezoidal. We know that when a function such as $f(x) = 9 - x2$ is integrated from -3 to 3, we expect 36 units, as shown in the following diagram:

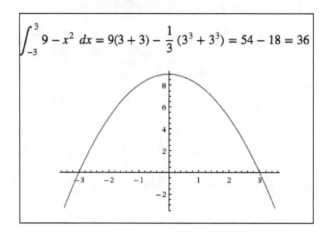

$$\int_{-3}^{3} 9 - x^2 \ dx = 9(3 + 3) - \frac{1}{3}(3^3 + 3^3) = 54 - 18 = 36$$

The preceding plot shows the *9-x2* function (which is symmetric along the *Y* axis). Mathematically, the integration from *-3* to *3* is twice that of the integration from *0* to *3*. How do we numerically integrate using SciPy? The following code shows one way to perform it using the trapezoidal method from NumPy:

```
import numpy as np
from scipy.integrate import simps, romberg

a = -3.0; b = 3.0;
N = 10

x = np.linspace(a, b, N)
y = 9-x*x
yromb = lambda x: (9-x*x)

t = np.trapz(y, x)
s = simps(y, x)
r = romberg(yromb, a, b)

#actual integral value
aiv = (9*b-(b*b*b)/3.0) - (9*a-(a*a*a)/3.0)

print 'trapezoidal = {0} ({1:%} error)'.format(t, (t - aiv)/aiv)
print 'simpsons = {0} ({1:%} error)'.format(s, (s - aiv)/aiv)
print 'romberg  = {0} ({1:%} error)'.format(r, (r - aiv)/aiv)
```

```
print 'actual value = {0}'.format(aiv)

trapezoidal = 35.5555555556 (-1.234568% error)
simpsons = 35.950617284 (-0.137174% error)
romberg  = 36.0 (0.000000% error)
actual value = 36.0
```

An example of linear equations

Let's try to solve a set of linear equations in three variables (x, y, and z) as follows:

- $x + 2y - z = 2$
- $2x - 3y + 2z = 2$
- $3x + y - z = 2$

NumPy offers a convenient method `np.linalg.solve()` to solve linear equations. However, the inputs are expected in vector form. The following program shows how one can solve linear equations.

```
import numpy as np

# Matrix A has coefficients of x,y and z
A = np.array([[1, 2, -1],
              [2, -3, 2],
              [3, 1, -1]])
#constant vector
b = np.array([2, 2, 2])

#Solve these equations by calling linalg.solve
v = np.linalg.solve(A, b)

# v is the vector that has solutions
print "The solution vector is "
print v
# Reconstruct Av to see if it produces identical values
print np.dot(A,v) == b

The solution vector is
[ 1.  2.  3.]
[ True  True  True]
```

Note that `np.dot(A,v)` is a matrix multiplication (not `A*v`). The solution vector `v = [1,2,3]` is the correct expected result.

The vectorized numerical derivative

Now as the last example in this section, we will take a look at the vectorized numeric derivatives that NumPy offers. We do know that the derivative is

$$\frac{d}{dx}\left(\frac{1}{1+cos^2(x)}\right) = \frac{sin2x}{(1+cos^2x)^2}$$ by applying the quotient rule of differentiation. However, by applying the vectorized methods in Python to compute the derivatives without loop, we will see the following code:

```
import numpy as np
import matplotlib.pyplot as plt

x = np.linspace(-np.pi/2, np.pi/2, 44)
y = 1/(1+np.cos(x)*np.cos(x))
dy_actual = np.sin(2*x)/(1+np.cos(x)*np.cos(x))**2

fig = plt.figure(figsize=(10,10))
ax=fig.add_subplot(111,axisbg='white')

# we need to specify the size of dy ahead because diff returns
dy = np.zeros(y.shape, np.float) #we know it will be this size
dy[0:-1] = np.diff(y) / np.diff(x)
dy[-1] = (y[-1] - y[-2]) / (x[-1] - x[-2])

plt.plot(x,y, linewidth=3, color='b', label='actual function')
plt.plot(x,dy_actual,label='actual derivative', linewidth=2,
color='r')
plt.plot(x,dy,label='forward diff', linewidth=2, color='g')
plt.legend(loc='upper center')
plt.show()
```

In the following example, we can see how you can plot the actual function, its derivative, and the forward difference in the same plot. The actual derivative is plugged into `dy_actual`, and the forward difference is calculated using `diff()` from NumPy.

The following plot diagram is the result of this program:

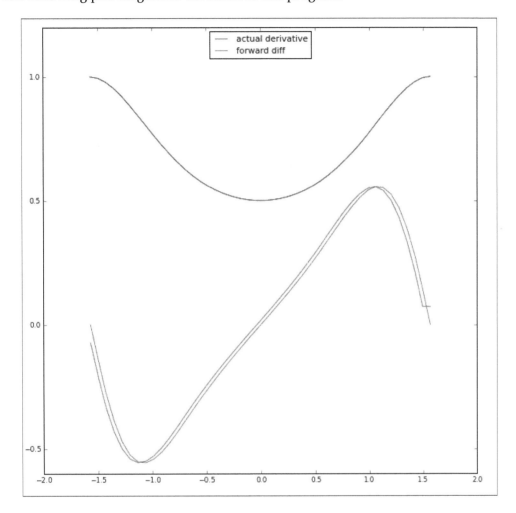

MKL functions

The MKL functions from Intel provide high-performance routines on vectors and matrices. In addition, they include FFT functions and vector statistical functions. These functions have been enhanced and optimized to work efficiently on Intel processors. For Anaconda users, Continuum has packaged these FFT functions into binary versions of Python libraries for MKL optimizations. However MKL optimizations are available as an add-on as part of the Anaconda Accelerate package. The graph here shows the difference in slowness without MKL:

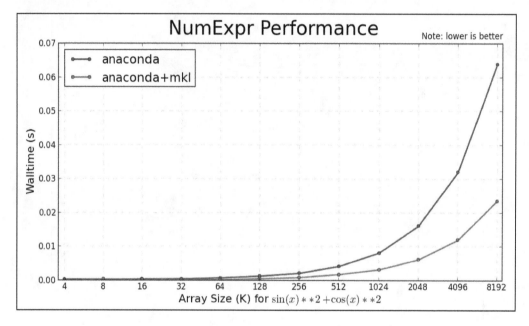

The preceding graph has been taken from
https://store.continuum.io/cshop/mkl-optimizations/.

For larger array inputs, MKL offers a significant improvement over performance, as shown in the following screenshot:

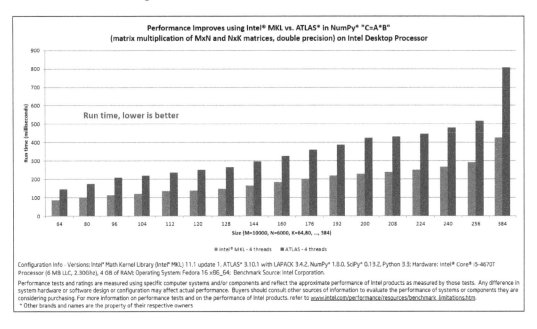

The preceding image has been taken from `https://software.intel.com/en-us/articles/numpyscipy-with-intel-mkl`.

The performance of Python

Python programmers often try to rewrite their innermost loops in C and call the compiled C functions from Python for performance reasons. There are many projects aimed at making this kind of optimization easier, such as Cython. However, it would be preferable to make their existing Python code faster without depending on another programming language.

There are few other options available to improve the performance of the computationally intensive programs in Python:

- **Use Numbapro**: This is a Python compiler from Continuum Analytics that can compile the Python code for execution on CUDA-capable GPUs or multicore CPUs. This compiled code runs the native compiled code and is several times faster than the interpreted code. Numbapro works by enabling compilation at runtime (this is **just-in-time** or the **JIT** compilation). With Numbapro, it is possible to write standard Python functions and run them on a CUDA-capable GPU. Numbapro is designed for array-oriented computing tasks, such as the widely used NumPy library. Numbapro is an enhanced version of Numba and is part of Anaconda Accelerate, a commercially licensed product from Continuum Analytics.

- **Use Scipy.weave**: This is a module that lets you insert snippets of the C code and seamlessly transports the arrays of NumPy into the C layer. It also has some efficient macros.

- **Use multicore approach**: The multiprocessing package of Python 2.6 or higher provides a relatively simple mechanism to create a subprocess. Even desktop computers these days have multicore processors; it makes sense to put all the processors to work. This is much simpler than using threading.

- **Use process pool called pool**: This is another class in the multiprocessing package. With pool, you can define the number of worker processes to be created in the pool and then pass an iterable object containing the parameters for each process.

- **Use Python in a distributed computing package (such as Disco)**: This is a lightweight, open source framework for distributed computing based on the MapReduce paradigm (`http://discoproject.org`). Other similar packages are Hadoop Streaming, mrjob, dumbo, hadoopy, and pydoop.

Scalar selection

Scalar selection is the simplest method to select elements from an array and is implemented using `[rowindex]` for one-dimensional arrays, `[rowindex, columnindex]` for two-dimensional arrays, and so on. The following is a simple code that shows an array element reference:

```
import numpy as np
x = np.array([[2.0,4,5,6], [1,3,5,9]])

x[1,2]
5.0
```

A pure scalar selection always returns a single element and not an array. The data type of the selected element matches the data type of the array used in the selection. Scalar selection can also be used to assign a value to an array element, as shown in the following code:

```
x[1,2] = 8

x
array([[2, 4, 5, 6],[1, 3, 8, 9]])
```

Slicing

Arrays can be sliced just like lists and tuples. Array slicing is identical to list slicing, except that the syntax is simpler. Arrays are sliced using the [: , :, ... :] syntax, where the number of dimensions of the arrays determine the size of the slice, except that these dimensions for which slices are omitted, all elements are selected. For example, if b is a three-dimensional array, b[0:2] is the same as b[0:2,:,:]. There are shorthand notations for slicing. Some common ones are:

- **: and:** are the same as *0:n:1*, where *n* is the length of the array
- **m: and m:n:** are the same as *m:n:1*, where *n* is the length of the array
- **:n:** is the same as *0:n:1*
- **::d:** is the same as *0:n:d*, where *n* is the length of the array

All these slicing methods have been referenced with the usage of arrays. This can also be applicable to lists. Slicing of one-dimensional arrays is identical to slicing a simple list (as one-dimensional arrays can be seen equivalent to a list), and the returned type of all the slicing operations matches the array being sliced. The following is a simple mechanism that shows array slices:

```
x = array([5,6,7,8,9,10,11,12,13,14,15,16,17,18,19,20])

# interpret like this - default start but end index is 2
y = x[:2]
array([5, 6])

# interpretation - default start and end, but steps of 2
y = x[::2]
array([5,7,9,11,13,15,17,19])
```

NumPy attempts to convert data type automatically if an element with one data type is inserted into an array with a different data type. For example, if an array has an integer data type, place a float into the array results in the float being truncated and store it as an integer. This can be dangerous; therefore in such cases, arrays should be initialized to contain floats unless a considered decision is taken to use a different data type for a good reason. This example shows that even if one element is float and the rest is integer, it is assumed to be the float type for the benefit of making it work properly:

```
a = [1.0, 2,3,6,7]
b = array(a)

b.dtype
dtype('float64')
```

Slice using flat

Data in matrices are stored in a row-major order, which means elements are indexed first by counting along the rows and then down the columns. For example, in the following matrix, there are three rows and three columns; the elements are read in the order 4,5,6,7,8,9,1,2,3 (for each row, column-wise):

$$A = \begin{bmatrix} 4 & 5 & 6 \\ 7 & 8 & 9 \\ 1 & 2 & 3 \end{bmatrix}$$

Linear slicing assigns an index to each element of the array in the order of the elements read. In two-dimensional arrays or lists, linear slicing works by first counting across the rows and then down the columns. In order to use linear slicing, you have to use the `flat` function, as shown in the following code:

```
a=array([[4,5,6],[7,8,9],[1,2,3]])
b = a.flat[:]

print b
[4, 5, 6, 7, 8, 9, 1, 2, 3]
```

Array indexing

Elements from NumPy arrays can be selected using four methods: scalar selection, slicing, numerical indexing, and logical (or Boolean) indexing. Scalar selection and slicing are the basic methods to access elements in an array, which has already been discussed here. Numerical indexing and logical indexing are closely related and allows more flexible selection. Numerical indexing uses lists or arrays of locations to select elements, whereas logical indexing uses arrays that contain Boolean values to select elements.

Numerical indexing

Numerical indexing is an alternative to slice notation. The idea in numerical indexing is to use coordinates to select elements. This is similar to slicing. Arrays created using numerical indexing create copies of data, whereas slices are only views of data, and not copies. For performance sake, slicing should be used. Slices are similar to one-dimensional arrays, but the shape of the slice is determined by the slice inputs.

Numerical indexing in one-dimensional arrays uses the numerical index values as locations in the array (0-based indexing) and returns an array with the same dimensions as the numerical index.

Note that the numerical index can be either a list or a NumPy array and must contain integer data, as shown in the following code:

```
a = 10 * arange(4.0)
array([0.,10.,20.,30.])

a[[1]]  # arrays index is list with first element
array([ 10.])

a[[0,3,2]] # arrays index are 0-th, 3-rd and 2-nd
array([  0.,   30.,   20.])

sel = array([3,1,4,2,3,3])  # array with repetition
a[sel]
array([ 30.  10.   0.  20.  30.  30.])

sel = array([4,1],[3,2]])
a[sel]
array([[ 30.,10.], [ 0.,20.]])
```

These examples show that the numerical indices determine the element location, and the shape of the numerical index array determines the shape of the output.

Similar to slicing, numerical indexing can be combined using the `flat` function to select elements from an array using the row-major ordering of the array. The behavior of numerical indexing with flat is identical to that of using numerical indexing on a flattened version of the underlying array. A few examples are shown here:

```
a = 10 * arange(8.0)
array([  0.,   10.,   20.,   30.,   40., 50., 60., 70.])

a.flat[[3,4,1]]
array([ 30., 40., 10.])

a.flat[[[3,4,7],[1,5,3]]]
array([[ 30., 40., 70.], [ 10., 50., 30.]])
```

Logical indexing

Logical indexing is different from slicing and numeric indexing; it rather uses logical indices to select elements, rows, or columns. Logical indices act as light switches and are either true or false. Pure logical indexing uses a logical indexing array with the same size as the array being used for selection and always returns a one-dimensional array, as shown in the following code:

```
x = arange(-4,5)

x < 0
array([True, True, True, True, False, False, False, False, False],
dtype=bool)

x[x>0]
array([1, 2, 3, 4])

x[abs(x) >= 2]
array([-4, -3, -2,  2,  3,  4])

#Even for 2-dimension it still does the same
x = reshape(arange(-8, 8), (4,4))
x
array([[-8, -7, -6, -5], [-4, -3, -2, -1], [ 0,  1,  2,  3], [ 4,  5,
6,  7]])

x[x<0]
array([-8, -7, -6, -5, -4, -3, -2, -1])
```

Here is another example to demonstrate logical indexing:

```
from math import isnan
a = [[3, 4, float('NaN')], [5, 9, 8], [3, 3, 2], [9, -1,
float('NaN')]]

list2 = [3, 4, 5, 6]
list1_valid = [elem for elem in list1 if not any([isnan(element) for
element in elem])]

list1_valid
[[3, 7, 8], [1, 1, 1]]

list2_valid = [list2[index] for index, elem in enumerate(list1) if not
any([isnan(element) for element in elem])]

list2_valid
 [4, 5]
```

Other data structures

Python has data structures such as stacks, lists, sets, sequences, tuples, lists, heaps, arrays, dictionaries, and deque. We have already discussed lists while attempting to understand arrays. Tuples are typically more memory efficient than lists because they are immutable.

Stacks

The `list` method is very convenient to be used as a stack, which is known to be an abstract data type with the principle of operation last-in, first-out. The known operations include adding of an item at the top of the stack using `append()`, extracting of the item from the top of the stack using `pop()`, and removing of the item using `remove(item-value)`, as shown in the following code:

```
stack = [5, 6, 8]
stack.append(6)
stack.append(8)

stack
[5, 6, 8, 6, 8]

stack.remove(8)
stack
[5, 6, 6, 8]

stack.pop()
8

stack.remove(8)
Traceback (most recent call last):
File "<ipython-input-339-61d6322e3bb8>", line 1, in <module>
stack.remove(8)
  ValueError: list.remove(x): x not in list
```

The `pop()` function is most efficient (constant-time) because all the other elements remain in their location. However, the parameterized version, `pop(k)`, removes the element that is at the $k < n$ index of a list, shifting all the subsequent elements to fill the gap that results from the removal. The efficiency of this operation is linear because the amount of shifting depends on the choice of index k, as illustrated in the following image:

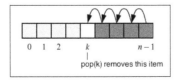

Tuples

A tuple is a sequence of immutable objects that look similar to lists. Tuples are heterogeneous data structures, which means that their elements have different meanings, whereas lists are a homogeneous sequence of elements. Tuples have structure, and lists have order. Some examples of tuples are days of the week, course names, and grading scales, as shown in the following code:

```
#days of the week
weekdays = ("Sunday", "Monday", "Tuesday", "Wednesday", "Thursday",
"Friday", "Saturday")

#course names
courses = ("Chemistry", "Physics", "Mathematics", "Digital Logic",
"Circuit Theory")

#grades
grades = ("A+", "A", "B+", "B", "C+", "C", "I")
```

Tuples have immutable objects. This means that you cannot change or remove them from tuple. However, the tuple can be deleted completely, for example, "del grades" will delete this tuple. After this, if an attempt is made to use that tuple, an error will occur. The following are the built-in tuple functions:

- `cmp(tup1, tup2)`: This function can be used to compare the elements of two tuples
- `len(tuple)`: This function can be used to get the total length of the tuple
- `max(tuple)`: This function can be used to determine the maximum value in the tuple
- `min(tuple)`: This function can be used to determine the minimum value in the tuple
- `tuple(lista)`: This function can be used to convert `lista` to `tuple`

Python has a `max()` function that behaves as expected for numerical values. However, if we pass a list of strings, `max()` returns the item that is the longest.

```
weekdays = ("Sunday", "Monday", "Tuesday", "Wednesday", "Thursday",
"Friday", "Saturday")
print max(weekdays)
Wednesday
```

Similarly `min()` has the same behavior for strings.

```
print min(weekdays)
Friday
```

When we need to find how many elements are in an array or list, `len()` is a convenient method that does the job.

```
len(weekdays)
7
```

Sets

Sets are similar to lists, but are different in two aspects. Firstly, they are an unordered collection as compared to lists (which are ordered by location or index). Secondly, they do not have duplicates (if you know the mathematical definition of sets). The notation used for a set is shown in the following command:

```
setoftrees = { 'Basswood', 'Red Pine', 'Chestnut', 'Gray Birch',
'Black Cherry'}

newtree = 'Tulip Tree'
if newtree not in setoftrees:  setoftrees.add(newtree)
```

Now with this command, you can see what is on `setoftrees`:

```
setoftrees  # typing this shows list of elements shown below
{'Basswood', 'Black Cherry', 'Chestnut', 'Gray Birch', 'Red Pine',
'Tulip Tree'}
```

Then, build `charsinmath` and `charsinchem` using the appropriate spelling, as shown in the following code

```
#example of set of operation on letters
charsinmath = set('mathematics')
charsinchem = set('chem')
```

Now, let's try to see what the values are in these sets:

```
Charsinmath # typing this shows letters in charsinmath
{'a', 'c', 'e', 'h', 'i', 'm', 's', 't'}

charsinchem # typing this shows letters in charsinchem
{'c', 'e', 'h', 'm'}
```

In order to find the set difference, we need to display `charsinmath - charsinchem` as follows:

```
# take away letters from charsinchem from charsinmath
charsinmath - charsinchem
{'a', 'i', 's', 't'}
```

Queues

Just like stacks, it is possible to use a list as a queue. However, the difference is that elements can be added or removed from the end of the list or from the beginning of the list. Although adding and removing from the end of a list is efficient, doing the same from the beginning is not efficient because in this case, elements have to be shifted.

Fortunately, Python has `deque` in its collections package that efficiently implements the adding and removing of elements from both ends using `append()`, `pop()`, `appendleft()`, and `popleft()`, as shown in the following code:

```
from collections import deque

queue = deque(["Daniel", "Sid", "Mathew",  "Michael"])
queue.append("Dirk")         # Dirk arrives
queue.append("Monte")     # Monte arrives queue

queue
deque(['Daniel', 'Sid', 'Mathew', 'Michael', 'Dirk', 'Monte'])

queue.popleft()
'Daniel'

queue.pop()
'Monte'

queue.appendleft('William')
queue
deque(['William', 'Sid', 'Mathew', 'Michael', 'Dirk'])

queue.append('Lastone')
queue
deque(['William', 'Sid', 'Mathew', 'Michael', 'Dirk', 'Lastone'])
```

Dictionaries

Dictionaries are a collection of unordered data values that are composed of a key/value pair, which has the unique advantage of accessing a value based on the key as an index. The question is that if the key is a string, then how does the indexing work? The key has to be hashable: a hash function is applied on the key to extract the location where the value is stored. In other words, the hash function takes a key value and returns an integer. Dictionaries then use these integers (or hash values) to store and retrieve the value. Some examples are shown here:

```
#example 1: Top 10 GDP of Africa
gdp_dict = { 'South Africa': 285.4, 'Egypt': 188.4, 'Nigeria': 173,
'Algeria': 140.6, 'Morocco': 91.4, 'Angola': 75.5, 'Libya': 62.3,
'Tunisia': 39.6, 'Kenya': 29.4, 'Ethiopia': 28.5, 'Ghana': 26.2,
'Cameron': 22.2}

gdp_dict['Angola']
75.5


#example 2: English to Spanish for numbers one to ten
english2spanish = { 'one' : 'uno', 'two' : 'dos', 'three': 'tres',
'four': 'cuatro', 'five': 'cinvo', 'six': 'seis', 'seven': 'seite',
'eight': 'ocho', 'nine': 'nueve', 'ten': 'diez'}

english2spanish['four']
'cuatro'
```

The keys should be immutable to have a predictable hash value; otherwise, the hash value change will result in a different location. Also, unpredictable things could occur. The default dictionary does not keep the values in the order they is inserted; therefore, by iterating after the insertion, the order of the key/value pair is arbitrary.

Python's collections package has an equivalent `OrderedDict()` function that keeps the order of pairs in the inserted order. One additional difference between the default dictionary and the ordered dictionary is that in the former, equality always returns `true` if they have an identical set of key/value pairs (not necessarily in the same order), and in the latter, equality returns `true` only when they have an identical set of key/value pairs and when they are in the same order. The following example demonstrates this:

```
# using default dictionary
dict = {}

dict['cat-ds1'] = 'Introduction to Data Structures'
dict['cat-ds2'] = 'Advanced Data Structures'
dict['cat-la1'] = 'Python Programming'
dict['cat-la2'] = 'Advanced Python Programming'
dict['cat-pda'] = 'Python for Data Analysis'
dict['cat-ps1'] = 'Data Science in Python'
dict['cat-ps2'] = 'Doing Data Science'

for key, val in dict.items():  print key,val

cat-ps1 Data Science in Python
cat-ps2 Doing Data Science
```

```
cat-pda Python for Data Analysis
cat-la2 Advanced Python Programming
cat-la1 Python Programming
cat-ds1 Introduction to Data Structures
cat-ds2 Advanced Data Structures

#using OrderedDict (inserting data the same way as before)
odict = OrderedDict()

odict['cat-ds1'] = 'Introduction to Data Structures'
odict['cat-ds2'] = 'Advanced Data Structures'
odict['cat-la1'] = 'Python Programming'
odict['cat-la2'] = 'Advanced Python Programming'
odict['cat-pda'] = 'Python for Data Analysis'
odict['cat-ps1'] = 'Data Science in Python'
odict['cat-ps2'] = 'Doing Data Science'

for key, val in odict.items():  print key,val

cat-ds1 Introduction to Data Structures
cat-ds2 Advanced Data Structures
cat-la1 Python Programming
cat-la2 Advanced Python Programming
cat-pda Python for Data Analysis
cat-ps1 Data Science in Python
cat-ps2 Doing Data Science
```

If you have to implement something similar to this, it is computationally better to use the ISBN as the key, rather than the catalog number as in a library. However, there may be old books that do not have an ISBN; therefore, an equivalent unique key/value has to be used to maintain consistency with other new books that have an ISBN number. A hash value is usually a number, and with a numeric key, the hash function might be much easier compared to an alphanumeric key.

Dictionaries for matrix representation

Usually, there are many examples where you can apply dictionaries when there is a key/value association. For example, state abbreviations and names; either one could be the key and the other the value, but it would be more efficient to have the abbreviation as the key. Other examples are word and word count or city names and population. One interesting area of computation where dictionaries could really be efficient is the representation of a sparse matrix.

Sparse matrices

Let's examine the space utilization of a matrix; for a *100 x 100* matrix represented using a list, each element occupies 4 bytes; therefore, the matrix would need 40,000 bytes, which is approximately 40 KB of space. However, among these 40,000 bytes, if only 100 of them have a nonzero value and the others are all zero, then the space is wasted. Now, let's consider a smaller matrix for the simplicity of discussion, as shown in the following image:

$$A = \begin{bmatrix} 0 & 0 & 0 & 0 & 2 & 0 & 0 & 1 & 0 & 2 \\ 0 & 4 & 0 & 3 & 0 & 0 & 0 & 0 & 1 & 0 \\ 6 & 0 & 1 & 0 & 0 & 7 & 0 & 0 & 0 & 0 \\ 0 & 0 & 0 & 0 & 0 & 0 & 0 & 0 & 0 & 1 \\ 0 & 0 & 0 & 0 & 0 & 0 & 0 & 0 & 0 & 0 \\ 3 & 0 & 2 & 0 & 0 & 0 & 0 & 0 & 3 & 0 \\ 0 & 0 & 0 & 2 & 0 & 0 & 1 & 0 & 0 & 0 \\ 0 & 0 & 0 & 0 & 0 & 0 & 0 & 0 & 1 & 0 \\ 3 & 0 & 2 & 0 & 0 & 0 & 0 & 0 & 0 & 1 \\ 0 & 3 & 0 & 0 & 0 & 0 & 0 & 0 & 0 & 0 \end{bmatrix}$$

This matrix has approximately 20 percent of nonzero values; therefore, finding an alternative way to represent the nonzero elements of the matrix would be a good start. There are seven values of *1*, five values of *2* and *3* each, and one value of *4*, *6*, and *7*. This could be represented as follows:

```
A = {1: [(2,2),(6,6),  (0,7),(1,8),(7,8),(3,9),(8,9)],
     2: [(5,2),(8,2),(6,3),(0,4),(0,9)],
     3: [(5,0),(8,0),(9,1),(1,3),(5,8)],
     4:[(1,1)], 6:[(2,0)], 7:[(2,5)]}
```

However, this representation makes it harder to access the $(i,j)^{th}$ value of *A*. There is a better way to represent this sparse matrix using dictionary, as shown in the following code:

```
def getElement(row, col):
    if (row,col) in A.keys():
        r = A[row,col]
    else:
        r = 0
    return r

A={(0,4): 2, (0,7): 1, (1,1): 4, (1,3):3, (1,8): 1, (2,0): 6, (0,9):
2, (2,2):1, (2,5): 7, (3,9): 1, (5,0): 3, (5,2): 2, (5,8): 3, (6,3):
2, (6,6):1, (7,8): 1, (8,0): 3, (8,2): 2, (8,9): 1, (9,1): 3}
```

```
print getElement(1,3)
3

print getElement(1,2)
0
```

To access an element at *(1, 3)* of the matrix *A*, we could use *A[(1, 3)]*, but if the key does not exist, it will throw an exception. In order to get the nonzero value using the key and return 0 if the key does not exist, we can use a function called getElement(), as shown in the preceding code.

Visualizing sparseness

We can visually see how sparse the matrix is with the help of SquareBox diagrams. The following image shows the sparseDisplay() function. This uses square boxes for each matrix entry that attempts to view the display. The black color represents sparseness, whereas the green color represents nonzero elements:

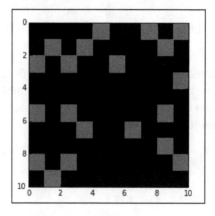

The following code demonstrates how one can display sparseness:

```
import numpy as np
import matplotlib.pyplot as plt

"""
    SquareBox diagrams are useful for visualizing values of a 2D array,
    Where black color representing sparse areas.
"""
def sparseDisplay(nonzero, squaresize, ax=None):
    ax = ax if ax is not None else plt.gca()

    ax.patch.set_facecolor('black')
    ax.set_aspect('equal', 'box')
    for row in range(0,squaresize):
        for col in range(0,squaresize):
```

```
        if (row,col) in nonzero.keys():
            el = nonzero[(row,col)]
            if el == 0:  color='black'
            else:  color = '#008000'
            rect = plt.Rectangle([col,row], 1, 1,
                    facecolor=color, edgecolor=color)
            ax.add_patch(rect)

    ax.autoscale_view()
    ax.invert_yaxis()

if __name__ == '__main__':
    nonzero={(0,4): 2, (0,7): 1, (1,1): 4, (1,3): 3, (1,8): 1,
(2,0): 6, (0,9): 2, (2,2): 1, (2,5): 7, (3,9): 1, (5,0): 3,
(5,2): 2, (5,8): 3, (6,3): 2, (6,6): 1, (7,8): 1, (8,0): 3, (8,2): 2,
(8,9): 1, (9,1): 3}

    plt.figure(figsize=(4,4))
    sparseDisplay(nonzero, 10)
    plt.show()
```

This is only a quick example to display the sparse matrix. Imagine that you have a *30 x 30* matrix with only a few nonzero values, then the display would look somewhat similar to the following image. The saving in this case is 97 percent as far as space utilization is concerned. In other words, the larger the matrix, the lesser the space utilized, as shown in the following image:

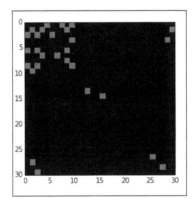

Having found a way to store the sparse matrix using dictionary, you may have to remember that there is no need to reinvent the wheel. Moreover, it makes sense to consider the possibility of storing the sparse matrix to understand the power of dictionary. However, what is really recommended is to take a look at the SciPy and pandas package for the sparse matrix. There may be further opportunities in this book to use these approaches in some examples.

Dictionaries for memoization

Memoization is an optimization technique in computational science that enables one to store intermediate results, which otherwise could be expensive. Not every problem needs memoization, but when there is a pattern of computing the same values by calling the function, it is often useful to use this approach. One example where this approach can be used is in the computation of the Fibonacci function using the dictionary to store the already computed value, so next time, you can just search for the value, rather than recompute it again, as shown in the following code:

```
fibvalues = {0: 0, 1: 1, 2:1, 3:2, 4:3, 5:5}

def fibonacci(n):
    if n not in fibvalues:
        sumvalue = fibonacci(n-1) + fibonacci(n-2)
        fibvalues[n] = sumvalue
    return fibvalues[n]

fibonacci(40)
102334155


print sorted(fibvalues.values())
[0, 1, 1, 2, 3, 5, 8, 13, 21, 34, 55, 89, 144, 233, 377, 610, 987,
1597, 2584, 4181, 6765, 10946, 17711, 28657, 46368, 75025, 121393,
196418, 317811, 514229, 832040, 1346269, 2178309, 3524578, 5702887,
9227465, 14930352, 24157817, 39088169, 63245986, 102334155]

#regular fibonacci without using dictionary
def fib(n):
    if n <= 1 : return 1
    sumval = fib(n-1)+fib(n-2)
    return sumval
```

The dictionary of `fibvalues` is very useful to prevent the recomputation of the values of Fibonacci, but `fibcalled` is used here only to demonstrate that by using dictionary, there cannot be more than one call to `fibonacci()` for a particular value of *n*. By comparing the ratio of the running times for `fib()` (without using dictionary to store the computed value) and `fibonacci()`, we can see that when plotted, it looks similar to the following screenshot:

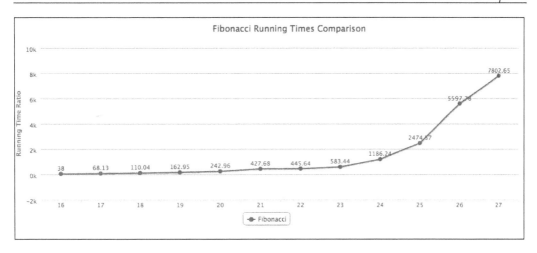

```
from time import time

for nval in range(16,27):
    fibvalues = {0: 0, 1: 1, 2:1, 3:2, 4:3, 5:5}
    t3 = time()
    fibonacci(nval)
    diftime1 = time()-t3
    t2 = time()
    fib(nval)
    diftime2 = time()-t2
    print "The ratio of time-2/time-1 :"+str(diftime2/diftime1)
```

Tries

Trie (pronounced trie or trai) is a data structure that has different names (*digital tree*, *radix tree*, or *prefix tree*). Tries are very efficient for search, insert, and delete functions. This data structure is very optimal for storage. For example, when the words *add*, *also*, *algebra*, *assoc*, *all*, *to*, *trie*, *tree*, *tea*, and *ten* are stored in the trie, it will look similar to the following diagram:

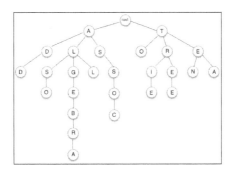

The characters are shown in uppercase just for clarity purposes in the preceding diagram, whereas in real storage, the characters are stored as they appear in words. In the implementation of trie, it makes sense to store the word count. The search functionality is very efficient and in particular when the pattern does not match, the results are even quicker. In other words, if the search is for *are*, then the failure is determined at the level when the letter *r* is not found.

One of the popular functionalities is *longest prefix matching*. In other words, if we were to find all the words in the dictionary that have the longest prefix match with a particular search string: *base* (for example). The results could be *base*, *based*, *baseline*, or *basement*, or even more words if they are found in the dictionary of words.

Python has many different implementations: `suffix_tree`, `pytire`, `trie`, `datrie`, and so on. There is a nice comparison study done by J. F. Sebastian that can be accessed at `https://github.com/zed/trie-benchmark`.

Most search engines have an implementation of trie called **inverted index**. This is the central component where space optimization is very important. Moreover, searching for this kind of structure is very efficient to find the relevance between the search string and the documents. Another interesting application of trie is IP routing, where the ability to contain large ranges of values is particularly suitable. It also saves space.

A simple implementation in Python (not necessarily the most efficient) is shown in the following code:

```python
_end = '_end_'

# to search if a word is in trie
def in_trie(trie, word):
    current_dict = trie
    for letter in word:
        if letter in current_dict:
            current_dict = current_dict[letter]
        else:
            return False
    else:
        if _end in current_dict:
            return True
        else:
            return False

#create trie stored with words
def create_trie(*words):
    root = dict()
```

```
    for word in words:
        current_dict = root
        for letter in word:
            current_dict = current_dict.setdefault(letter, {})
        current_dict = current_dict.setdefault(_end, _end)
    return root

def insert_word(trie, word):
    if in_trie(trie, word): return

    current_dict = trie
    for letter in word:
            current_dict = current_dict.setdefault(letter, {})
    current_dict = current_dict.setdefault(_end, _end)

def remove_word(trie, word):
    current_dict = trie
    for letter in word:
        current_dict = current_dict.get(letter, None)
        if current_dict is None:
            # the trie doesn't contain this word.
            break
    else:
        del current_dict[_end]

dict = create_trie('foo', 'bar', 'baz', 'barz', 'bar')
print dict
print in_trie(dict, 'bar')
print in_trie(dict, 'bars')
insert_word(dict, 'bars')
print dict
print in_trie(dict, 'bars')
```

Visualization using matplotlib

matplotlib has been a popular plotting package besides a few other that are available today. The capability of matplotlib is now being realized by the Python community. John Hunter, the creator and project leader of this package summed it up as *matplotlib tries to make easy things easy and hard things possible.* You can generate very high-quality, publication-ready graphs with very little effort. In this section, we will pick a few interesting examples to illustrate the power of matplotlib.

Word clouds

Word clouds give greater prominence to words that appear more frequently in any given text. They are also called tag clouds or weighted words. You can tweak word clouds with different fonts, layouts, and color schemes. The significance of a word's strength in terms of the number of occurrences visually maps to the size of their appearance. In other words, the word that appears the largest in visualization is the one that has appeared the most in the text.

Beyond the obvious map to their occurrences, word clouds have several useful applications for social media and marketing. Some of the applications are as follows:

- Businesses can get to know their customers and how they view their products. Some organizations have used a very creative method of asking their fans or followers to post words about what they think of their brand, taking all these words into a word cloud to better understand the most common impressions of their product brand.

- Finding ways to learn about their competitors by identifying a brand whose online presence is popular. Creating a word cloud from their content to better understand what words and themes hook the product target market.

In order to create a word cloud, you can write the Python code or use something that already exists. Andreas Mueller from the NYU Center for Data Science created a pretty simple and easy-to-use word cloud in Python. It can be installed with the instructions given in the next section.

Installing word clouds

For faster installation, you can just use `pip` with `sudo` access, as shown in the following code:

```
sudo pip install git+git://github.com/amueller/word_cloud.git
```

Alternatively, you can obtain the package via `wget` on Linux or `curl` on Mac OS with the following code:

```
wget https://github.com/amueller/word_cloud/archive/master.zip
unzip master.zip
rm master.zip
cd word_cloud-master
sudo pip install -r requirements.txt
```

For the Anaconda IDE, you will have to install it using conda with the following three steps:

```
#step-1 command
conda install wordcloud


Fetching package metadata: ....
Error: No packages found in current osx-64 channels matching: wordcloud


You can search for this package on Binstar with
# This only means one has to search the source location
binstar search -t conda wordcloud


Run 'binstar show <USER/PACKAGE>' to get more details:
Packages:
                         Name | Access       | Package Types   |
     ------------------------- | ------------ | --------------- |
            derickl/wordcloud | public       | conda           |
Found 1 packages


# step-2 command
binstar show derickl/wordcloud


Using binstar api site https://api.binstar.org
Name:    wordcloud
Summary:
Access:  public
Package Types:  conda
Versions:
   + 1.0


To install this package with conda run:
conda install --channel https://conda.binstar.org/derickl wordcloud


# step-3 command
conda install --channel https://conda.binstar.org/derickl wordcloud
```

```
Fetching package metadata: ......
Solving package specifications: .
Package plan for installation in environment /Users/MacBook/anaconda:

The following packages will be downloaded:

    package                    |                build
    ---------------------------|-----------------
    cython-0.22                |             py27_0      2.2 MB
    django-1.8                 |             py27_0      3.2 MB
    pillow-2.8.1               |             py27_1      454 KB
    image-1.3.4                |             py27_0       24 KB
    setuptools-15.1            |             py27_1      435 KB
    wordcloud-1.0              |         np19py27_1       58 KB
    conda-3.11.0               |             py27_0      167 KB
    ------------------------------------------------------------
                                            Total:      6.5 MB

The following NEW packages will be INSTALLED:
    django:     1.8-py27_0
    image:      1.3.4-py27_0
    pillow:     2.8.1-py27_1
    wordcloud:  1.0-np19py27_1

The following packages will be UPDATED:
    conda:      3.10.1-py27_0 --> 3.11.0-py27_0
    cython:     0.21-py27_0   --> 0.22-py27_0
    setuptools: 15.0-py27_0   --> 15.1-py27_1

The following packages will be DOWNGRADED:

    libtiff:    4.0.3-0       --> 4.0.2-1

Proceed ([y]/n)? y
```

Input for word clouds

In this section, there will be two sources where you can extract words to construct word clouds. The first example shows how to extract text from the web feeds of some known websites and how to extract the words from its description. The second example shows how to extract text from tweets with the help of search keywords. The two examples will need the `feedparser` package and the `tweepy` package, and by following similar steps (as mentioned for other packages previously), you can easily install them.

Our approach will be to collect words from both these examples and use them as the input for a common word cloud program.

Web feeds

There are well grouped and structured RSS or atom feeds in most of the news and technology service websites today. Although our aim is to restrict the context to technology alone, we can determine a handful of feed lists, as shown in the following code. In order to be able to parse these feeds, the `parser()` method of `feedparser` comes in handy. Word cloud has its own `stopwords` list, but in addition to this, we can also use one while collecting the data, as shown here (`stopwords` here is not complete, but you can gather more from any known resource on the Internet):

```
import feedparser
from os import path
import re

d = path.dirname(__file__)
mystopwords = [ 'test', 'quot', 'nbsp']

feedlist = ['http://www.techcrunch.com/rssfeeds/',
'http://www.computerweekly.com/rss',
'http://feeds.twit.tv/tnt.xml',
'https://www.apple.com/pr/feeds/pr.rss',
'https://news.google.com/?output=rss'
'http://www.forbes.com/technology/feed/'                'http://rss.
nytimes.com/services/xml/rss/nyt/Technology.xml',         'http://www.
nytimes.com/roomfordebate/topics/technology.rss',
'http://feeds.webservice.techradar.com/us/rss/reviews'
'http://feeds.webservice.techradar.com/us/rss/news/software',
'http://feeds.webservice.techradar.com/us/rss',
'http://www.cnet.com/rss/',
'http://feeds.feedburner.com/ibm-big-data-hub?format=xml',
'http://feeds.feedburner.com/ResearchDiscussions-DataScien
ceCentral?format=xml',        'http://feeds.feedburner.com/
BdnDailyPressReleasesDiscussions-BigDataNews?format=xml',
```

```
'http://http://feeds.feedburner.com/ibm-big-data-hub-
galleries?format=xml',                'http://http://feeds.feedburner.com/
PlanetBigData?format=xml',
'http://rss.cnn.com/rss/cnn_tech.rss',
'http://news.yahoo.com/rss/tech',
'http://slashdot.org/slashdot.rdf',
'http://bbc.com/news/technology/']


def extractPlainText(ht):
    plaintxt=''
    s=0
    for char in ht:
        if char == '<': s = 1
        elif char == '>':
            s = 0
            plaintxt += ' '
        elif s == 0: plaintxt += char
    return plaintxt


def separatewords(text):
    splitter = re.compile('\\W*')
    return [s.lower() for s in splitter.split(text) if len(s) > 3]


def combineWordsFromFeed(filename):
    with open(filename, 'w') as wfile:
      for feed in feedlist:
        print "Parsing " + feed
        fp = feedparser.parse(feed)
        for e in fp.entries:
          txt = e.title.encode('utf8') +
                extractPlainText(e.description.encode('utf8'))
          words = separatewords(txt)

          for word in words:
            if word.isdigit() == False and word not in mystopwords:
              wfile.write(word)
              wfile.write(" ")
          wfile.write("\n")
    wfile.close()
    return


combineWordsFromFeed("wordcloudInput_FromFeeds.txt")
```

The Twitter text

In order to access the Twitter API, you will need the access token and consumer credentials that consist of four parameters: `access_token`, `access_token_secret`, `consumer_key`, and `consumer_secret`. In order to obtain these keys, you will have to use a Twitter account. The steps involved in obtaining these keys are available on the Twitter website. The steps involved are:

1. Log in to the Twitter account.
2. Navigate to `developer.twitter.com` and use **Manage My Apps** to follow through and obtain the parameters mentioned before.

Assuming that these parameters are ready, with the `tweepy` package, you can access tweets via Python. The following code displays a simple custom stream listener. Here, as the tweets are streamed, there is a listener that listens to the status and writes the state to a file. This can be used later to create word clouds.

The stream uses a filter to narrow the Twitter text that is focused on *the Python program*, *data visualization*, *big data*, *machine learning*, and *statistics*. The `tweepy` stream provides the tweets that are extracted. This can run forever because there is unlimited data available out there. How do we set it to stop? The accessing speed may be slower than you would expect, and for the purposes of creating a word cloud, you would imagine that extracting a certain number of tweets is probably sufficient. We therefore set a limit and called it `MAX_TWEETS` to be `50`, as shown in the following code:

```
import tweepy
import json
import sys
import codecs

counter = 0
MAX_TWEETS = 500

#Variables that contains the user credentials to access Twitter API
access_token = "Access Token"
access_token_secret = "Access Secret"
consumer_key = "Consumer Key"
consumer_secret = "Consumer Secret"

fp = codecs.open("filtered_tweets.txt", "w", "utf-8")

class CustomStreamListener(tweepy.StreamListener):

    def on_status(self, status):
        global counter
```

```
            fp.write(status.text)
            print "Tweet-count:" +str(counter)
            counter += 1
            if counter >= MAX_TWEETS: sys.exit()

        def on_error(self, status):
            print status

    if __name__ == '__main__':

        auth = tweepy.OAuthHandler(consumer_key, consumer_secret)
        auth.set_access_token(access_token, access_token_secret)
        streaming_api = tweepy.streaming.Stream(auth,
                CustomStreamListener(), timeout=60)

        streaming_api.filter(track=['python program', 'statistics',
                'data visualization', 'big data', 'machine learning'])
```

Using any bag of words, you can write fewer than 20 lines of the Python code to generate word clouds. A word cloud generates an image, and using `matplotlib.pyplot`, you can use `imshow()` to display the word cloud image. The following word cloud can be used with any input file of words:

```
from wordcloud import WordCloud, STOPWORDS
import matplotlib.pyplot as plt
from os import path

d = path.dirname("__file__")
text = open(path.join(d, 'filtered_tweets.txt')).read()

wordcloud = WordCloud(
    font_path='/Users/MacBook/kirthi/RemachineScript.ttf',
    stopwords=STOPWORDS,
    background_color='#222222',
    width=1000,
    height=800).generate(text)

# Open a plot of the generated image.
plt.figure(figsize=(13,13))
plt.imshow(wordcloud)
plt.axis("off")
plt.show()
```

The required font file can be downloaded from any of a number of sites (one specific resource for this font is available at `http://www.dafont.com/remachine-script.font`). Wherever the font file is located, you will have to use this exact path set to `font_path`. For using the data from feeds, there is only one line that changes, as shown in the following code:

```
text = open(path.join(d, 'wordcloudInput_fromFeeds.txt')).read()
```

Using the similar idea of extracting text from tweets to create word clouds, you could extract text within the context of mobile phone vendors with keywords, such as *iPhone*, *Samsung Galaxy*, *Amazon Fire*, *LG Optimus*, *Nokia Lumia*, and so on, to determine the sentiments of consumers. In this case, you may need an additional set of information, that is, the positive and negative sentiment values associated with words.

There are a few approaches that you can follow in a sentiment analysis on tweets in a restricted context. First, a very naïve approach would be to just associate weights to words that correspond to a positive sentiment as w_p and a negative sentiment as w_n, applying the following notation $p(+)$ as the probability of a positive sentiment and $p(-)$ for a negative sentiment:

$$p(+) = e^{\frac{1}{w_p - w_n + 1}}$$
$$p(-) = 1 - p(+)$$

The second approach would be to use a natural language processing tool and apply trained classifiers to obtain better results. **TextBlob** is a text processing package that also has sentiment analysis (`http://textblob.readthedocs.org/en/dev`).

TextBlob builds a text classification system and creates a training set in the JSON format. Later, using this training and the Naïve Bayes classifier, it performs the sentiment analysis. We will attempt to use this tool in later chapters to demonstrate our working examples.

Plotting the stock price chart

The two biggest stock exchanges in the U.S. are the **New York Stock Exchange** (**NYSE**), founded in 1792 and the NASDAQ founded in 1971. Today, most stock market trades are executed electronically. Even the stocks themselves are almost always held in the electronic form, not as physical certificates. There are numerous other websites that also provide real-time stock price data, apart from NASDAQ and NYSE.

Obtaining data

One of the websites to obtain data is Yahoo, which provides data via the API, for example, to obtain the stock price (low, high, open, close, and volume) of Amazon, the URL is `http://chartapi.finance.yahoo.com/instrument/1.0/amzn/chartdata;type=quote;range=3y/csv`. Depending on the plotting method you select, there is some data conversion that is required. For instance, the data obtained from this resource includes date in a format that does not have any format, as shown in the following code:

```
uri:/instrument/1.0/amzn/chartdata;type=quote;range=3y/csv
ticker:amzn
Company-Name:Amazon.com, Inc.
Exchange-Name:NMS
unit:DAY
timestamp:
first-trade:19970516
last-trade:20150430
currency:USD
previous_close_price:231.9000
Date:20120501,20150430
labels:20120501,20120702,20121001,20130102,20130401,20130701,20131001,
20140102,20140401,20140701,20141001,20150102,20150401
values:Date,close,high,low,open,volume
close:208.2200,445.1000
high:211.2300,452.6500
low:206.3700,439.0000
open:207.4000,443.8600
volume:984400,23856100
20120501,230.0400,232.9700,228.4000,229.4000,6754900
20120502,230.2500,231.4400,227.4000,227.8200,4593400
20120503,229.4500,232.5300,228.0300,229.7400,4055500
...
...
20150429,429.3700,434.2400,426.0300,426.7500,3613300
20150430,421.7800,431.7500,419.2400,427.1100,3609700
```

We will discuss three approaches in creating the plots. Each one has its own advantages and limitations.

In the first approach, with the `matplotlib.cbook` package and the `pylab` package, you can create a plot with the following lines of code:

```
from pylab import plotfile show, gca
import matplotlib.cbook as cbook
fname = cbook.get_sample_data('/Users/MacBook/stocks/amzn.csv',
asfileobj=False)
plotfile(fname, ('date', 'high', 'low', 'close'), subplots=False)
show()
```

This will create a plot similar to the one shown in the following screenshot:

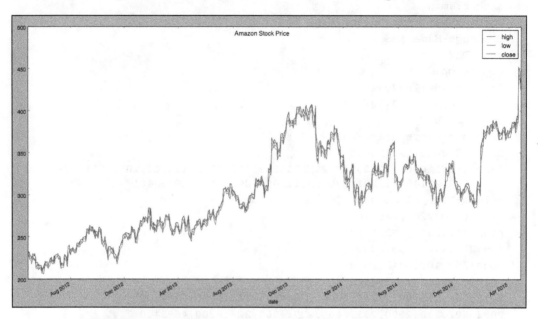

There is one additional programming effort that is required before attempting to plot using this approach. The date values have to be formatted to represent *20150430* as `%d-%b-%Y`. With this approach, the plot can also be split into two, one showing the stock price and the other showing the volume, as shown in the following code:

```
from pylab import plotfile show, gca
import matplotlib.cbook as cbook
fname = cbook.get_sample_data('/Users/MacBook/stocks/amzn.csv',
asfileobj=False)
plotfile(fname, (0,1,5), plotfuncs={f:'bar'})
show()
```

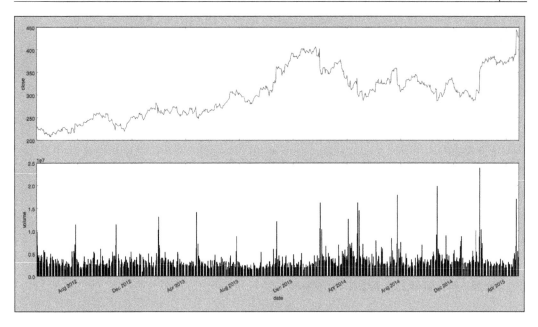

The second approach is to use the subpackages of `matplotlib.mlab` and `matplotlib.finance`. This has convenient methods to fetch the stock data from `http://ichart.finance.yahoo.com/table.csv?s=GOOG&a=04&b=12&c=2014&d=06&e=20&f=2015&g=d`, and to just show a sample, here is a code snippet:

```
ticker='GOOG'

import matplotlib.finance as finance
import matplotlib.mlab as mlab
import datetime

startdate = datetime.date(2014,4,12)
today = enddate = datetime.date.today()

fh = finance.fetch_historical_yahoo(ticker, startdate, enddate)
r = mlab.csv2rec(fh); fh.close()
r.sort()
print r[:2]

[ (datetime.date(2014, 4, 14), 538.25, 544.09998, 529.56, 532.52002,
2568000, 532.52002)  (datetime.date(2014, 4, 15), 536.82001,
538.45001, 518.46002, 536.44, 3844500, 536.44)]
```

When you attempt to plot the stock price comparison, it does not make sense to display the volume information because for each stock ticker, the volumes are different. Also, it becomes too cluttered to view the stock chart.

`matplotlib` already has a working example to plot the stock chart, which is elaborate enough and includes **Relative Strength Indicator (RSI)** and **Moving Average Convergence/Divergence (MACD)**, and is available at http://matplotlib.org/examples/pylab_examples/finance_work2.html. For details on RSI and MACD, you can find many resources online, but there is one interesting explanation at http://easyforextrading.co/how-to-trade/indicators/.

In an attempt to use the existing code, modify it, and make it work for multiple charts, a function called `plotTicker()` was created. This helps in plotting each ticker within the same axis, as shown in the following code:

```python
import datetime
import numpy as np

import matplotlib.finance as finance
import matplotlib.dates as mdates
import matplotlib.mlab as mlab
import matplotlib.pyplot as plt

startdate = datetime.date(2014,4,12)
today = enddate = datetime.date.today()

plt.rc('axes', grid=True)
plt.rc('grid', color='0.75', linestyle='-', linewidth=0.5)
rect = [0.4, 0.5, 0.8, 0.5]

fig = plt.figure(facecolor='white', figsize=(12,11))

axescolor = '#f6f6f6' # the axes background color

ax = fig.add_axes(rect, axisbg=axescolor)
ax.set_ylim(10,800)

def plotTicker(ticker, startdate, enddate, fillcolor):
    """
    matplotlib.finance has fetch_historical_yahoo() which fetches
    stock price data the url where it gets the data from is
    http://ichart.yahoo.com/table.csv stores in a numpy record
    array with fields:
      date, open, high, low, close, volume, adj_close
    """

    fh = finance.fetch_historical_yahoo(ticker, startdate, enddate)
    r = mlab.csv2rec(fh);
    fh.close()
    r.sort()
```

```
### plot the relative strength indicator
### adjusted close removes the impacts of splits and dividends
prices = r.adj_close

### plot the price and volume data

ax.plot(r.date, prices, color=fillcolor, lw=2, label=ticker)
ax.legend(loc='top right', shadow=True, fancybox=True)

# set the labels rotation and alignment
for label in ax.get_xticklabels():
    # To display date label slanting at 30 degrees
    label.set_rotation(30)
    label.set_horizontalalignment('right')

ax.fmt_xdata = mdates.DateFormatter('%Y-%m-%d')

#plot the tickers now
plotTicker('BIDU', startdate, enddate, 'red')
plotTicker('GOOG', startdate, enddate, '#1066ee')
plotTicker('AMZN', startdate, enddate, '#506612')

plt.show()
```

When you use this to compare the stock prices of Bidu, Google, and Amazon, the plot would look similar to the following screenshot:

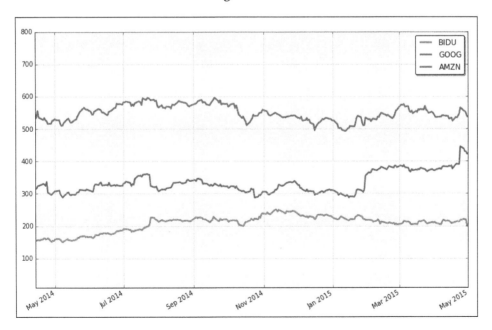

Use the following code to compare the stock prices of Twitter, Facebook, and LinkedIn:

```
plotTicker('TWTR', startdate, enddate, '#c72020')
plotTicker('LNKD', startdate, enddate, '#103474')
plotTicker('FB', startdate, enddate, '#506612')
```

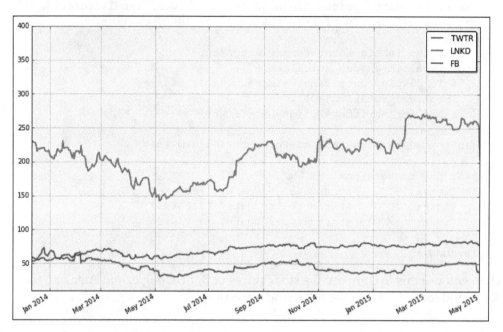

Now, you can add the volume plot as well. For a single ticker plot with volume, use the following code:

```
import datetime

import matplotlib.finance as finance
import matplotlib.dates as mdates
import matplotlib.mlab as mlab
import matplotlib.pyplot as plt

startdate = datetime.date(2013,3,1)
today = enddate = datetime.date.today()

rect = [0.1, 0.3, 0.8, 0.4]

fig = plt.figure(facecolor='white', figsize=(10,9))
ax = fig.add_axes(rect, axisbg='#f6f6f6')
```

```
def plotSingleTickerWithVolume(ticker, startdate, enddate):

    global ax

    fh = finance.fetch_historical_yahoo(ticker, startdate, enddate)

    # a numpy record array with fields:
    #     date, open, high, low, close, volume, adj_close
    r = mlab.csv2rec(fh);
    fh.close()
    r.sort()

    plt.rc('axes', grid=True)
    plt.rc('grid', color='0.78', linestyle='-', linewidth=0.5)

    axt = ax.twinx()
    prices = r.adj_close

    fcolor = 'darkgoldenrod'

    ax.plot(r.date, prices, color=r'#1066ee', lw=2, label=ticker)
    ax.fill_between(r.date, prices, 0, prices, facecolor='#BBD7E5')
    ax.set_ylim(0.5*prices.max())

    ax.legend(loc='upper right', shadow=True, fancybox=True)

    volume = (r.close*r.volume)/1e6  # dollar volume in millions
    vmax = volume.max()

    axt.fill_between(r.date, volume, 0, label='Volume',
                facecolor=fcolor, edgecolor=fcolor)

    axt.set_ylim(0, 5*vmax)
    axt.set_yticks([])

    for axis in ax, axt:
        for label in axis.get_xticklabels():
            label.set_rotation(30)
            label.set_horizontalalignment('right')

        axis.fmt_xdata = mdates.DateFormatter('%Y-%m-%d')

plotSingleTickerWithVolume ('MSFT', startdate, enddate)
plt.show()
```

With the single ticker plot along with volume and the preceding changes in the earlier code, the plot will look similar to the following screenshot:

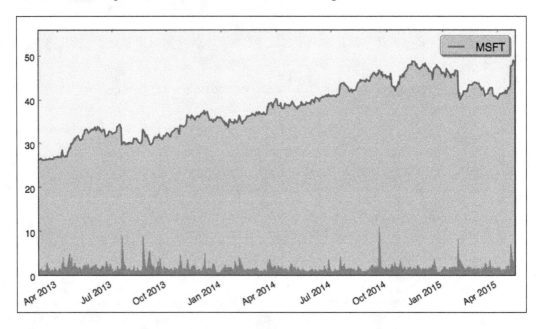

You may also have the option of using the *third approach*: using the `blockspring` package. In order to install `blockspring`, you have to use the following `pip` command:

pip install blockspring

Blockspring's approach is to generate the HTML code. It autogenerates data for the plots in the JavaScript format. When this is integrated with D3.js, it provides a very nice interactive plot. Amazingly, there are only two lines of code:

```
import blockspring
import json

print blockspring.runParsed("stock-price-comparison",
    { "tickers": "FB, LNKD, TWTR",
    "start_date": "2014-01-01", "end_date": "2015-01-01" }).params
```

Depending on the operating system, when this code is run, it generates the HTML code in a default area.

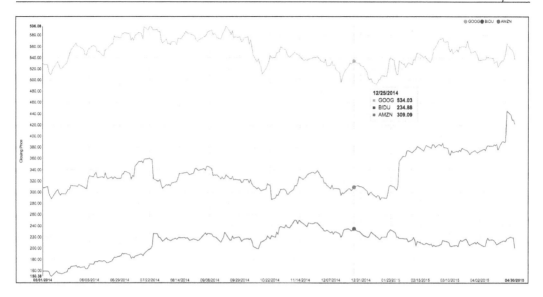

The visualization example in sports

Let's consider a different example here to illustrate the various different approaches to visualizing data. Instead of choosing a computational problem, we will restrict ourselves to a simple set of data, and show how many different analyses can be done that ultimately result in visualizations, to help in clarifying these analyses.

There are several major league sports in North American sports, and we will compare four of them: **The National Football League (NFL)**, **Major League Baseball (MLB)**, **National Basketball Association (NBA)**, and **National Hockey League**. NFL has a combined team value of 9.13 billion dollars and a total revenue of 9.58 billion dollars. We will select this sport with the following data of team values and their championships (only part of the data is shown here):

	Team.name	Team.value	Years.Completed	Num.Championships	Championships.yr.average
1	Dallas Cowboys	3210	55	5	23.18
2	Washington Redskins	2400	83	3	12.22
3	New York Giants	2100	90	4	13.88
4	Houston Texans	1850	13	0	5.00
5	New York Jets	1810	55	1	8.63
6	Philadelphia Eagles	1750	82	0	5.00
7	Chicago Bears	1700	96	1	7.08
8	New England Patriots	1635	55	4	15.90
9	San Francisco 49ers	1600	69	5	19.49
10	Baltimore Ravens	1500	19	2	26.05

The team value is one significant factor in comparing different teams, but championships also have a value. A simple plot of this data with *years completed* along the *x* axis, the *number of championships* along the *y* axis, and the bubble size representing the *number of championship per year average* would give us something similar to the following image:

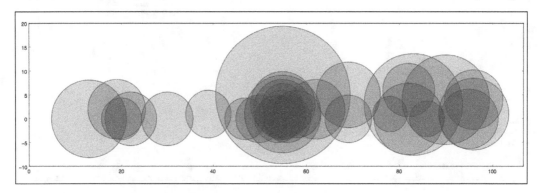

However, unless you can make it interactive by displaying the labels or details, the preceding plot may not be very useful. The preceding plot is possible with matplotlib, as shown in the following code:

```
import matplotlib.pyplot as plt
fig = plt.figure(figsize=(15,10), facecolor='w')

def plotCircle(x,y,radius,color, alphaval):
  circle = plt.Circle((x, y), radius=radius, fc=color,\
   alpha=alphaval)
  fig.gca().add_patch(circle)
  nofcircle = plt.Circle((x, y), radius=radius, ec=color, \
   fill=False)
  fig.gca().add_patch(nofcircle)

x = [55,83,90,13,55,82,96,55,69,19,55,95,62,96,82,30,22,39, \
  54,50,69,56,58,55,55,47,55,20,86,78,56]
y = [5,3,4,0,1,0,1,3,5,2,2,0,2,4,6,0,0,1,0,0,0,0,1,1,0,0,3,0, \
  0,1,0]
r = [23,17,15,13,13,12,12,11,11,10,10,10,10,10,9,9,9,8,8,8,8, \
   8,8,8,7,7,7,7,6,6,6]
for i in range(0,len(x)):
  plotCircle(x[i],y[i],r[i],'b', 0.1)


plt.axis('scaled')
plt.show()
```

You can even use this numeric data to convert into a format that JavaScript can understand (JSON format) so that when integrated with an SVG map, it is possible to display the valuation on the map, as shown in the following screenshot:

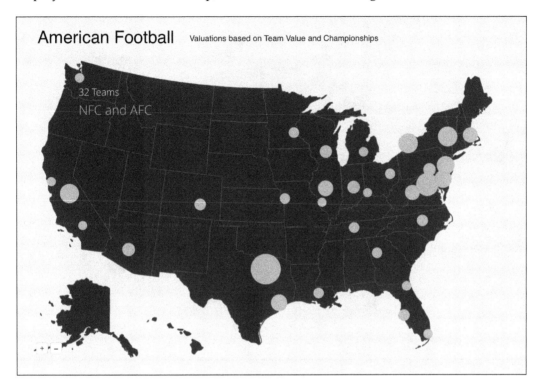

The preceding map with bubbles would be better if there were associated labels displayed. However, due to the lack of space in certain regions of the map, it would make much more sense to add an interactive implementation to this map and have the information displayed via navigation.

You can refer to the original data source at `http://tinyurl.com/oyxk72r`.

An alternate source is available at `http://www.knapdata.com/python/nfl_franch.html`.

There are several other visualization methods you could apply, apart from the plain bubble chart and the bubble chart on maps. One of the visual formats that will look cluttered when displaying the statistics of 32 teams would be a pie chart or a bar chart.

It not only looks cluttered, the labels are hardly readable. The whole point in showing this pie chart is to illustrate that in this sort of data, one has to seek alternate methods of visualization, as shown in the following image:

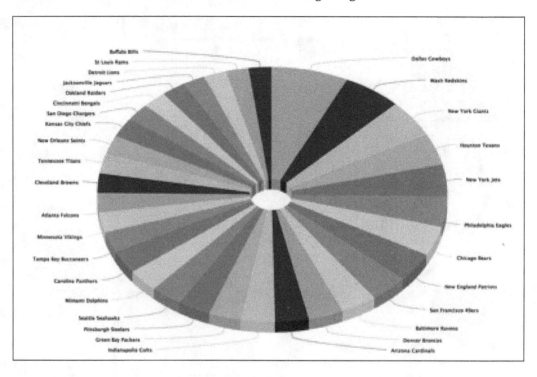

If we combine a set of teams within a certain range of their team value, then by reducing them, we may be able to show them in a more organized fashion, as shown in the following image:

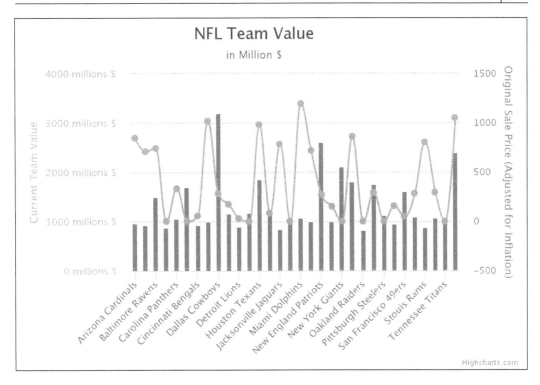

The preceding image is one alternative to display the value of teams by segregating them into groups, for example, denote 2300 million dollars for $2300,000,000, which means 2300 million dollars. This way, the data labels are readable.

Summary

During the last several decades, computing has emerged as a very important part of many fields. In fact, the curriculum of computer science in many schools, such as Stanford, UC-Berkeley, MIT, Princeton, Harvard, Caltech, and so on, has been revised to accommodate interdisciplinary courses because of this change. In most scientific disciplines, computational work is an important complement to experiments and theory. Moreover, a vast majority of experimental and theoretical papers involve some numerical calculations, simulations, or computer modeling.

Python has come a long way, and today the community of Python has grown to the extent that there are sources and tools to help write minimal code to accomplish almost everything that one may need in computing very efficiently. We could only pick a few working examples in this chapter, but in the following chapters, we will take a look at more examples.

The rendering image, can also use the R display, the value of range be telling the... the entire picture, for example, denote... 2000 million dollars for $2,000,000,000 with a... figure 2000 million... just as this is the data that is the rendering.

SUMMARY

During the last couple of decades, computing has emerged as a very important part of many building... of the principal tools of computer scientists to resolve problems... such as within a... Berkeley, MIT, Princeton, Harvard... allied and given the... has been used to accumulate... for most any courses, technical or the branches of... more specific disciplines, computable logic work is an important complement to... experiments and theory. Moreover, a vast majority of experimental and theoretical purposes give some numerical calculations, simulations, or computer modelling.

Python has come a long way, and today the community of Python has grown... to the extent that they are growing and... tools to be... with a initial and code in some... them as... that, also, everything that one may need for compiling very efficiently. We could only... a token few work by examples in this chapter, but in the following chapters, we will take a look at more examples.

5
Financial and Statistical Models

Financial and economic models primarily help in the simplification and abstraction of data and make extensive use of probability and statistics. It's always important to take a look at the data; the first step in data analysis should be plotting the data. Problems such as bad data, outliers, and missing data can often be detected by visualizing data. Bad data should be corrected whenever possible or otherwise discarded. However, in some unusual cases, such as in a stock market, outliers are good data and should be retained. To summarize, it is important to detect the bad data and outliers and to understand them so that appropriate action can be taken. The choice of data variables plays an important role in these models.

The selection of variables is important because the nature of a model will often determine the facts that are being looked at. For instance, in order to measure inflation, a model of behavior is required so that you can understand the real changes in price, and the changes in price that directly connect to inflation.

There are many interesting models and their applications that we can discuss, but to stay within the scope of this book, we will select some examples. In some cases, such as Monte Carlo, we will also select some application in sports. In the later sections, we will discuss the following topics:

- Monte Carlo simulation—examples applicable in many areas
- Price models with examples
- Understanding volatility measures with examples
- The threshold model—Shelling's model of segregation
- Bayesian regression methods with plotting options

- Geometric Brownian, diffusion-based simulation, and portfolio valuation
- Profiling and creating real-time interactive plots
- Statistical and machine learning overview

Computational finance is a field in computer science and deals with the data and algorithms that arise in financial modeling. For some readers, the contents of this chapter may be well understood, but for others, looking at these concepts will be useful for learning some new insights that may likely be useful in their lives or be applicable in their areas of interests.

Before you learn about the applications of Monte Carlo simulation methods, let's take a look at a very simple example of investment and gross returns over a period of time.

The deterministic model

The ultimate goal of investment is to make a profit, and the revenue from investing or loss depends on both the change in prices and the number of assets being held. Investors are usually interested in revenues that are highly relative to the size of the initial investments. Returns measure this mainly because returns are an asset. For example, a stock, a bond, or a portfolio of stocks and bonds are by definition expressed as changes, and price is expressed as a fraction of the initial price. Let's take a look at the gross returns example.

Gross returns

Let's assume that P_t is the investment amount at time t. A simple gross return is expressed as follows:

$$\frac{P_{t+1}}{P_t} = 1 + R_{t+1}$$

Here, P_{t+1} is the returned investment value and the return is R_{t+1}. For example, if $P_t = 10$ and $P_{t+1} = 10.6$, then $R_{t+1} = 0.06 = 6\%$. Returns are scale-free, meaning that they do not depend on the units, but returns are dependent on the units of t (hour, day, and so on). In other words, if t is measured in years, then, as stated more precisely, this net return is 6 percent per year.

The gross return over the most recent k years is the product of k single year gross returns (from $t\text{-}k$ to t), as shown here:

$$1 + R_t(k) = \frac{P_t}{P_{t-k}}$$

$$= \left(\frac{P_t}{P_{t-1}}\right)\left(\frac{P_{t-1}}{P_{t-2}}\right)\cdots\left(\frac{P_{t-k+1}}{P_{t-k}}\right)$$

$$= (1 + R_t)(1 + R_{t-1})\cdots(1 + R_{t-k+1})$$

This is an example of a deterministic model, except that there is one caveat that we did not mention: you have to incorporate the inflation rate in the equation per year. If we include this in the preceding equation by assuming F_t is the inflation that corresponds to the return R_t, we will get the following equation:

$$1 + R_t(k) = \frac{(1 + R_t)}{(1 + F_t)}\frac{(1 + R_{t-1})}{(1 + F_{t-1})}\cdots\frac{(1 + R_{t-k+1})}{(1 + F_{t-k+1})}$$

If we assume $F_t = 0$, then the previous equation would be applicable. Assume that we do not include inflation and ask this question: "with an initial investment of $10,000 in 2010 and a return rate of 6%, after how many years will my investment double?"

Let's try to find the answer with the Python program. In this program, we also have to add a straight line that is almost similar to $y = 2x$ and see where it intersects the curve of the return values plotted on the y axis with the year running on the x axis. First, we will plot without the line to determine whether the invested value is almost doubled in 12 years. Then, we will calculate the slope of the line $m = 10,000/12 = 833.33$. Therefore, we included this slope value of 833.33 in the program to display both the return values and the straight line. The following code compares the return value overlap with the straight line:

```
import matplotlib.pyplot as plt

principle_value=10000   #invested amount
grossReturn = 1.06      # Rt

return_amt = []
x = []
y = [10000]
year=2010
return_amt.append(principle_value)
x.append(year)
```

```
for i in range(1,15):
    return_amt.append(return_amt[i-1] * grossReturn)
    print "Year-",i," Returned:",return_amt[i]

    year += 1
    x.append(year)
    y.append(833.33*(year-2010)+principle_value)

# set the grid to appear
plt.grid()

# plot the return values curve
plt.plot(x,return_amt, color='r')
plt.plot(x,y, color='b')

Year- 1 Returned: 10600.0
Year- 2 Returned: 11236.0
Year- 3 Returned: 11910.16
Year- 4 Returned: 12624.7696
Year- 5 Returned: 13382.255776
Year- 6 Returned: 14185.1911226
Year- 7 Returned: 15036.3025899
Year- 8 Returned: 15938.4807453
Year- 9 Returned: 16894.78959
Year- 10 Returned: 17908.4769654
Year- 11 Returned: 18982.9855834
Year- 12 Returned: 20121.9647184
Year- 13 Returned: 21329.2826015
Year- 14 Returned: 22609.0395575
```

After looking at the plot, you would wonder whether there is a way to find out how much money the banks that provide mortgage loans make. We'll leave this to you.

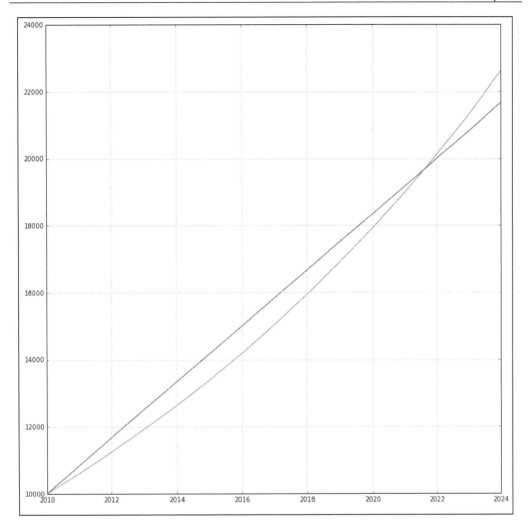

An interesting fact is that the curve intersects the line before 2022. At this point, the return value is exactly $20,000. However, in 2022, the return value will be approximately $20,121. Having looked at the gross returns, is it similar in stocks? Many stocks, especially of mature companies, pay dividends that must be accounted for in the equation.

If a dividend (or interest) D_t is paid prior to time t, then the gross return at time t is defined as follows:

$$1 + R_t = \frac{P_t + D_t}{P_{t-1}}$$

Another example is a mortgage loan, where a certain amount of loan is borrowed from a financial institution at an interest rate. Here, for the purposes of understanding the nature of the business, we will select a loan amount of $350,000 at an interest rate of 5 percent on a 30-year term. This is a typical example of American Mortgage Loan
(the loan amount and interest rate varies depending on the credit history and the market rate of interest of a loan seeker).

A simple interest calculation is known to be $P\ (1 + rt)$, where P is the principal amount, r is the interest rate, and t is the term, so the total amount accrued at the end of 30 years is:

$$350,000 \times \left(1 + \frac{5}{100} \times 30\right) = 350,000 \times \frac{5}{2} = 875,000$$

It turns out that by the end of 30 years, you would have paid more than twice the loan amount (we have not taken the real estate taxes into account in this calculation):

```python
from decimal import Decimal
import matplotlib.pyplot as plt

colors = [(31, 119, 180),(174, 199, 232),(255,128,0),(255, 15, 14),
          (44, 160, 44),(152, 223, 138),(214, 39, 40),(255,173, 61),
          (148, 103, 189),(197, 176, 213),(140, 86, 75),(196, 156, 148),
          (227, 119, 194),(247, 182, 210),(127, 127, 127),
          (199, 199, 199),(188, 189, 34), (219, 219, 141),
          (23, 190, 207), (158, 218, 229)]

# Scale the RGB values to the [0, 1] range, which is the format
matplotlib accepts.
for i in range(len(colors)):
    r, g, b = colors[i]
    colors[i] = (r / 255., g / 255., b / 255.)

def printHeaders(term, extra):
    # Print headers
    print "\nExtra-Payment: $"+str(extra)+" Term:"+str(term)+" years"
    print "------------------------------------------------------------"
    print 'Pmt no'.rjust(6), ' ', 'Beg. bal.'.ljust(13), ' ',
```

```
        print 'Payment'.ljust(9), ' ', 'Principal'.ljust(9), ' ',
        print 'Interest'.ljust(9), ' ', 'End. bal.'.ljust(13)
        print ''.rjust(6, '-'), ' ', ''.ljust(13, '-'), ' ',
        print ''.rjust(9, '-'), ' ', ''.ljust(9, '-'), ' ',
        print ''.rjust(9, '-'), ' ', ''.ljust(13, '-'), ' '

def amortization_table(principal, rate, term, extrapayment,
printData=False):
    xarr=[]
    begarr = []

    original_loan = principal
    money_saved=0
    total_payment=0
    payment = pmt(principal, rate, term)
    begBal = principal

    # Print data
    num=1
    endBal=1
    if printData == True: printHeaders(term, extrapayment)
    while  (num < term + 1) and (endBal >0):

        interest = round(begBal * (rate / (12 * 100.0)), 2)
        applied = extrapayment+round(payment - interest, 2)
        endBal = round(begBal - applied, 2)
        if (num-1)%12 == 0 or (endBal < applied+extrapayment):
          begarr.append(begBal)
          xarr.append(num/12)
          if printData == True:
              print '{0:3d}'.format(num).center(6), ' ',
              print '{0:,.2f}'.format(begBal).rjust(13), ' ',
              print '{0:,.2f}'.format(payment).rjust(9), ' ',
              print '{0:,.2f}'.format(applied).rjust(9), ' ',
              print '{0:,.2f}'.format(interest).rjust(9), ' ',
              print '{0:,.2f}'.format(endBal).rjust(13)
        total_payment += applied+extrapayment
        num +=1
        begBal = endBal
    if extrapayment > 0 :
      money_saved = abs(original_loan - total_payment)
      print '\nTotal Payment:','{0:,.2f}'.format(total_payment).
rjust(13)
      print '  Money Saved:','{0:,.2f}'.format(money_saved).rjust(13)
    return xarr, begarr, '{0:,.2f}'.format(money_saved)

def pmt(principal, rate, term):
```

```
        ratePerTwelve = rate / (12 * 100.0)

        result = principal * (ratePerTwelve / (1 - (1 + ratePerTwelve) **
(-term)))

        # Convert to decimal and round off to two decimal
        # places.
        result = Decimal(result)
        result = round(result, 2)
        return result

plt.figure(figsize=(18, 14))

#amortization_table(150000, 4, 180, 500)
i=0
markers = ['o','s','D','^','v','*','p','s','D','o','s','D','^','v','*
','p','s','D']
markersize=[8,8,8,12,8,8,8,12,8,8,8,8,8,8,8,8,8,8,8,8,8,8,8,8,8]

for extra in range(100,1700,100):
  xv, bv, saved = amortization_table(450000, 5, 360, extra, False)
  if extra == 0:
    plt.plot(xv, bv, color=colors[i], lw=2.2, label='Principal only',
marker=markers[i], markersize=markersize[i])
  else:
    plt.plot(xv, bv, color=colors[i], lw=2.2, label="Principal
plus\$"+str(extra)+str("/month, Saved:\$")+saved, marker=markers[i],
markersize=markersize[i])
  i +=1


plt.grid(True)
plt.xlabel('Years', fontsize=18)
plt.ylabel('Mortgage Balance', fontsize=18)
plt.title("Mortgage Loan For $350,000 With Additional Payment Chart",
fontsize=20)
plt.legend()
plt.show()
```

When this program is run, you would get the amortized schedule for every 12 months for all the cases of extra payment, starting from $100 to $1600. Here is just one of those cases:

```
Extra-Payment: $800 Term: 30 years
----------------------------------------------------------------Pmt
no   Beg. bal.   Payment   Principal   Interest   End. bal.    -----
-    --------    -------   ---------   ---------   ------
  1     350,000.00  1,878.88* 1,220.55   1,458.33   348,779.45
 13     335,013.07  1,878.88  1,282.99   1,395.89   333,730.08
```

25	319,259.40	1,878.88	1,348.63	1,330.25	317,910.77
37	302,699.75	1,878.88	1,417.63	1,261.25	301,282.12
49	285,292.85	1,878.88	1,490.16	1,188.72	283,802.69
61	266,995.41	1,878.88	1,566.40	1,112.48	265,429.01
73	247,761.81	1,878.88	1,646.54	1,032.34	246,115.27
85	227,544.19	1,878.88	1,730.78	948.10	225,813.41
97	206,292.20	1,878.88	1,819.33	859.55	204,472.87
109	183,952.92	1,878.88	1,912.41	766.47	182,040.51
121	160,470.74	1,878.88	2,010.25	668.63	158,460.49
133	135,787.15	1,878.88	2,113.10	565.78	133,674.05
145	109,840.70	1,878.88	2,221.21	457.67	107,619.49
157	82,566.78	1,878.88	2,334.85	344.03	80,231.93
169	53,897.49	1,878.88	2,454.31	224.57	51,443.18
181	23,761.41	1,878.88	2,579.87	99.01	21,181.54
188	5,474.98	1,878.88	2,656.07	22.81	2,818.91
189	2,818.91	1,878.88	2,667.13	11.75	151.78

```
* $1878.88 includes $1078.88 plus $800 extra payment towards principal
Total Payment: $504,526.47 Money Saved: $154,526.47
Approximately after 15 years 10 months, one can pay off in half the
time.
```

The Python code results in the following plot that compares the additional savings with principal savings on a mortgage payment:

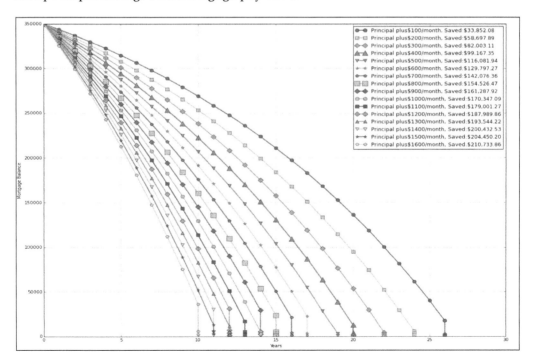

The preceding plot shows the mortgage balance dropping earlier than the 30 years by paying an additional amount against the principal amount.

The monthly payment for a fixed rate mortgage is the amount paid by the borrower every month to ensure that the loan is paid in full with interest at the end of its term. The monthly payment depends on the interest rate (r) as a fraction, the number of monthly payments (N), which is called the loan's term, and the amount borrowed (P), which is called the loan's principal; when you rearrange the formula for the present value of an ordinary annuity, we get the formula for the monthly payment. However, every month, if an extra amount is paid along with the fixed monthly payment, then the loan amount can be paid off in a much shorter time.

In the following chart, we have attempted to use the money saved from the program and plot that money against the additional amount in the range of $500 to $1300. If we see carefully, with an additional amount of $800, you can save almost half the loan amount and pay off the loan in half the term.

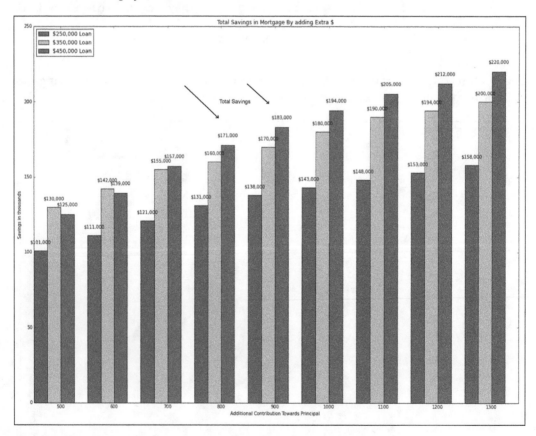

The preceding plot shows the savings for three different loan amounts, where the additional contribution is shown along the *x* axis and savings in thousands is shown along the *y* axis. The following code uses a bubble chart that also visually shows savings toward additional amount toward the principal on a mortgage loan:

```
import matplotlib.pyplot as plt

# set the savings value from previous example
yvals1 = [101000,111000,121000,131000,138000,
143000,148000,153000,158000]
yvals2 = [130000,142000,155000,160000,170000,
180000,190000,194000,200000]
yvals3 = [125000,139000,157000,171000,183000,
194000,205000,212000,220000]
xvals = ['500','600','700', '800', '900','1000','1100','1200','1300']

#initialize bubbles that will be scaled
bubble1 = []
bubble2 = []
bubble3 = []

# scale it on something that can be displayed
# It should be scaled to 1000, but display will be too big
# so we choose to scale by 5% (divide these by 20 again to relate
# to real values)

for i in range(0,9):
  bubble1.append(yvals1[i]/20)
  bubble2.append(yvals2[i]/20)
  bubble3.append(yvals3[i]/20)

#plot yvalues with scaled by bubble sizes
#If bubbles are not scaled, they don't fit well
fig, ax = plt.subplots(figsize=(10,12))
plt1 = ax.scatter(xvals,yvals1, c='#d82730', s=bubble1, alpha=0.5)
plt2 = ax.scatter(xvals,yvals2, c='#2077b4', s=bubble2, alpha=0.5)
plt3 = ax.scatter(xvals,yvals3, c='#ff8010', s=bubble3, alpha=0.5)

#Set the labels and title
ax.set_xlabel('Extra Dollar Amount', fontsize=16)
ax.set_ylabel('Savings', fontsize=16)
ax.set_title('Mortgage Savings (Paying Extra Every Month)',
        fontsize=20)

#set x and y limits
ax.set_xlim(400,1450)
```

```
ax.set_ylim(90000,230000)

ax.grid(True)
ax.legend((plt1, plt2, plt3), ('$250,000 Loan', '$350,000 Loan',
    '$450,000 Loan'), scatterpoints=1, loc='upper left',
    markerscale=0.17, fontsize=10, ncol=1)

fig.tight_layout()
plt.show()
```

By creating a scatter plot, it is much easier to view which loan category would offer more savings compared to others, but to keep it simple, we will compare only three loan amounts: $250,000, $350,000, and $450,000.

The following plot is the result of a scatter plot that demonstrates the savings by paying extra every month:

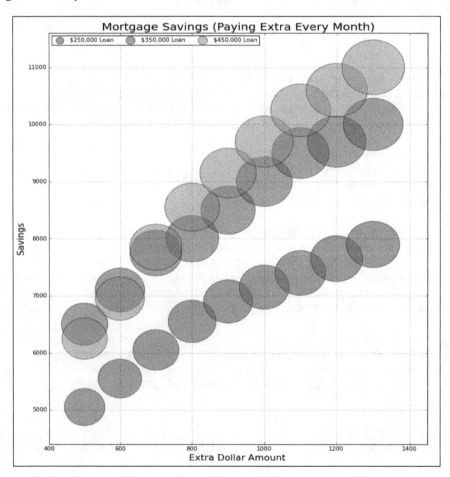

The stochastic model

We have discussed the deterministic model, where a single outcome with quantitative input values has no randomness. The word stochastic is derived from the Greek word called Stochastikos. It means skillful at guessing or chance. The antonym of this is "certain", "deterministic", or "sure". A stochastic model predicts a set of possible outcomes weighted by their likelihoods or probabilities. For instance, a coin when flipped in the air will "surely" land on earth eventually, but whether it lands heads or tails is "random".

Monte Carlo simulation

Monte Carlo simulation, which is also viewed as a probability simulation, is a technique used to understand the impact of risk and uncertainty in any forecasting model. The Monte Carlo method was invented in 1940 by Stanislaw Ulam when he was working on several nuclear weapon projects at the Los Alamos National Laboratory. Today, with computers, you can generate random numbers and run simulations pretty fast, but he amazingly found this method many years ago when computing was really hard.

In a forecasting model or any model that plans ahead for the future, there are assumptions made. These may be assumptions about the investment return on a portfolio, or how long it will take to complete a certain task. As these are future projections, the best thing to do is estimate the expected value.

What exactly is Monte Carlo simulation?

Monte Carlo simulation is a method to iteratively evaluate a deterministic model with sets of random numbers as inputs. This method is often used when the model is complex, nonlinear, or involves more than just a couple of uncertain parameters. A simulation can typically involve more than 100,000 or even a million evaluations of the model. Let's take a look at the difference between a deterministic model and a stochastic model. A deterministic model will have actual inputs that are deterministic to produce consistent results, as shown in the following image:

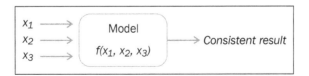

Let's see how a probabilistic model is different from the deterministic model.

Stochastic models have inputs that are probabilistic and come from a probabilistic density function, producing a result that is also probabilistic. Here is how a stochastic model looks:

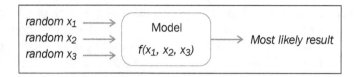

Now, how do we describe the preceding diagram in words?

First, create a model. Let's say that you have determined three random inputs: $x1$, $x2$, and $x3$, determined a method: $f(x1, x2, x3)$, and generated a set of 10,000 random values of inputs (in some cases, it could be less or more). Evaluate the model for these inputs, repeat it for these 10,000 random inputs, and record these as yi, where i runs from 1 to 10,000. Analyze the results and pick one that is most likely.

For instance, if we were to find an answer to the question, that is, "what is the probability that the Los Angeles Clippers will win the seventh game?" With some random inputs in the context of basketball that make reasonable sense to the question, you can find an answer by running Monte Carlo simulation and obtain an answer: there is a 45 percent chance that they will win. Well, actually they lost.

Monte Carlo simulation depends heavily on random number generators; therefore, it makes sense to figure out what is the fastest and efficient way to perform Monte Carlo simulation? Hans Petter Langtangen has performed an outstanding task that shows that Monte Carlo simulation can be made much more efficient by porting the code to Cython at `http://hplgit.github.io/teamods/MC_cython/sphinx/main_MC_cython.html`, where he also compares it with pure C implementation.

Let's consider several examples to illustrate Monte Carlo simulation. The first example shows an inventory problem. Later, we will discuss an example in sports (Monte Carlo simulation is applicable to many sports analytics.

An inventory problem in Monte Carlo simulation

A fruit retail salesman sells some fruit and places an order for Y units everyday. Each unit that is sold gives a profit of 60 cents and units not sold at the end of the day are thrown out at a loss of 40 cents per unit. The demand, D, on any given day is uniformly distributed on [80, 140]. How many units should the retailer order to maximize the expected profit?

Let's denote the profit as P. When you attempt to create equations based on the preceding problem description, s denotes the number of units sold, whereas d denotes the demand, as shown in the following equation:

$$P = \begin{cases} 0.6s & \text{if } d \geq s \\ 0.6d - 0.4(s-d) & \text{if } s > d \end{cases}$$

Using this representation of profit, the following Python program shows maximum profit:

```
import numpy as np
from math import log

import matplotlib.pyplot as plt

x=[]
y=[]

#Equation that defines Profit
def generateProfit(d):

    global s

    if d >= s:
        return 0.6*s
    else:
        return 0.6*d - 0.4*(s-d)

# Although y comes from uniform distribution in [80,140]
# we are running simulation for d in [20,305]

maxprofit=0

for s in range (20, 305):

    # Run a simulation for n = 1000
    # Even if we run for n = 10,000 the result would
    # be almost the same
    for i in range(1,1000):

        # generate a random value of d
        d = np.random.randint(10,high=200)
```

```
        # for this random value of d, find profit and
        # update maxprofit
        profit = generateProfit(d)
        if profit > maxprofit:
            maxprofit = profit


    #store the value of s to be plotted along X axis
    x.append(s)


    #store the value of maxprofit plotted along Y axis
    y.append(log(maxprofit)) # plotted on log scale

plt.plot(x,y)
print "Max Profit:",maxprofit

# Will display this
Max Profit: 119.4
```

The following plot shows that the profit increases when the number of units are sold, but when the demand is met, the maximum profit stays constant:

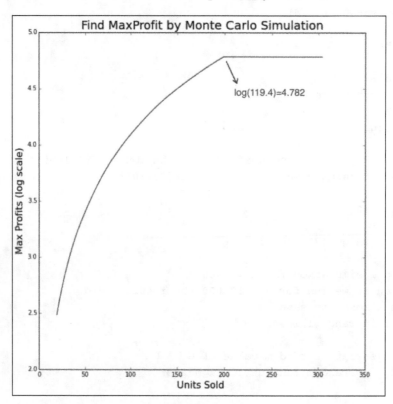

The preceding plot is shown on the log scale, which means that the maximum profit was 119.4 from a simulation run for *n=1000*. Now, let's try to take a look at an analytical solution and see how close the simulation result is to the one from the analytical method.

As the demand (*D*) is uniformly distributed in [80,140], the expected profit is derived from the following integral:

$$Profit = \int_{s}^{140} \frac{0.6s}{60} dx + \int_{80}^{s} \frac{0.6x - 0.4(s-x)}{60} dx$$

$$= \int_{s}^{140} \frac{0.6s}{60} dx + \int_{80}^{s} \frac{(x - 0.4s)}{60} dx$$

$$= \frac{s}{100}(140 - s) + \frac{s^2}{600} + \frac{8}{15}s - \frac{160}{3}$$

$$= \frac{7}{5}s - \frac{s^2}{100} + \frac{s^2}{600} + \frac{8}{15}s - \frac{160}{3}$$

$$= -\frac{5}{600}s^2 + \frac{29}{15}s - \frac{160}{3}$$

$$-\frac{s}{60} + \frac{29}{15} = 0 \Rightarrow s = \frac{29 \times 60}{15} = 116$$

The answer using the analytical method is 116, and Monte Carlo simulation also produces somewhere around this figure: 119. Sometimes, it produces 118 or 116. This depends on the number of trials.

Let's consider another simple example and seek an answer to the question: "in a classroom full of 30 students, what is the probability that more than one person will have the same birthday?" We will assume that it is not a leap year and instead of using the month and day, we will just use the days in the calendar year, that is, 365 days. The logic is pretty simple. The following code shows how one can calculate the probability of more than one person having the same birthday in a room of 30 students:

```
import numpy as np
numstudents = 30
numTrials = 10000
numWithSameBday = 0

for trial in range(numTrials):
    year = [0]*365

    for i in range(numstudents):
        newBDay = np.random.randint(365)
        year[newBDay] = year[newBDay] + 1

    haveSameBday = False
```

```
    for num in year:
        if num > 1:
            haveSameBday = True

    if haveSameBday == True:
        numWithSameBday = numWithSameBday + 1

prob = float(numWithSameBday) / float(numTrials)
print("The probability of a shared birthday in a class of ",
numstudents, " is ", prob)

('The probability of a shared birthday in a class of ', 30, ' is ',
0.7055)
```

In other words, there is a 70 percent chance that two people have the same birthday in a class of 30 students. The following example illustrates how Monte Carlo simulation can be applied to know the likelihood of winning the game in a situation that continues to occur more often today than in the past.

Monte Carlo simulation in basketball

Let's consider an example in a basketball game that is being addressed at the Khan Academy using JavaScript. The question was, "when down by three and left with only 30 seconds, is it better to attempt a hard 3-point shot or an easy 2-point shot and get another possession?"(asked by Lebron James).

Most readers may understand the basketball game, but we will only highlight some of the important rules. Each team has a 24-second possession of the ball. Within this time, if they score (even in less time), the opposing team gets possession for the next 24 seconds. However, as there is only 30 seconds left, if a player can make a quick 3-point shot in probably less than 10 seconds, then there is about 20 seconds left for the opposing team. Basketball, similar to any other sport, is very competitive, and since the player's goal is to reduce the trailing points, it is in their best interest to get a 3-point score. Let's try to write a Python program to answer the question.

Before showing the simulation program, let's take a look at some of the parameters that are involved in this problem domain. In order to determine whether shooting a 3-point shot is better in terms of the probability of winning, the following statistics of the player and also the opposing team is very important. The threePtPercent and twoPtPercent of the player not only determines his strength, but also determines the opposing team's percentage of scoring a 2-point labeled oppTwoPtPercent, and the opposing team's strength in a free throw percentage which is labeled oppFtPercent.

There are other combinations too, but to keep it simple, we will stop here. The higher the opposing team's free throw percentage, the more our answer is inclined towards making a 3-point shot. You can lower the value of `oppFtPercent` and see what is being discussed here. For this example, we will show snippets in different bits and pieces, and you can put them together in whichever way you are comfortable and use them to run. First, we will need the NumPy package because here, we intend to use the random number generator from this package, and `matplotlib` is required to plot, as shown in the following code:

```
import numpy as np
import matplotlib.pyplot as plt
```

In many examples, we will use colors that are standard colors used in tableau, and you may want to put this in a separate file. The following array of color codes can be used in any visualization plot:

```
colors = [(31, 119, 180), (174, 199, 232), (255, 127,  14),
    (255, 187, 120), (44, 160, 44), (214,  39,  40), (148,103,189),
    (152, 223, 138), (255,152,150), (197, 176, 213), (140, 86, 75),
    (196, 156, 148), (227,119,194), (247, 182, 210), (127,127,127),
    (199, 199, 199),(188,189, 34),(219, 219, 141), (23, 190,207),
    (158, 218, 229),(217,217,217)]

# Scale RGB values to the [0, 1] range, format matplotlib accepts.
for i in range(len(colors)):
  r, g, b = colors[i]
  colors[i] = (r / 255., g / 255., b / 255.)
```

Let's take a look at the three-point attempt. If `threePtPercent` is larger than the random number and there is more probability of an overtime, then a win is guaranteed. Take a look at the following code:

```
def attemptThree():
  if np.random.randint(0, high=100) < threePtPercent:
    if np.random.randint(0, high=100) < overtimePercent:
      return True #We won!!
  return False #We either missed the 3 or lost in OT
```

The logic for the two-point attempt is a little bit involved because it is all about how much time is left and who has the possession of the ball. Assuming that on an average, it takes only 5 seconds to attempt a two-point shot and the two-point scoring percent labeled `twoPtPercent` of the player is pretty high, then they score a two-point shot, which will be deducted from the value in the `pointsDown` variable. The following function is for a two-point scoring attempt:

```
def attemptTwo():
  havePossession = True
  pointsDown = 3
```

```
timeLeft = 30
while (timeLeft > 0):
  #What to do if we have possession
  if (havePossession):
    #If we are down by 3 or more, we take the
    #2 quickly.  If we are down by 2 or less
    #We run down the clock first
    if (pointsDown >= 3):
      timeLeft -= timeToShoot2
    else:
      timeLeft = 0


    #Do we make the shot?
    if (np.random.randint(0, high=100) < twoPtPercent):
      pointsDown -= 2
      havePossession = False
  else:
    #Does the opponent team rebound?
    #If so, we lose possession.
    #This doesn't really matter when we run
    #the clock down
    if (np.random.randint(0, high=100) >= offenseReboundPercent):
      havePossession = False
    else:   #cases where we don't have possession
      if (pointsDown > 0):  #foul to get back possession

        #takes time to foul
        timeLeft -= timeToFoul

        #opponent takes 2 free throws
        if (np.random.randint(0, high=100) < oppFtPercent):
          pointsDown += 1

        if (np.random.randint(0, high=100) < oppFtPercent):
          pointsDown += 1
          havePossession = True
      else:
        if (np.random.randint(0, high=100) >= ftReboundPercent):
          #you were able to rebound the missed ft
          havePossession = True
        else:
          #tied or up so don't want to foul;
          #assume opponent to run out clock and take
          if (np.random.randint(0, high=100) < oppTwoPtPercent):
```

```
                pointsDown += 2 #They made the 2
            timeLeft = 0


    if (pointsDown > 0):
      return False
    else:
      if (pointsDown < 0):
        return True
      else:
        if (np.random.randint(0, high=100) < overtimePercent):
          return True
        else:
          return False
```

For the sake of comparison, we will choose five players who have either a good 3-point average or a 2-point average or both, as shown in the following code:

```
plt.figure(figsize=(14,14))
names=['Lebron James', 'Kyrie Irving', 'Steph Curry',
       'Kyle Krover', 'Dirk Nowitzki']
threePercents = [35.4,46.8,44.3,49.2, 38.0]
twoPercents = [53.6,49.1,52.8, 47.0,48.6]
colind=0

for i in range(5):  # can be run individually as well
  x=[]
  y1=[]
  y2=[]
  trials = 400 #Number of trials to run for simulation
  threePtPercent = threePercents[i] # % chance of making 3-pt shot
  twoPtPercent = twoPercents[i] # % chance of making a 2-pt shot
  oppTwoPtPercent = 40 #Opponent % chance making 2-pter
  oppFtPercent = 70 #Opponent's FT %
  timeToShoot2 = 5 #How many seconds elapse to shoot a 2
  timeToFoul = 5 #How many seconds elapse to foul opponent
  offenseReboundPercent = 25 #% of regular offense rebound
  ftReboundPercent = 15 #% of offense rebound after missed FT
  overtimePercent = 50 #% chance of winning in overtime

  winsTakingThree = 0
  lossTakingThree = 0
  winsTakingTwo = 0
  lossTakingTwo = 0
```

```
        curTrial = 1

    while curTrial < trials:
      #run a trial take the 3
      if (attemptThree()):
        winsTakingThree += 1
      else:
        lossTakingThree += 1
        #run a trial taking a 2
        if attemptTwo() == True :
          winsTakingTwo += 1
        else:
          lossTakingTwo += 1

        x.append(curTrial)
        y1.append(winsTakingThree)
        y2.append(winsTakingTwo)
        curTrial += 1


    plt.plot(x,y1, color=colors[colind], label=names[i]+" Wins Taking
  Three Point", linewidth=2)
    plt.plot(x,y2, color=colors[20], label=names[i]+" Wins Taking Two
  Point", linewidth=1.2)
    colind += 2

  legend = plt.legend(loc='upper left', shadow=True,)
  for legobj in legend.legendHandles:
      legobj.set_linewidth(2.6)
  plt.show()
```

This was run for individual players by setting the range 1 and only including that player's name and statistics. In all the cases, as the opponent team's 2-point percent was high (70 percent), for all the players, Monte Carlo simulation resulted in suggesting wins by taking a 3-point score. Let's take a look at the results when one of them is plotted individually and all together.

We have picked players with a reasonably good 3-point percentage from the latest statistics available at `http://www.basketball-reference.com/teams/`. The statistics is current as of May 12, 2015. In all the cases, taking an attempt to score 3 points has a better chance of winning. If the opposing team has a lower average of free point throws, then the result will be different.

The following two plots shows the results for an individual player and five chosen players from the NBA League (2015):

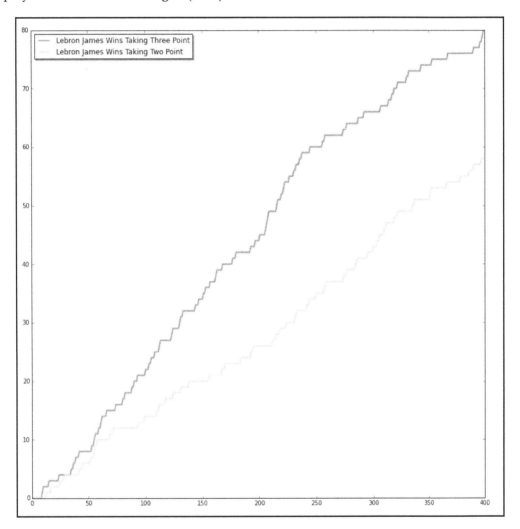

The preceding screenshot shows the three-point and two-point attempts by Lebron. The following plot shows the attempts of the other four players for comparison:

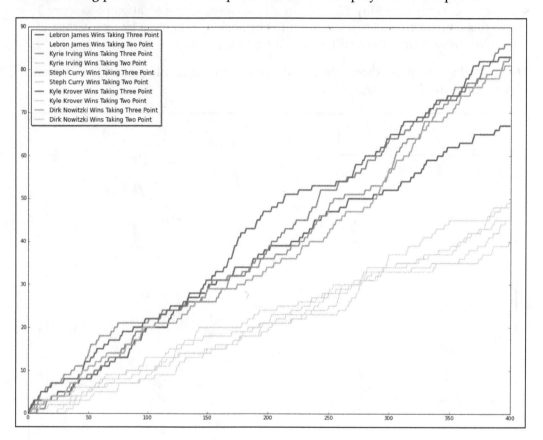

The volatility plot

We have seen many useful Python packages so far. Time and again, we have seen the use of matplotlib, but here, we will show the use of pandas with a very few lines of code so that you can achieve financial plots quickly. Standard deviation is a statistical term that measures the amount of variation or dispersion around an average. This is also a measure of volatility.

By definition, dispersion is the difference between the actual value and the average value. For plotting volatility along with the closed values, this example illustrates how you can see from a given start date, how a particular stock (such as IBM) is performing, and take a look at the volatility with the following code:

```
import pandas.io.data as stockdata
import numpy as np
```

```
r,g,b=(31,  119, 180)
colornow=(r/255.,g/255.,b/255.)
ibmquotes = stockdata.DataReader(name='IBM', data_source='yahoo', 
start='2005-10-1')
ibmquotes['Volatility'] = np.log(ibmquotes['Close']/ 
    ibmquotes['Close'].shift(1))
ibmquotes[['Close', 'Volatility']].plot(figsize=(12,10), \
    subplots=True, color=colornow)
```

The following screenshot is a result of the volatility plot:

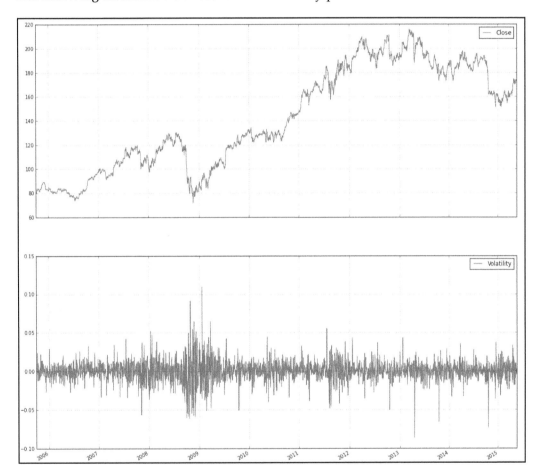

Now, let's see how our volatility is measured. Volatility is the measure of variation of price, which can have various peaks. Moreover, the exponential function lets us plug in time and gives us growth; logarithm (inverse of exponential) lets us plug in growth and gives us the time measure. The following snippet shows logarithm plot of measuring volatility:

```
%time
ibmquotes['VolatilityTest'] = 0.0
for I in range(1, len(ibmquotes)):
    ibmquotes['VolatilityTest'] =
        np.log(ibmquotes['Close'][i]/ibmquotes['Close'][i-1])
```

If we time this, the preceding snippet will take the following:

```
CPU times: user 1e+03 ns, sys: 0 ns, total: 1e+03 ns Wall time: 5.01
µs
```

To break down and show how we did is using `%time` and assigning volatility measure using the ratio of close value against the change in close value, as shown here:

```
%time
ibmquotes['Volatility'] = np.log(ibmquotes['Close']/
ibmquotes['Close'].shift(1))
```

If we time this, the preceding snippet will take the following:

```
CPU times: user 2 µs, sys: 3 µs, total: 5 µs Wall time: 5.01 µs.
```

The higher the variance in their values, the more volatile it turns out. Before we attempt to plot some of the implied volatility of volatility against the exercise price, let's take a look at the VSTOXX data. This data can be downloaded from `http://www.stoxx.com` or `http://www.eurexchange.com/advanced-services/`. Sample rows of the VSTOXX data is shown here:

Date	V2TX	V6I1	V6I2	V6I3	V6I4	V6I5	V6I6	V6I7	V6I8
2015-05-18	21.01	21.01	21.04	NaN	21.12	21.16	21.34	21.75	21.84
2015-05-19	20.05	20.06	20.15	17.95	20.27	20.53	20.83	21.38	21.50
2015-05-20	19.57	19.57	19.82	20.05	20.22	20.40	20.63	21.25	21.44
2015-05-21	19.53	19.49	19.95	20.14	20.39	20.65	20.94	21.38	21.55
2015-05-22	19.63	19.55	20.07	20.31	20.59	20.83	21.09	21.59	21.73

This data file consists of Euro Stoxx volatility indices, which can all be plotted via one simple filter mechanism of dates between Dec 31, 2011 to May 1, 2015. The following code can be used to plot the VSTOXX data:

```
import pandas as pd

url = 'http://www.stoxx.com/download/historical_values/h_vstoxx.txt'
vstoxx_index = pd.read_csv(url, index_col=0, header=2,
                           parse_dates=True, dayfirst=True,
                           sep=',')
vstoxx_short = vstoxx_index[('2011/12/31' < vstoxx_index.index)
                            & (vstoxx_index.index < '2015/5/1')]
# to plot all together
vstoxx_short.plot(figsize=(15,14))
```

When the preceding code is run, it creates a plot that compares Euro Stoxx volatility index:

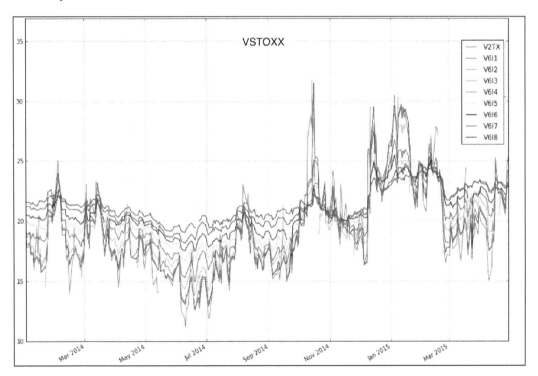

The preceding plot shows all the indices plot together, but if they are to be plotted on separate subplots, you may have to set the following subplots to `True`:

```
# to plot in subplots separately
vstoxx_short.plot(subplots=True, grid=True, color='r',
    figsize=(20,20), linewidth=2)
```

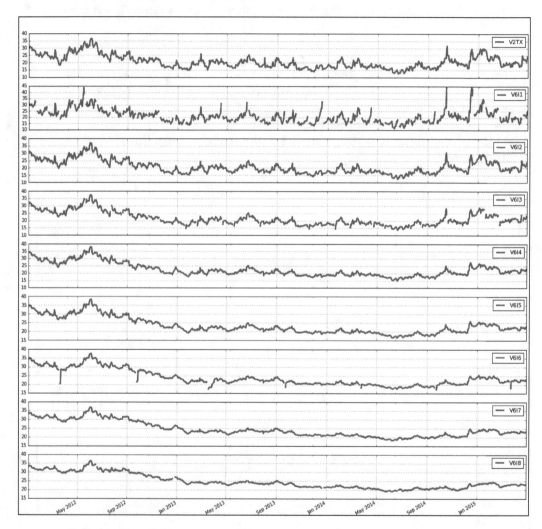

Implied volatilities

The Black–Scholes–Merton model is a statistical model of a financial market. From this model, one can find an estimate of the price of European style options. This formula is widely used, and many empirical tests have shown that the Black–Scholes price is "fairly close" to the observed prices. Fischer Black and Myron Scholes first published this model in their 1973 paper, *The Pricing of Options and Corporate Liabilities*. The main idea behind the model is to hedge the option by buying and selling the underlying asset in just the right way.

In this model, the price of a European call option on a nondividend paying stock is as follows:

$$C_o = S_o N(d_1) - Xe^{-rT} N(d_2)$$

$$d_1 = \frac{ln\left(\frac{S_o}{X}\right) + \left(r + \frac{\sigma^2}{T}\right)T}{\sigma\sqrt{T}}$$

$$d_2 = \frac{ln\left(\frac{S_o}{X}\right) + \left(r - \frac{\sigma^2}{T}\right)T}{\sigma\sqrt{T}}$$

$N(d)$ *is standard Normal Distribution*

where

S_o = *the stock price* T = *time to expiration*

X = *exercise price or strike price* r = *risk free interest rate*

σ = *standard deviation of log returns* (*volatility*)

For a given European call option, C_g, the implied volatility is calculated from the preceding equation (the standard deviation of log returns). The partial derivative of the option pricing formula with respect to the volatility is called **Vega**. This is a number that tells in what direction and to what extent the option price will move if there is a positive 1 percent change in the volatility and only in the volatility, as shown in the following equation:

$$Vega = \frac{\partial C_o}{\partial \sigma} = S_o N'(d_1)\sqrt{T}$$

The volatility model (such as BSM) forecasts the volatility and what the financial uses of this model entail, forecasting the characters of the future returns. Such forecasts are used in risk management and hedging, market timing, portfolio selection, and many other financial activities. American Call or Put Option provides you the right to exercise at any time, but for European Call or Put Option, one can exercise only on the expiration date.

There is no closed form solution to **Black–Scholes–Merton (BSM)**, but with the Newton's method (also known as the Newton-Raphson method), one can obtain an approximate value by iteration. Whenever an iterative method is involved, there is a certain amount of threshold that goes in to determine the terminating condition of the iteration. Let's take a look at the Python code to find the values by iteration (Newton's method) and plot them:

$$\frac{\partial C(\sigma_n)}{\partial \sigma_n} = -\left(\frac{C_{n+1} - C^*}{\sigma_{n+1} - \sigma_n}\right)$$

$$\Rightarrow \sigma_{n+1} - \sigma_n = -\frac{C_{n+1} - C^*}{\dfrac{\partial C(\sigma_n)}{\partial \sigma_n}}$$

$$\Rightarrow \sigma_{n+1} = \sigma_n - \left(\frac{C_{n+1} - C^*}{vega}\right)$$

```
from math import log, sqrt, exp
from scipy import stats
import pandas as pd
import matplotlib.pyplot as plt

colors = [(31, 119, 180), (174, 199, 232), (255,128,0),
  (255, 15, 14), (44, 160, 44), (152, 223, 138), (214, 39, 40),
  (255, 152, 150),(148, 103, 189), (197, 176, 213), (140, 86, 75),
 (196, 156, 148),(227, 119, 194), (247, 182, 210), (127, 127, 127),
 (199, 199, 199),(188, 189, 34), (219, 219, 141), (23, 190, 207),
 (158, 218, 229)]

# Scale the RGB values to the [0, 1] range, which is the format
matplotlib accepts.
for i in range(len(colors)):
  r, g, b = colors[i]
  colors[i] = (r / 255., g / 255., b / 255.)

def black_scholes_merton(S, r, sigma, X, T):
```

```
    S = float(S) # convert to float
    logsoverx = log (S/X)
    halfsigmasquare = 0.5 * sigma ** 2
    sigmasqrtT = sigma * sqrt(T)

    d1 = logsoverx + ((r + halfsigmasquare) * T) / sigmasqrtT
    d2 = logsoverx + ((r - halfsigmasquare) * T) / sigmasqrtT

    # stats.norm.cdf -> cumulative distribution function
    value = (S * stats.norm.cdf(d1, 0.0, 1.0) -
        X * exp(-r * T) *   stats.norm.cdf(d2, 0.0, 1.0))

    return value

def vega(S, r, sigma, X, T):

    S = float(S)
    logsoverx = log (S/X)
    halfsigmasquare = 0.5 * sigma ** 2
    sigmasqrtT = sigma * sqrt(T)
    d1 = logsoverx + ((r + halfsigmasquare) * T) / sigmasqrtT
    vega = S * stats.norm.cdf(d1, 0.0, 1.0) * sqrt(T)

    return vega

def impliedVolatility(S, r, sigma_est, X, T, Cstar, it):

    for i in range(it):
        numer = (black_scholes_merton(S, r, sigma_est, X, T) - Cstar)
        denom = vega(S,r, sigma_est, X, T)
        sigma_est -= numer/denom

    return sigma_est
```

We have these functions ready to be used, which can either be used in a separate file and imported, or to run this only once, be embedded in code altogether. The input file is obtained from stoxx.com in a file called vstoxx_data.h5, as shown in the following code:

```
h5 = pd.HDFStore('myData/vstoxx_data_31032014.h5', 'r')

futures_data = h5['futures_data'] # VSTOXX futures data
options_data = h5['options_data'] # VSTOXX call option data

h5.close()

options_data['IMP_VOL'] = 0.0
```

```
V0 = 17.6639   # the closing value of the index
r=0.04         # risk free interest rate
sigma_est=2
tol = 0.5      # tolerance level for moneyness
```

Now, let's run the iteration with the `options_data` and `futures_data` values form:

```
for option in options_data.index:
  # iterating over all option quotes
  futureval = futures_data[futures_data['MATURITY'] ==
      options_data.loc[option]['MATURITY']]['PRICE'].values[0]

  # picking the right futures value
  if (futureval * (1 - tol) < options_data.loc[option]['STRIKE']
    < futureval * (1 + tol)):
    impliedVol = impliedVolatility(V0,r,sigma_est,
          options_data.loc[option]['STRIKE'],
          options_data.loc[option]['TTM'],
          options_data.loc[option]['PRICE'],   #Cn
          it=100)                              #iterations
      options_data['IMP_VOL'].loc[option] = impliedVol

plot_data = options_data[options_data['IMP_VOL'] > 0]
maturities = sorted(set(options_data['MATURITY']))

plt.figure(figsize=(15, 10))

i=0
for maturity in maturities:

  data = plot_data[options_data.MATURITY == maturity]

  # select data for this maturity
  plot_args = {'lw':3, 'markersize': 9}
  plt.plot(data['STRIKE'], data['IMP_VOL'], label=maturity.date(),
      marker='o', color=colors[i], **plot_args)
  i += 1

plt.grid(True)

plt.xlabel('Strike rate $X$', fontsize=18)
plt.ylabel(r'Implied volatility of $\sigma$', fontsize=18)
plt.title('Short Maturity Window (Volatility Smile)', fontsize=22)

plt.legend()
plt.show()
```

The following plot is the result of running the preceding program that demonstrates implied volatility against the strike rate with data downloaded from `http://vstoxx.com`. Alternatively, this can be downloaded at `http://knapdata.com/python/vstoxx_data_31032014.h5`. The following plot shows implied volatility against the strike rate of Euro Stoxx:

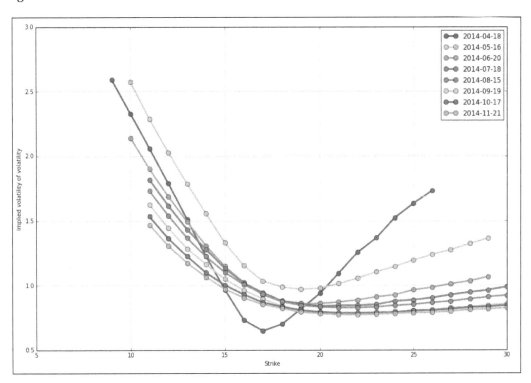

The portfolio valuation

The common sense of portfolio valuation of an entity is to estimate its current worth. Valuations are usually applicable on a financial asset or liability and can be performed on stocks, options, business enterprises, or intangible assets. For the purposes of understanding valuation and their visualization methods, we will pick mutual funds and plot them, compare them, and find the correlation.

Let's assume that we value all the portfolios denominated in a single currency. This simplifies the aggregation of values in a portfolio significantly.

We will pick three funds from the Vanguard, such as Vanguard US Total (`vus.to`), Vanguard Canadian Capped (`vre.to`), and Vanguard Emerging Markets (`vee.to`). The following code shows the comparison of three Vanguard funds.

```
import pandas as pd    #gets numpy as pd.np
```

```
from pandas.io.data import get_data_yahoo
import matplotlib.pyplot as plt

# get data
data = get_data_yahoo(["vus.to","vre.to","vee.to"],
  start = '2014-01-01')['Adj Close']

data.plot(figsize=(10,10), lw=2)
plt.show()
```

There is also another alternative to obtain data using `get_data_yahoo()` from `pandas.io.data`, as shown in the following screenshot:

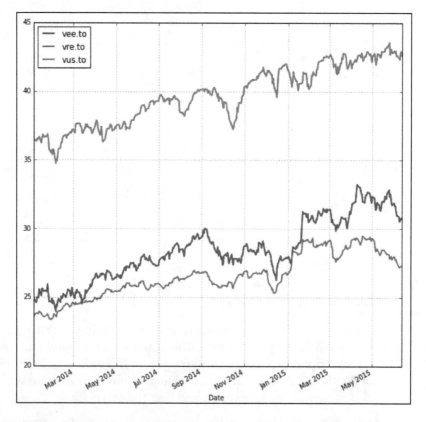

Besides plotting them, one may also get the correlation matrix after converting prices to log returns in order to scale the values, as shown in the following code:

```
#convert prices to log returns
retn=data.apply(pd.np.log).diff()

# make corr matrix
```

```
retn.corr()

#make scatterplot to show correlation
pd.tools.plotting.scatter_matrix(retn, figsize=(10,10))
plt.show()

# some more stats
retn.skew()
retn.kurt()
# Output
vee.to     0.533157
vre.to     3.717143
vus.to     0.906644
dtype: float64
```

The correlation plot is shown in the following image. This was obtained using the scatter_matrix function from pandas after applying the skew() and kurt() correlation:

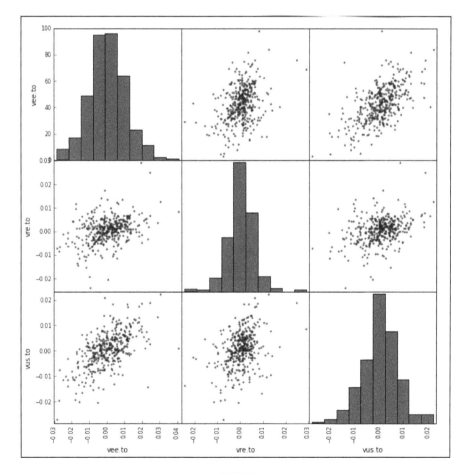

The simulation model

A model is a representation of a construction and system's functions. A model is similar to the system it represents and is easier to understand. A simulation of a system is a working model of the system. The model is usually reconfigurable to allow frequent experimentation. The operation of the model can be useful to study the model. Simulation is useful before an existing system is built to reduce the possibility of failure in order to meet specifications.

When is a particular system suitable for the simulation model? In general, whenever there is a need to model and analyze randomness in a system, simulation is the tool of choice.

Geometric Brownian simulation

Brownian motion is an example of a random walk, which is widely used to model physical processes, such as diffusion and biological processes and social and financial processes (such as the dynamics of a stock market).

Brownian motion is a sophisticated method. This is based on a process in plants discovered by R. Brown in 1827. It has a range of applications, including modeling noise in images, generating fractals, the growth of crystals, and the stock market simulation. For the purposes of the relevance of the contents here, we will pick the latter, that is, the stock market simulation.

M.F.M Osborne studied the logarithms of common stock prices and the value of money and showed that they have an ensemble of impact in statistical equilibrium. Using statistics and the prices of stock choice at random times, he was able to derive a distribution function that closely resembles the distribution for a particle in Brownian motion.

Definition of geometric Brownian motion:

A stochastic process (S_t) is said to follow a geometric Brownian motion if it satisfies the following stochastic differential equation:

$$dS_t = uS_t dt + \sigma S_t dW_t$$

$$\frac{dS_t}{S_t} = udt + \sigma dW_t$$

Integrating both sides and applying the initial condition: $S_t = S_0$, the solution to the preceding equation can be arrived at as follows:

$$S_t = S_o exp^{\left(\left(u - \frac{\sigma^2}{2}\right)t + \sigma W_t\right)}$$

Using the preceding derivation, we can plug in the values to obtain the following Brownian motion:

```python
import matplotlib.pyplot as plt
import numpy as np


'''
Geometric Brownian Motion with drift!
u=drift factor
sigma: volatility
T: time span
dt: length of steps
S0: Stock Price in t=0
W: Brownian Motion with Drift N[0,1]
'''
rect = [0.1, 5.0, 0.1, 0.1]
fig = plt.figure(figsize=(10,10))

T = 2
mu = 0.1
sigma = 0.04
S0 = 20
dt = 0.01
N = round(T/dt)
t = np.linspace(0, T, N)

# Standare normal distrib
W = np.random.standard_normal(size = N)
W = np.cumsum(W)*np.sqrt(dt)

X = (mu-0.5*sigma**2)*t + sigma*W

#Brownian Motion
S = S0*np.exp(X)

plt.plot(t, S, lw=2)
plt.xlabel("Time t", fontsize=16)
```

```
plt.ylabel("S", fontsize=16)
plt.title("Geometric Brownian Motion (Simulation)",
    fontsize=18)
plt.show()
```

The result of the Brownian motion simulation is shown in the following screenshot:

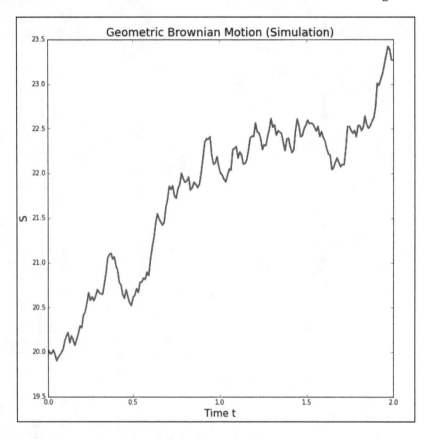

The simulating stock prices using Brownian motion is also shown in the following code:

```
import pylab, random

class Stock(object):
    def __init__(self, price, distribution):
        self.price = price
        self.history = [price]
        self.distribution = distribution
        self.lastChange = 0
```

```
    def setPrice(self, price):
        self.price = price
        self.history.append(price)

    def getPrice(self):
        return self.price

    def walkIt(self, marketBias, mo):
        oldPrice = self.price
        baseMove = self.distribution() + marketBias
        self.price = self.price * (1.0 + baseMove)
        if mo:
            self.price = self.price + random.gauss(.5, .5)*self.
lastChange
        if self.price < 0.01:
            self.price = 0.0
        self.history.append(self.price)
        self.lastChange = oldPrice - self.price

    def plotIt(self, figNum):
        pylab.figure(figNum)
        pylab.plot(self.history)
        pylab.title('Closing Price Simulation Run-' + str(figNum))
        pylab.xlabel('Day')
        pylab.ylabel('Price')


def testStockSimulation():
    def runSimulation(stocks, fig, mo):
        mean = 0.0
        for s in stocks:
            for d in range(numDays):
                s.walkIt(bias, mo)
            s.plotIt(fig)
            mean += s.getPrice()
        mean = mean/float(numStocks)
        pylab.axhline(mean)
    pylab.figure(figsize=(12,12))
    numStocks = 20
    numDays = 400
    stocks = []
    bias = 0.0
    mo = False
    startvalues = [100,500,200,300,100,100,100,200,200, 300,300,400,50
0,00,300,100,100,100,200,200,300]
    for i in range(numStocks):
        volatility = random.uniform(0,0.2)
```

```
        d1 = lambda: random.uniform(-volatility, volatility)
        stocks.append(Stock(startvalues[i], d1))
    runSimulation(stocks, 1, mo)

testStockSimulation()
pylab.show()
```

The results of the closing price simulation using random data from the uniform distribution is shown in the following screenshot:

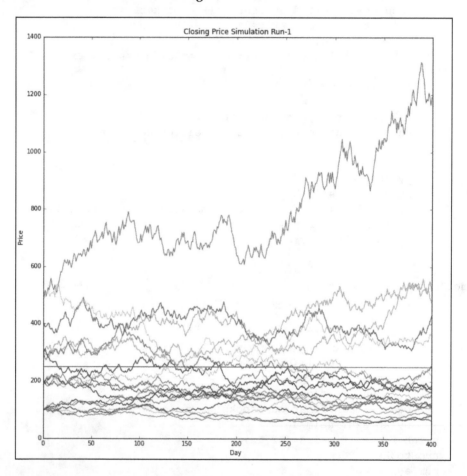

The diffusion-based simulation

Stochastic models provide a more detailed understanding of the reaction diffusion processes. Such a description is often necessary for the modeling of biological systems. There are a variety of simulation models that have been studied, and to restrict ourselves within the context of this chapter, we will consider the square-root diffusion.

The square-root diffusion, popularized for finance by Cox, Ingersoll, and Ross (1985) is used to model mean reverting quantities (such as interest rates and volatility). The stochastic differential equation of this process is as follows:

$$dx_t = \underbrace{k\left(\theta - x_t\right)dt}_{\text{Drift part}} + \underset{\text{Diffusion}}{\sigma\sqrt{x_t}\,dW_t}$$

The values of x_t have chi-squared distribution, but in the discrete version, they can be approximated by normal distribution. By discrete version, we mean applying Euler's numerical method of approximation using the iterative approach, as shown in the following equation:

$$x_t^{new} = x_s^{new} + k\left(\theta - x_s^+\right)\Delta t + \sigma\sqrt{x_s^+\Delta t}\,w_t$$

$$x_t = x_t^+$$

$$where\ x_s^+ = \max\left(x_s, 0\right) and\ x_t^+ = \max\left(x_t, 0\right)$$

```
import numpy as np
import matplotlib.pyplot as plt
import numpy.random as npr

S0 = 100 # initial value
r = 0.05
sigma = 0.25
T = 2.0

x0=0
k=1.8
theta=0.24
i = 100000
M = 50
dt = T / M
def srd_euler():
  xh = np.zeros((M + 1, i))
  x1 = np.zeros_like(xh)
  xh[0] = x0
  x1[0] = x0
  for t in range(1, M + 1):
   xh[t] = (xh[t - 1]
     + k * (theta - np.maximum(xh[t - 1], 0)) * dt
     + sigma * np.sqrt(np.maximum(xh[t - 1], 0)) * np.sqrt(dt)
    * npr.standard_normal(i))
  x1 = np.maximum(xh, 0)
  return x1
```

```
x1 = srd_euler()

plt.figure(figsize=(10,6))
plt.hist(x1[-1], bins=30, color='#98DE2f', alpha=0.85)
plt.xlabel('value')
plt.ylabel('frequency')
plt.grid(False)

plt.figure(figsize=(12,10))
plt.plot(x1[:, :10], lw=2.2)
plt.title("Square-Root Diffusion - Simulation")
plt.xlabel('Time', fontsize=16)
plt.ylabel('Index Level', fontsize=16)
#plt.grid(True)
plt.show()
```

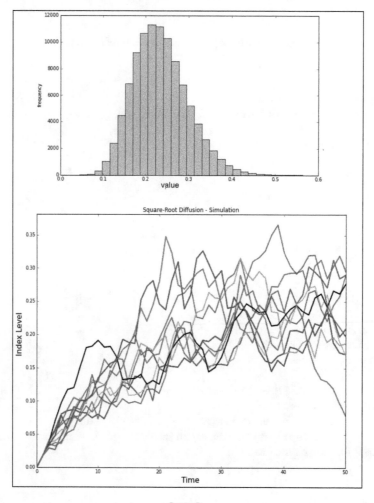

The threshold model

A threshold model is any model where some threshold value(s) is/are used to distinguish the ranges of values, where the behavior predicted by the model converges in some important way. Schelling attempted to model the dynamics of segregation, which was motivated when individual interactions by constructing two simulation models.

Schelling's Segregation Model

Schelling's Segregation Model (SSM) was first developed by Thomas C. Schelling. This model is one of the first constructive models of a system that is capable of self-organization.

Schelling experimented by placing pennies and dimes on a chessboard and moving them around according to various rules. In his experiment, he used a board analogous to a city, a board square to a domicile, and squares to a neighborhood. The pennies and dimes (visually different as well) could represent smokers, nonsmokers, male, female, executives, nonexecutives, students, or teachers for two groups.

The simulation rules specify the termination condition as *none of the agents moved from their current position because they are happy*, which means that agents will move if they are *not happy*.

The Schelling Model is used to simulate the segregation of a classroom, where the model shows that segregated patterns can occur even for weak preferences on neighboring classmates.

Suppose we have three types of student categories based on their number one priority: *sports*, *advanced proficiency academics*, and *regular*, each with type *0, 1,* and *2* respectively.

For the purpose of illustration here, we will assume that there are 250 students of each type in a high school. Each agent represents a student. These agents all live on a single unit square (this can be visualized as a high school building). The position of an agent is just a point *(x, y)*, where *0 < x ,y <1*. An agent is happy if half or more of her 12 nearest neighbors are of the same type (nearest in terms of Euclidean distance). The initial position of each agent is an independent draw from a bivariate uniform distribution, as shown in the following code:

```python
from random import uniform, seed
from math import sqrt
import matplotlib.pyplot as plt


num = 250               # These many agents of a particular type
numNeighbors = 12       # Number of agents regarded as neighbors
requireSameType = 8     # At least this many neighbors to be same type


seed(10)  # for reproducible random numbers


class StudentAgent:

    def __init__(self, type):
        #Students of different type will be shown in colors
        self.type = type
        self.show_position()

    def show_position(self):
        # position changed by using uniform(x,y)
        self.position = uniform(0, 1), uniform(0, 1)

    def get_distance(self, other):
        #returns euclidean distance between self and other agent.
        a = (self.position[0] - other.position[0])**2
        b = (self.position[1] - other.position[1])**2
        return sqrt(a + b)

    def happy(self, agents):
        "returns True if reqd number of neighbors are the same type."
        distances = []

        for agent in agents:
            if self != agent:
                distance = self.get_distance(agent)
                distances.append((distance, agent))
        distances.sort()
```

```
        neighbors = [agent for d, agent in distances[:numNeighbors]]
        numSameType = sum(self.type == agent.type
            for agent in neighbors)
        return numSameType >= requireSameType

    def update(self, agents):
        "If not happy, randomly choose new positions until happy."
        while not self.happy(agents):
            self.show_position()


def plot_distribution(agents, cycle_num):

    x1,y1 = [],[]
    x2,y2 = [],[]
    x3,y3 = [],[]

    for agent in agents:
        x, y = agent.position
        if agent.type == 0:
            x1.append(x); y1.append(y)
        elif agent.type == 1:
            x2.append(x); y2.append(y)
        else:
            x3.append(x); y3.append(y)

    fig, ax = plt.subplots(figsize=(10,10))
    plot_args = {'markersize' : 8, 'alpha' : 0.65, 'markersize': 14}
    ax.set_axis_bgcolor('#ffffff')
    ax.plot(x1, y1, 'o', markerfacecolor='#1b62a5',   **plot_args)
    ax.plot(x2, y2, 'o', markerfacecolor='#279321', **plot_args)
    ax.plot(x3, y3, 'D', markerfacecolor='#fd6610', **plot_args)
    ax.set_title('Iteration {}'.format(cycle_num))
    plt.show()

agents = [StudentAgent(0) for i in range(num)]
agents.extend(StudentAgent(1) for i in range(num))
agents.extend(StudentAgent(2) for i in range(num))
count = 1
terminate=False
while terminate == False:
    plot_distribution(agents, count)
    count += 1
    no_one_moved = True
```

```
for agent in agents:
    old_position = agent.position
    agent.update(agents)
    if agent.position != old_position:
        no_one_moved = False
if no_one_moved:
    terminate=True
```

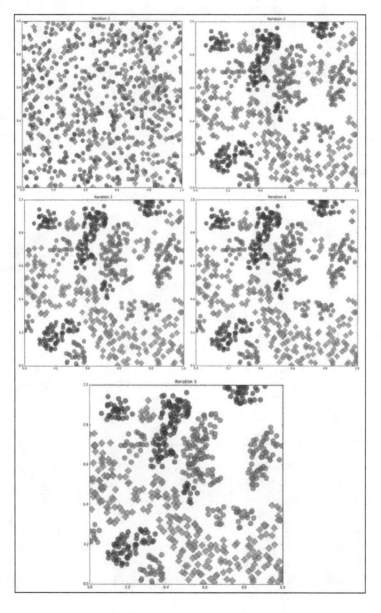

An overview of statistical and machine learning

The field of **Artificial Intelligence** (**AI**) is not new, and if we remember thirty years ago when we studied AI, except for robotics, there was very little understanding of the future this field held back then. Now, especially in the last decade, there has been a considerable growth of interest in Artificial Intelligence and machine learning. In the broadest sense, these fields aim to 'discover and learn something useful' about the environment. The gathered information leads to the discovery of new algorithms, which then leads to the question, "how to process high-dimensional data and deal with uncertainty"?

Machine learning aims to generate classifying expressions that are simple enough to follow by humans. They must mimic human reasoning sufficiently to provide insights into the decision process. Similar to statistical approaches, background knowledge may be exploited in the development phase. Statistical learning plays a key role in many areas of science, and the science of learning plays a key role in the fields of statistics, data mining, and artificial intelligence, which intersect with areas of engineering and other disciplines.

The difference between statistical and machine learning is that statistics emphasizes *inference*, whereas machine learning emphasizes *prediction*. When one applies statistics, the general approach is to infer the process by which data was generated. For machine learning, one would want to know how to predict the future characteristics of the data with respect to some variable. There is a lot of overlap between statistical learning and machine learning, and often one side of the experts argues one way versus the other. Let's leave this debate to the experts and select a few areas to discuss in this chapter. Later in the following chapter, there will be elaborate examples of machine learning. Here are some of the algorithms:

- Regression or forecasting
- Linear and quadratic discriminant analysis
- Classification
- Nearest neighbor
- Naïve Bayes
- Support vector machines
- Decision trees
- Clustering

The algorithms of machine learning are broadly categorized as supervised learning, unsupervised learning, reinforced learning, and deep learning. The supervised learning method of classification is where the test data is labeled, and like a teacher, it gives the classes supervision. Unsupervised learning does not have any labeled training data, whereas supervised learning has completely labeled training data. Semisupervised learning falls between supervised and unsupervised learning. This also makes use of the unlabeled data for training.

As the context of this book is data visualization, we will only discuss a few algorithms in the following sections.

K-nearest neighbors

The first machine learning algorithm that we will look at is **k-nearest neighbors (k-NN)**. k-NN does not build the model from the training data. It compares a new piece of data without a label to every piece of existing data. Then, take the most similar pieces of data (the nearest neighbors) and view their labels. Now, look at the top k most similar pieces of data from the known dataset (k is an integer and is usually less than 20). The following code demonstrates k-nearest neighbors plot:

```
from numpy import random,argsort,sqrt
from pylab import plot,show
import matplotlib.pyplot as plt

def knn_search(x, data, K):

    """ k nearest neighbors """

    ndata = data.shape[1]
    K = K if K < ndata else ndata
    # euclidean distances from the other points
    sqd = sqrt(((data - x[:,:ndata])**2).sum(axis=0))
    idx = argsort(sqd) # sorting
    # return the indexes of K nearest neighbors
    return idx[:K]

data = random.rand(2,200) # random dataset
x = random.rand(2,1) # query point

neig_idx = knn_search(x,data,10)

plt.figure(figsize=(12,12))

# plotting the data and the input point
plot(data[0,:],data[1,:],'o',  x[0,0],x[1,0],'o', color='#9a88a1',
```

```
      markersize=20)

# highlighting the neighbors
plot(data[0,neig_idx],data[1,neig_idx],'o',
  markerfacecolor='#BBE4B4',markersize=22,markeredgewidth=1)

show()
```

The approach to k-Nearest Neighbors is as follows:

- Collecting data using any method
- Preparing numeric values that are needed for a distance calculation
- Analyzing with any appropriate method
- Training none (there is no training involved)
- Testing to calculate the error rate
- The application takes some action on the calculated k-nearest neighbor search and identifies the top *k* nearest neighbors of a query

In order to test out a classifier, you can start with some known data so that you can hide the answer from the classifier and ask the classifier for its best guess.

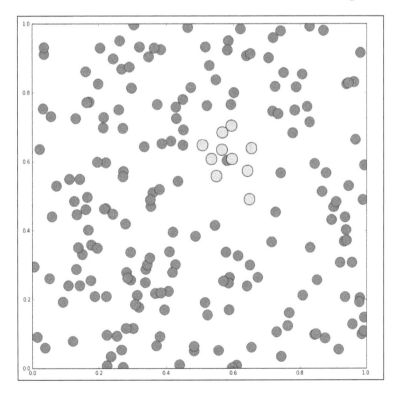

Generalized linear models

Regression is a statistical process to estimate the relationships among variables. More specifically, regression helps you understand how the typical value of the dependent variable changes when any one of the independent variables is varied.

Linear regression is the oldest type of regression that can apply interpolation, but it is not suitable for predictive analytics. This kind of regression is sensitive to outliers and cross-correlations.

Bayesian regression is a kind of penalized estimator and is more flexible and stable than traditional linear regression. It assumes that you have some prior knowledge about the regression coefficients, and statistical analysis is applicable in the context of the Bayesian inference.

We will discuss a set of methods in which the target value (y) is expected to be a linear combination of some input variables (x_1, x_2, and … x_n). In other words, representing the target values using notations is as follows:

Predicted value $\hat{y}$ is given by

$$\hat{y}(w,x) = w_o + w_1 x_1 + w_2 x_2 + \ldots + w_n x_n = w_o + \sum_{i=0}^{n} w_i x_i$$

Now, let's take a look at the Bayesian linear regression model. A logical question one may ask is "why Bayesian?" The answer being:

- Bayesian models are more flexible
- The Bayesian model is more accurate in small samples (may depend on priors)
- Bayesian models can incorporate prior information

Bayesian linear regression

First, let's take a look at a graphical model for linear regression. In this model, let's say we are given data values— $D = ((x_1, y_1), (x_2, y_2), \ldots (x_n, y_n))$ —and our goal is to model this data and come up with a function, as shown in the following equation:

$$f(x) = w^T \phi(x)$$
$$w \sim N(0, \sigma_0^2 I)$$
$$Y_i \sim N(w^T \phi(x_i), \sigma^2)$$

Here, w is a weight vector and each Y_i is normally distributed, as shown in the preceding equation. Y_i are random variables, and with a new variable x to condition each of the random variable $Y_i = y_i$ from the data, we can predict the corresponding y for the new variable x, as shown in the following code:

```python
import numpy as np
import matplotlib.pyplot as plt
from scipy import stats

from sklearn.linear_model import BayesianRidge
from sklearn.linear_model import LinearRegression

np.random.seed(0)
n_samples, n_features = 200, 200

X = np.random.randn(n_samples, n_features)  # Gaussian data
# Create weights with a precision of 4.
theta = 4.
w = np.zeros(n_features)

# Only keep 8 weights of interest
relevant_features = np.random.randint(0, n_features, 8)
for i in relevant_features:
    w[i] = stats.norm.rvs(loc=0, scale=1. / np.sqrt(theta))

alpha_ = 50.
noise = stats.norm.rvs(loc=0, scale=1. / np.sqrt(alpha_), size=n_
samples)
y = np.dot(X, w) + noise

# Fit the Bayesian Ridge Regression
clf = BayesianRidge(compute_score=True)
clf.fit(X, y)

# Plot weights and estimated and histogram of weights
plt.figure(figsize=(11,10))
plt.title("Weights of the model", fontsize=18)
plt.plot(clf.coef_, 'b-', label="Bayesian Ridge estimate")
plt.plot(w, 'g-', label="Training Set Accuracy")
plt.xlabel("Features", fontsize=16)
plt.ylabel("Values of the weights", fontsize=16)
plt.legend(loc="best", prop=dict(size=12))
plt.figure(figsize=(11,10))
```

```
plt.title("Histogram of the weights", fontsize=18)
plt.hist(clf.coef_, bins=n_features, log=True)
plt.plot(clf.coef_[relevant_features], 5 * np.ones(len(relevant_
features)),
         'ro', label="Relevant features")
plt.ylabel("Features", fontsize=16)
plt.xlabel("Values of the weights", fontsize=16)
plt.legend(loc="lower left")
plt.show()
```

The following two plots are the results of the program:

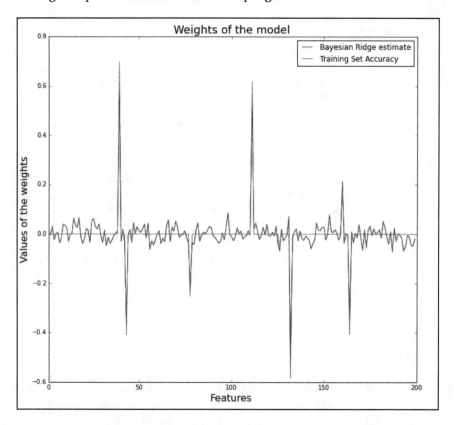

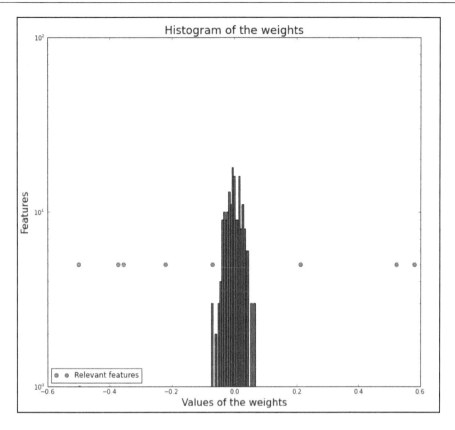

Creating animated and interactive plots

There are a few tools for interactive plots that one may choose from, such as Bokeh, Plotly, and VisPy.

Bokeh allows you to plot matplotlib objects via JavaScript, which enables the interactive part easily. For instance, if one needs a map plot that is interactive, Bokeh can be used. Bokeh uses JavaScript and enables D3.js style plots and targets the visualization via modern web browsers. Bokeh delivers good performance over a large dataset. You can easily install bokeh either via conda or pip, as shown in the following code:

```
conda install bokeh
```

```
   OR
```

```
pip install bokeh
```

```
    import collections
```

```python
from bokeh.sampledata import us_counties, unemployment
from bokeh.plotting import figure, show, output_file
from bokeh.models import HoverTool

county_coordinate_xs=[
us_counties.data[code]['lons'] for code in us_counties.data
if us_counties.data[code]['state'] == 'ca'
]
county_coordinate_ys=[
us_counties.data[code]['lats'] for code in us_counties.data
if us_counties.data[code]['state'] == 'ca'
]

colors = ["#e6f2ff", "#cce5ff", "#99cbff", "#b2d8ff", "#73abe5",
"#5985b2"]
county_colors = []
for county_id in us_counties.data:
  if us_counties.data[county_id]['state'] != 'ca':
    continue
  try:
    rate = unemployment.data[county_id]
    idx = min(int(rate/2), 5)
    county_colors.append(colors[idx])
  except KeyError:
    county_colors.append("black")

output_file("california.html", title="california.py example")

TOOLS="pan,wheel_zoom,box_zoom,reset,hover,save"
p = figure(title="California Unemployment 2009", width=1000,
height=1000, tools=TOOLS)

p.patches(county_coordinate_xs, county_coordinate_ys,
fill_color=county_colors, fill_alpha=0.7,
line_color="white", line_width=0.5)

mouse_hover = p.select(dict(type=HoverTool))
mouse_hover.point_policy = "follow_mouse"
mouse_hover.tooltips = collections.OrderedDict([
("index", "$index"), ("(x,y)", "($x, $y)"),
("fill color", "$color[hex, swatch]:fill_color"),
])
show(p)
```

In order to view the results, you may have to use a browser to open
`California.html`:

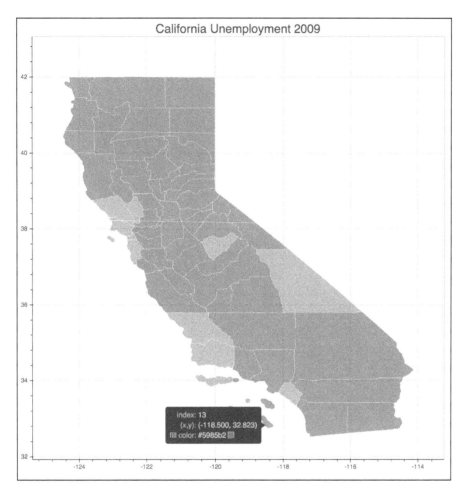

Plotly is another option that allows interactive plots, but requires one to be online
and have a Plotly account. The plots using Plotly look very nice and is interactive.
The following code shows how one can create interactive plots using `plotly`:

```
from pylab import *
import plotly
#py = plotly.plotly('me', 'mykey')


def to_plotly(ax=None):
    if ax is None:
        ax = gca()
```

```
        lines = []
        for line in ax.get_lines():
            lines.append({'x': line.get_xdata(),
                          'y': line.get_ydata(),
                          'name': line.get_label(),
                          })

        layout = {'title':ax.get_title(),
                  'xaxis':{'title':ax.get_xlabel()},
                  'yaxis':{'title':ax.get_ylabel()}
                  }
        filename = ax.get_title()  if ax.get_title() != '' else 'Untitled'
        print filename
        close('all')
        #return lines, layout
        return py.iplot(lines,layout=layout, filename = filename)

plot(rand(100), label = 'trace1')
plot(rand(100)+1, label = 'trace2')
title('Title')
xlabel('X label')
ylabel('Y label ')

response = to_plotly()
response
```

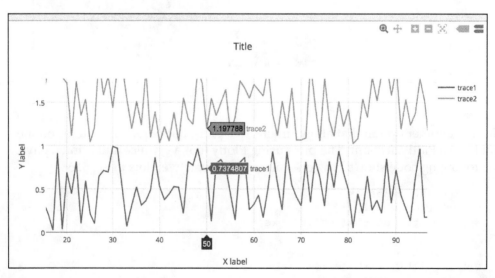

VisPy is another high performance interactive tool built using Python and OpenGL; therefore, it delivers the power of modern GPU's. It is fairly new, and as it matures, it leaves users with another good visualization library to choose from. The following example shows that using `vispy` one can create an image that can be zoomed interactively:

```
import sys

from vispy import scene
from vispy import app
import numpy as np

canvas = scene.SceneCanvas(keys='interactive')
canvas.size = 800, 800
canvas.show()

# Set up a viewbox to display the image with interactive pan/zoom
view = canvas.central_widget.add_view()

# Create the image
img_data = np.random.normal(size=(100, 100, 3), loc=128,
                            scale=40).astype(np.ubyte)
image = scene.visuals.Image(img_data, parent=view.scene)

# Set 2D camera (the camera will scale to the contents in the scene)
view.camera = scene.PanZoomCamera(aspect=1)

if __name__ == '__main__' and sys.flags.interactive == 0:
    app.run()
```

The preceding image shows the plot that appears the first time, but as we move the mouse and zoom in on it, it appears as follows:

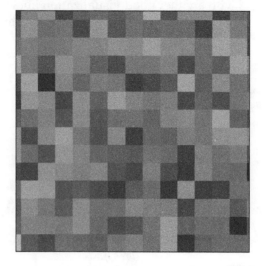

Summary

This chapter discussed typical financial examples and looked at machine learning towards the end. A brief introduction to the deterministic model using gross profit analysis and savings in mortgage payments was discussed.

Using real-world data in the form of options, the implied volatilities of European call options on the VSTOXX volatility index was also discussed. We also looked at Monte Carlo simulation. Using different implementation approaches, we showed simulation methods using the Monte Carlo method, the inventory problem, and a basketball situation.

Further, you learned simulation models (such as geometric Brownian and the diffusion-based simulation) with the example of the stock market model. The chapter also focused on how diffusion can be used to show drift and volatility.

We also looked at Bayesian linear regression and interactive plotting methods that one can choose from. Then, we discussed the k-nearest neighbors algorithm, instance-based learning performance, and the machine learning algorithm. This example was just touched to generate an interest about the subject and give you an idea about these algorithms. However, in the following chapter, we will look at more interesting statistical and machine learning algorithms.

6
Statistical and Machine Learning

Machine learning enables you to create and use computer algorithms, learn from these algorithms, correct them, and improve them to draw any new patterns that were unknown in the past. You can also extract insights from these new patterns that were found from the data. For instance, one may be interested in teaching a computer how to recognize ZIP codes value in an image. Another example is if we have a specific task, such as to determine spam messages, then instead of writing a program to solve this directly, in this paradigm, you can seek methods to learn and become better at getting accurate results using a computer.

Machine learning has become a significant part of artificial intelligence in recent years. With the power of computing, it is very likely that we will be able to build intelligent systems using machine learning methods. With the power of computing that we have today, these tasks have become far simpler than they were two decades ago. The primary goal of machine learning is to develop algorithms that have promising value in the real world. Besides time and space efficiency, the amount of data that is required by these learning algorithms also plays a challenging role. As machine learning algorithms are driven by data, you can see why there are so many different algorithms already today in this subject area. In the following sections of this chapter, we will discuss the following topics with examples:

- Classification methods – decision tree and linear and k-nearest neighbors
- Naïve Bayes, linear regression, and logistic regression
- Support vector machines
- Tree-based regression and unsupervised learning
- Principal component analysis
- Clustering based on similarity
- Measuring performance for classification

Classification methods

Machine learning algorithms are useful in many real-world applications, for example, if someone is interested in making accurate predictions about the climate or in the diagnosis of a disease. The learning is usually based on some known behavior or observations. This means that machine learning is about learning to improve on something in the future based on the experience or observations of the past.

Machine learning algorithms are broadly categorized as supervised learning, unsupervised learning, reinforced learning, and deep learning. The supervised learning method of classification (where the test data is labeled) is similar to a teacher who supervises different classes. Supervised learning relies on the algorithm to learn from data when we specify a target variable. Building an accurate classifier requires the following features:

- A good set of training examples
- A reasonably good performance on the training set
- A classifier method that is closely related to prior expectations

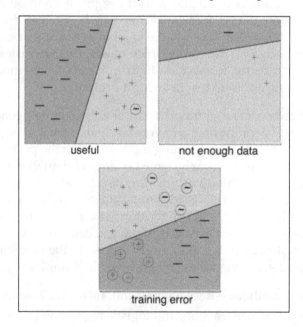

A binary classifier takes the data items and places them in one of the two classes (for higher dimensions, the data items are placed in k classes). The examples of a binary classifier determines whether a person's results can be diagnosed with the possibility of being positive on some disease or negative. The classifier algorithm is probabilistic. With some margin of error, someone can be diagnosed as either positive or negative. In any of these algorithms, there is a general approach to accomplish this, which goes in the following order:

- Collecting data from a reliable source.
- Preparing or reorganizing data with a specific structure. For a binary classifier, a distance calculation is required.
- Analyzing data with any appropriate method.
- Training (this is not applicable for a binary classifier).
- Testing (calculating the error rate).

In this chapter, the discussion will be to focus on what tools are available to visualize the input and results, but there is not much focus on the machine learning concepts. For greater depth on this subject, you can refer to the appropriate material. Let's take a look at an example and gradually walk through to see the various options to choose from.

Understanding linear regression

A simple scenario would be where one would like to predict whether a student is likely to be accepted into a college undergraduate program (such as Princeton University) based on the data of the GPA score and the SAT score with sample data as follows:

	SAT.Score	GPA	Accepted
1	2400	4.4	Y
2	2350	4.5	Y
3	2400	4.2	Y
4	2290	4.3	N
5	2100	4.0	N
6	2380	4.1	Y
7	2300	3.9	N
8	2280	4.0	N
9	2210	4.3	Y
10	2390	4.5	Y

In order to be able to consider the acceptance versus some score that is a combination of the SAT score and the GPA score, just for the purposes of illustrating an example here (note that this does not resemble the actual admissions process), we will attempt to figure out the line of separation. As the SAT scores vary from *2100* to *2390* along the *x* axis, we can try five values from *y=2490 – 2*i*2000*. In the following example, we have 2150 instead of 2000. GPA along the *y* axis has extreme values as *3.3* and *5.0*; therefore, we use the incremental values starting with *3.3* using *3.3+0.2i* from one extreme and *5.0-0.2i* from the other extreme (with a step size of *0.2*).

As a first attempt to see how the data visually looks, we will attempt to explore it with matplotlib and numpy. Using the SAT and GPA scores in the *x* and *y* axes and applying the scatter plot, we will attempt to find the line of separation in the following example:

```python
import matplotlib.pyplot as plt
import matplotlib as mpl
import numpy as np

mpl.rcParams['axes.facecolor']= '#f8f8f8'
mpl.rcParams['grid.color'] = '#303030'
mpl.rcParams['grid.color']= '#303030'
mpl.rcParams['lines.linestyle'] = '--'
#SAT Score
x=[2400,2350,2400,2290,2100,2380,2300,2280,2210,2390]

#High school GPA
y=[4.4,4.5,4.2,4.3,4.0,4.1,3.9,4.0,4.3,4.5]

a = '#6D0000'
r = '#00006F'
#Acceptance or rejections core
z=[a,a,a,r,r,a,r,r,a,a]

plt.figure(figsize=(11,11))
plt.scatter(x,y,c=z,s=600)

# To see where the separation lies
for i in range(1,5):
    X_plot = np.linspace(2490-i*2,2150+i*2,20)
    Y_plot = np.linspace(3.3+i*0.2,5-0.2*i,20)
    plt.plot(X_plot,Y_plot, c='gray')

plt.grid(True)

plt.xlabel('SAT Score', fontsize=18)
```

```
plt.ylabel('GPA', fontsize=18)
plt.title("Acceptance in College", fontsize=20)
plt.legend()

plt.show()
```

In the preceding code, we will not perform any regression or classification. This is just an attempt to understand how the data visually looks. You can also draw several lines of separation to get an intuitive understanding of how linear regression works.

You can see that there is not enough data to apply an accurate way to predict with the test data. However, if we attempt to get more data and use some well-known packages to apply machine learning algorithms, we can get a better understanding of the results. For instance, adding extracurricular activities (such as sports and music).

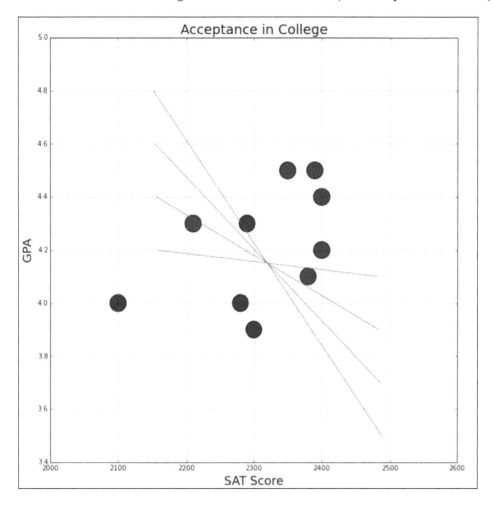

Linear regression

The main goal of using linear regression is to predict a numeric target value. One way to do this is to write an equation for the target value with respect to the inputs. For example, assume that we are trying to forecast the acceptance rate of a fully rounded student who participates in sports and music, but belongs to a low-income family.

One possible equation is *acceptance = 0.0015*income + 0.49*(participation_score)*; this is a regression equation. This uses a simple linear regression to predict a quantitative response with a single feature. It takes the following form:

$$y = \beta_0 + \beta_1 x$$
where y is the response
x = feature
β_0 = intercept
β_1 = is the coefficient for x

Together, β_0 and β_1 are called the model coefficients. To create our model, you must learn the values of these coefficients. Once you've learned these coefficients, you can use the model to predict the acceptance rate reasonably.

These coefficients are estimated using the least squares criteria, which means that we will find the separating line mathematically and minimize the sum of squared residuals. The following is a portion of the data that is used in the following example:

	X	academic	sports	music	acceptance
1	1	230.1	37.8	62.9090909	81.851852
2	2	44.5	39.3	41.0000000	38.518519
3	3	17.2	45.9	63.0000000	34.444444
4	4	151.5	41.3	68.5185185	68.518519
5	5	180.8	10.8	53.0909091	47.777778
6	6	8.7	48.9	68.1818182	26.666667
7	7	57.5	32.8	21.3636364	43.703704
8	8	120.2	19.6	10.5454545	48.888889
9	9	8.6	2.1	0.9090909	17.777778
10	10	199.8	2.6	19.2727273	39.259259
11	11	66.1	5.8	22.0000000	31.851852
12	12	214.7	24.0	64.4444444	64.444444
13	13	23.8	35.1	59.9090909	34.074074
14	14	97.5	7.6	6.5454545	35.925926
15	15	204.1	32.9	70.3703704	70.370370
16	16	195.4	47.7	82.9629630	82.962963
17	17	67.8	36.6	103.6363636	46.296296
18	18	281.4	39.6	90.3703704	90.370370
19	19	69.2	20.5	16.6363636	41.851852
20	20	147.3	23.9	17.3636364	54.074074

The following Python code shows how one can attempt scatter plots to determine the correlation between variables:

```
from matplotlib import pyplot as pplt

import pandas as pds

import statsmodels.formula.api as sfapi

df = pds.read_csv('/Users/myhomedir/sports.csv', index_col=0)
fig, axs = plt.subplots(1, 3, sharey=True)
df.plot(kind='scatter', x='sports', y='acceptance', ax=axs[0],
figsize=(16, 8))
df.plot(kind='scatter', x='music', y='acceptance', ax=axs[1])
df.plot(kind='scatter', x='academic', y='acceptance', ax=axs[2])

# create a fitted model in one line
lmodel = sfapi.ols(formula='acceptance ~ music', data=df).fit()

X_new = pd.DataFrame({'music': [df.music.min(), df.music.max()]})
predictions = lmodel.predict(X_new)

df.plot(kind='scatter', x='music', y='acceptance', figsize=(12,12),
s=50)

plt.title("Linear Regression - Fitting Music vs Acceptance Rate",
fontsize=20)
plt.xlabel("Music", fontsize=16)
plt.ylabel("Acceptance", fontsize=16)

# then, plot the least squares line
```

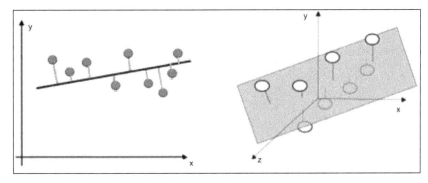

As shown in the preceding image, the blue dots are the observed values of *(x,y)*, the line that crosses diagonally is the least square fit based on the *(x,y)* values, and the orange lines are the residuals, which are the distances between the observed values and the least squares line.

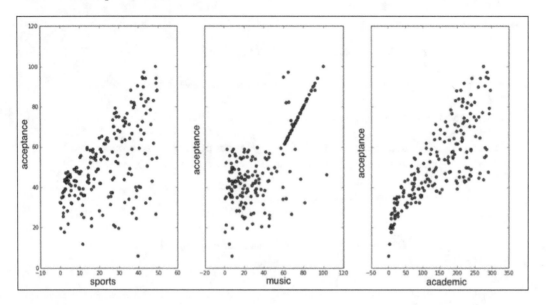

Using `statsmodels`, `pandas`, and `matplotlib` (as shown in the preceding image), we can assume that there is some sort of scoring based on how a university rates its students' contribution to academics, sports, and music.

To test a classifier, we can start with some known data and not knowing the answer, we will seek the answer from the classifier for its best guess. In addition, we can add the number of times the classifier was wrong and divide it by the total number of tests conducted to get the error rate.

The following is a plot of linear regression derived from the previous Python code.

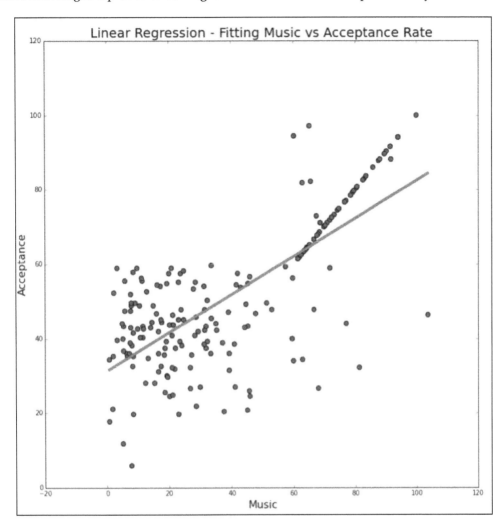

There are numerous other Python libraries that one can use for linear regression, and `scikit-learn`, `seaborn`, `statsmodels`, and `mlpy` are some of the notable and popular libraries among them. There are numerous examples already on the Web that explains linear regression with these packages. For details on the `scikit-learn` package, refer to `http://scikit-learn.org/stable/modules/generated/sklearn.linear_model.LinearRegression.html`.

There is another interesting machine learning model called **decision tree learning**, which can sometimes be referred to as **classification tree**. Another similar model is **regression tree**. Here, we will see the differences between them and whether one makes sense over the other.

Decision tree

Classification trees are used to separate the data into classes belonging to the response variable. The response variable usually has two classes: *Yes* or *No* (1 or 0) and sunny or rain. If the target variable has more than two categories, then C4.5 can be applicable. C4.5 improves the ID3 algorithm for the continuous attributes, the discrete attributes, and the post construction process.

Similar to most learning algorithms, the classification tree algorithm analyzes a training set and then builds a classifier based on that training so that with new data in the future, it can classify the training as well as the new data correctly. A test example is an input object, and the algorithm must predict an output value. Classification trees are used when the response or target variable is categorical in nature.

On the contrary, regression trees are needed when the response variable is continuous and not discrete. For example, the predicted price of a product. A regression tree is built through binary partitioning. This is an iterative process that splits the data into partitions or branches and then continues splitting each partition into smaller groups as the method moves up each partition or branch. In other words, regression trees are applicable when the problem involves prediction as opposed to classification. For more details on this, we recommend you refer to books on classification and regression trees.

When the relationship between predictors and response is linear, a standard regression tree is more appropriate, and when the relationship between predictors and response is nonlinear, then C4.5 should be used. Furthermore, to summarize, when the response variable has only two categories, the classification tree algorithm should be used.

An example

For a decision tree algorithm to play tennis or golf, one can easily sort down the decision process by asking a question, that is, is it raining out there or is it sunny? and draw the decision diagram branching out at every question based on the answers. The playing nature of the games are almost the same — tennis versus golf — and in any sporting event, if it is windy and raining, chances are that there is not going to be a game.

For tennis, if the outlook is sunny, but the humidity is high, then it is recommended to not play. Similarly, if it is raining and windy, then the whole dynamics of the tennis game will be pretty bad. Therefore, chances are that it is no fun playing tennis under these conditions as well. The following diagram shows all the possible conditions:

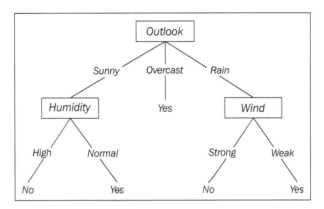

We can also add discrete attributes (such as temperature); for what range of temperatures does it not make sense to play tennis? Probably, if the temperature is greater than 70 degrees Fahrenheit, that is, if the temperature is hot. We can write the rules combining all these as follows:

```
If (Outlook = Sunny) and (Humidity = High) then play=No
If (Outlook = Rain) and (Wind = Strong) then play=No
If (Outlook = Sunny) and (Humidity = Normal) or
   (Outlook = Overcast) or (Outlook=Rain and Wind=Weak) then play=Yes
```

With the following training set, we can run the algorithm to select the next best classifier:

Outlook	Temperature	Humidity	Wind	Play?
Sunny	Hot	High	Weak	No
Sunny	Hot	High	Strong	No
Overcast	Hot	High	Weak	Yes
Overcast	Cool	Normal	Strong	Yes
Sunny	Mild	High	Weak	No
Sunny	Cool	Normal	Weak	Yes
Rain	Mild	High	Weak	Yes
Rain	Cool	Normal	Weak	Yes
Rain	Cool	Normal	Strong	No
Rain	Mild	Normal	Weak	Yes

Outlook	Temperature	Humidity	Wind	Play?
Sunny	Mild	Normal	Strong	Yes
Overcast	Mild	High	Strong	Yes
Overcast	Hot	Normal	Weak	Yes
Rain	Mild	High	Strong	No

The top down **induction of decision trees (ID3)** is a method that follows these rules:

- Iterate over leaf nodes until stopping condition:
    1. Identify the best decision attribute for the next node in the traversal.
    2. Assign that best node from step 1 as the decision attribute.
    3. For each value of those best nodes, create new descendants of those nodes.
    4. Sort the training data into leaf nodes.
    5. Stopping condition for iteration:
       If the training data is classified within the threshold

One clear distinction between a linear regression and a decision tree algorithm is that the decision boundaries are parallel to the axes, for example, if we have two features (x_1 and x_2), then it can only create rules, such as x_1 >=5.2, x_2 >= 7.2. The advantage the decision tree algorithm has is that it is robust to errors, which means that the training set could have errors. Also, it doesn't affect the algorithm much.

Using the `sklearn` package from `scikit-learn` (`scikit-learn.org`) and the following code, we can plot the decision tree classifier:

```
from sklearn.externals.six import StringIO
from sklearn import tree
import pydot


# Four columns from the table above with values
# 1st col - 1 for Sunny, 2 for Overcast, and 3 for Rainy
# 2nd col - 1 for Hot, 2 for Mild, 3 for Cool
# 3rd col - 1 for High and 2 for Normal
# 4th col - 0 for Weak and 1 for Strong

X=[[1,1,1,0],[1,1,1,1],[2,1,1,0],[2,3,2,1],[1,2,1,0],[1,3,2,0],\
[3,2,1,0],[3,3,2,0],[3,3,2,1],[3,2,2,0],[1,2,2,1],[2,2,1,1],\
[2,1,2,0],[3,2,1,0]]
```

```
# 1 for Play and 0 for Don't Play
Y=[0,0,1,1,0,1,1,1,0,1,1,1,1,0]

clf = tree.DecisionTreeClassifier()
clf = clf.fit(X, Y)

dot_data = StringIO()
tree.export_graphviz(clf, out_file=dot_data)

graph = pydot.graph_from_dot_data(dot_data.getvalue())
graph.write_pdf("game.pdf")
```

Use the export functionality of `sklearn` to be able to convert the tree diagram in the form of a graph that looks similar to the following diagram:

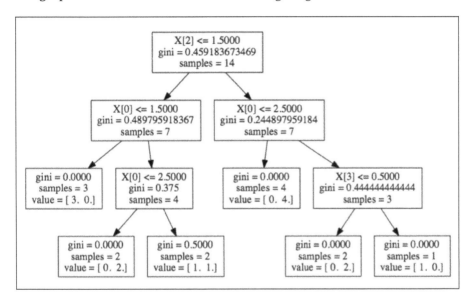

In order to create your own tree structure, there is an option of using plotting methods from `matplotlib`. In order to display a tree-like diagram, `matplotlib` has annotation that allows you to create a tree-shaped structure with labels, as shown in the following code:

```
import matplotlib.pyplot as plt

#create nodes here
branchNode = dict(boxstyle="sawtooth", fc="0.8")
leafNode = dict(boxstyle="round4", fc="0.8")
startNode = dict(boxstyle="sawtooth", fc="0.9")
```

```
def createPlot():
    fig = plt.figure(1, facecolor='white')
    fig.clf()
    createPlot.ax1 = plt.subplot(111, frameon=False) #ticks for demo
purposes
    plotNode('from here', (0.3,0.8), (0.3, 0.8), startNode)
    plotNode('a decision node', (0.5, 0.1), (0.3, 0.8), branchNode)
    plotNode('a leaf node', (0.8, 0.1), (0.3, 0.8), leafNode)
    plt.show()
...
```

This is usually an idea of how you can create a tree structure from scratch using `matplotlib`. Basically the preceding example shows the creation of three nodes and connecting them to form a small tree. The results of this code are shown as follows:

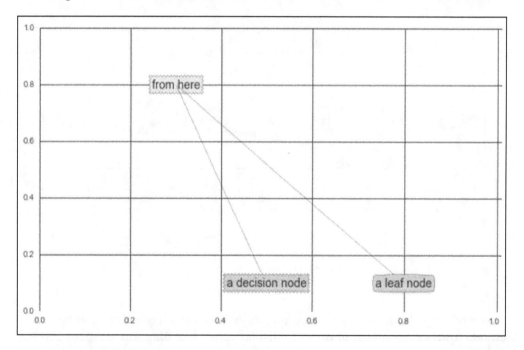

The Bayes theorem

In order to understand the Bayes theorem first, before we attempt to take a look at the Naïve Bayes classification method, we should consider this example. Let's assume that among all the people in the U universe, the set of people who have breast cancer is set A, and set B is the set of people who had a screening test and were unfortunately diagnosed with the result positive for breast cancer. This is shown as the overlap region $A \cap B$ in the following diagram:

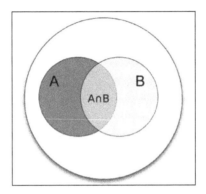

There are two unusual areas that need focus: $B - A \cap B$ or people without breast cancer and with a positive test on diagnosis and the event $A - A \cap B$ or people with breast cancer and with a negative test on diagnosis. Now, let's attempt to answer whether we know that the test is positive for a randomly selected person. Then, what is the probability that the person has breast cancer? This visually translates to whether we know that a person is visible in the B area, then what is the probability that the same person appears in $A \cap B$? Mathematically, this translates to what is *probability (A given B)*. Conditional probability equation is shown here:

$$P(A|B) = \frac{|A \cap B|}{|B|} = \frac{\dfrac{|A \cap B|}{|U|}}{\dfrac{|B|}{|U|}}$$

$$P(A|B) = \frac{P(A \cap B)}{P(B)}$$

Similarly, if we know that a randomly selected person has cancer, what is the probability that the diagnosis test came out positive? This translates to *probability (B given A)*, as shown in the following code:

$$P(B \mid A) = \frac{|A \cap B|}{|B|} = \frac{\frac{|A \cap B|}{|U|}}{\frac{|A|}{|U|}}$$

$$P(B \mid A) = \frac{P(A \cap B)}{P(A)}$$

$$\Rightarrow P(A \cap B) = P(B \mid A)P(A) = P(A \mid B)P(B)$$

$$P(A \mid B) = \frac{P(B \mid A)P(A)}{P(B)}$$

Thus, we derive at the Bayes theorem, where A and B are events with $P(B)$ nonzero.

The Naïve Bayes classifier

The Naive Bayes classifier technique is based on the Bayesian theorem and is appropriate when the dimensionality of the input is high. Although it appears to be very simple, it is technically better performed than the other classification methods.

(More information is available at `http://scikit-learn.org/stable/modules/naive_bayes.html` and `http://sebastianraschka.com/Articles/2014_naive_bayes_1.html`).

Let's take a look at the following example that shows objects in red and blue. As indicated, the objects shown in red represent the set of people who have breast cancer, and the objects shown in blue represent the set of people diagnosed positive for breast cancer. Our task is to be able to label any new data, which in this case is a new person as they emerge that is based on the existing structure or category of objects and identify the group or class that the new data or person belongs to.

In Bayesian, the prior probability is more inclined to be close to the pattern or behavior of how the objects are currently characterized. This is mainly due to the fact that the word prior is synonymous to previous experience here; therefore, if there is a greater percentage of red than blue objects, then this gives us an advantage in expecting that the predicted outcome should be higher for it to be red.

The method here is a combination of Naïve Bayes and the k-nearest neighbor algorithm. For a pure Naïve Bayes classification, we will discuss another example using `TextBlob` (`http://textblob.readthedocs.org/en/dev/`).

The following image visually shows a new person as unclassified yet:

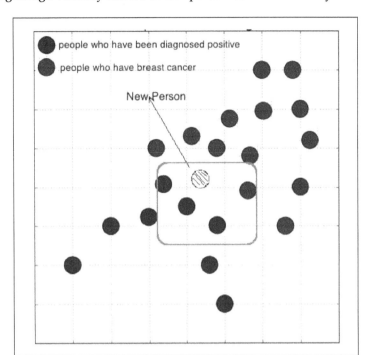

Using the prior probability of red and blue, you can calculate the posterior probability of x being red or blue, as shown in the following code:

$$prior\ probability\ of\ red = \frac{13}{21}$$

$$prior\ probability\ of\ blue = \frac{8}{21}$$

$$likelihood\ of\ x\ given\ red = \frac{Number\ of\ red\ \text{in the vicinity}}{Total\ number\ of\ reds} = \frac{1}{13}$$

$$likelihood\ of\ x\ given\ blue = \frac{Number\ of\ blue\ \text{in the vicinity}}{Total\ number\ of\ blue} = \frac{3}{8}$$

$$posterior\ probability\ of\ x\ being\ red = \frac{1}{13} \times \frac{13}{21} = \frac{1}{21}$$

$$posterior\ probability\ of\ x\ being\ blue = \frac{3}{8} \times \frac{8}{21} = \frac{3}{21} = \frac{1}{7}$$

The new person is most likely to be classified as one who is diagnosed positive with breast cancer.

The Naïve Bayes classifier using TextBlob

`TextBlob` is an interesting library that has a collection of tools for text processing purposes. It comes with the API for **natural language processing (NLP)** tasks, such as classification, noun phrase extraction, part-of-speech tagging, and sentiment analysis.

There are a few steps involved to make sure that one can use `TextBlob`. Any library that works with NLP needs some corpora; therefore, the following sequence of installation and configuration needs to be done before attempting to use this interesting library:

- Installing `TextBlob` (either via `conda` or `pip`)
- Downloading corpora

Installing TextBlob

Using `binstar search -t conda textblob`, one can find where to install it for anaconda users. More details can be found in *Appendix, Go Forth and Explore Visualization*.

Downloading corpora

The following command will let one download `corpora`:

```
$ python -m textblob.download_corpora

[nltk_data] Downloading package brown to
[nltk_data]     /Users/administrator/nltk_data...
[nltk_data]   Unzipping corpora/brown.zip.
[nltk_data] Downloading package punkt to
[nltk_data]     /Users/administrator/nltk_data...
[nltk_data]   Unzipping tokenizers/punkt.zip.
[nltk_data] Downloading package wordnet to
[nltk_data]     /Users/administrator/nltk_data...
[nltk_data]   Unzipping corpora/wordnet.zip.
[nltk_data] Downloading package conll2000 to
[nltk_data]     /Users/administrator/nltk_data...
[nltk_data]   Unzipping corpora/conll2000.zip.
[nltk_data] Downloading package maxent_treebank_pos_tagger to
[nltk_data]     /Users/administrator/nltk_data...
[nltk_data]   Unzipping taggers/maxent_treebank_pos_tagger.zip.
[nltk_data] Downloading package movie_reviews to
[nltk_data]     /Users/administrator/nltk_data...
[nltk_data]   Unzipping corpora/movie_reviews.zip.
Finished.
```

The Naïve Bayes classifier using TextBlob

TextBlob makes it easy to create custom text classifiers. In order to understand this better, one may need to do some experimentation with their training and test data. In the TextBlob 0.6.0 version, the following classifiers are available:

- BaseClassifier
- DecisionTreeClassifier
- MaxEntClassifier
- NLTKClassifier *
- NaiveBayesClassifier
- PositiveNaiveBayesClassifier

The classifier marked with * is the abstract class that wraps around the nltk.classify module.

For sentiment analysis, one can use the Naive Bayes classifier and train the system with this classifier and textblob.en.sentiments.PatternAnalyzer. A simple example is as follows:

```
from textblob.classifiers import NaiveBayesClassifier
from textblob.blob import TextBlob

from textblob.classifiers import NaiveBayesClassifier
from textblob.blob import TextBlob

train = [('I like this new tv show.', 'pos'),
  # similar train sentences with sentiments goes here]
test = [ ('I do not enjoy my job', 'neg'),
  # similar test sentences with sentiments goes here]
]

cl = NaiveBayesClassifier(train)
cl.classify("The new movie was amazing.") # shows if pos or neg


cl.update(test)

# Classify a TextBlob
blob = TextBlob("The food was good. But the service was horrible. "
                "My father was not pleased.", classifier=cl)
print(blob)
print(blob.classify())
```

```
for sentence in blob.sentences:
    print(sentence)
    print(sentence.classify())
```

Here is the result that will be displayed when the preceding code is run:

```
pos
neg
The food was good.
pos
But the service was horrible.
neg
My father was not pleased.
pos
```

One can read the training data from a file either in the text format or the JSON format. The sample data in the JSON file is shown here:

```
[
    {"text": "mission impossible three is awesome btw","label": "pos"},
    {"text": "brokeback mountain was beautiful","label":"pos"},
    {"text": " da vinci code is awesome so far","label":"pos"},
    {"text": "10 things i hate about you + a knight's tale * brokeback
mountain","label":"neg"},
    {"text": "mission impossible 3 is amazing","label":"pos"},

        {"text": "harry potter = gorgeous","label":"pos"},
        {"text": "i love brokeback mountain too: ]","label":"pos"},
]

from textblob.classifiers import NaiveBayesClassifier
from textblob.blob import TextBlob
from nltk.corpus import stopwords

stop = stopwords.words('english')

pos_dict={}
neg_dict={}
with open('/Users/administrator/json_train.json', 'r') as fp:
    cl = NaiveBayesClassifier(fp, format="json")
print "Done Training"

rp = open('/Users/administrator/test_data.txt','r')
res_writer = open('/Users/administrator/results.txt','w')
for line in rp:
    linelen = len(line)
```

```
        line = line[0:linelen-1]
        sentvalue = cl.classify(line)
        blob = TextBlob(line)
        sentence = blob.sentences[0]
        for word, pos in sentence.tags:
            if (word not in stop) and (len(word)>3 \
                and sentvalue == 'pos'):
              if pos == 'NN' or pos == 'V':
                pos_dict[word.lower()] = word.lower()
            if (word not in stop) and (len(word)>3 \
                and sentvalue == 'neg'):
              if pos == 'NN' or pos == 'V':
                neg_dict[word.lower()] = word.lower()

        res_writer.write(line+" => sentiment "+sentvalue+"\n")

        #print(cl.classify(line))
    print "Lengths of positive and negative sentiments",len(pos_dict),
    len(neg_dict)

Lengths of positive and negative sentiments 203 128
```

We can add more training data from the corpus and evaluate the accuracy of the classifier with the following code:

```
test=[
("mission impossible three is awesome btw",'pos'),
("brokeback mountain was beautiful",'pos'),
("that and the da vinci code is awesome so far",'pos'),
("10 things i hate about you =",'neg'),
("brokeback mountain is a spectacularly beautiful movie",'pos'),
("mission impossible 3 is amazing",'pos'),
("the actor who plays harry potter sucks",'neg'),
("harry potter = gorgeous",'pos'),
('The beer was good.', 'pos'),
('I do not enjoy my job', 'neg'),
("I ain't feeling very good today.", 'pos'),
("I feel amazing!", 'pos'),
('Gary is a friend of mine.', 'pos'),
("I can't believe I'm doing this.", 'pos'),
("i went to see brokeback mountain, which is beautiful(",'pos'),
("and i love brokeback mountain too: ]",'pos')
]

print("Accuracy: {0}".format(cl.accuracy(test)))
```

```
from nltk.corpus import movie_reviews

reviews = [(list(movie_reviews.words(fileid)), category)
for category in movie_reviews.categories()
for fileid in movie_reviews.fileids(category)]
new_train, new_test = reviews[0:100], reviews[101:200]

cl.update(new_train)
accuracy = cl.accuracy(test + new_test)
print("Accuracy: {0}".format(accuracy))

# Show 5 most informative features
cl.show_informative_features(4)
```

The output would be as follows:

```
Accuracy: 0.973913043478
Most Informative Features
contains(awesome) = True          pos : neg     =      51.9 : 1.0
contains(with) = True             neg : pos     =      49.1 : 1.0
contains(for) = True              neg : pos     =      48.6 : 1.0
contains(on) = True               neg : pos     =      45.2 : 1.0
```

First, the training set had 250 samples with an accuracy of 0.813 and later it added another 100 samples from movie reviews. The accuracy went up to 0.974. We therefore attempted to use different test samples and plotted the sample size versus accuracy, as shown in the following graph:

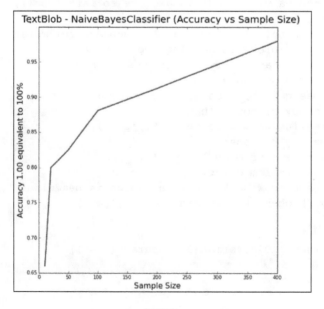

Viewing positive sentiments using word clouds

Word clouds give greater prominence to words that appear more frequently in any given text. They are also called tag clouds or weighted words. The significance of a word's strength in terms of its number of occurrences visually maps to the size of its appearance. In other words, the word that appears the largest in visualization is the one that has appeared the most in the text.

Beyond showing the occurrences of the words in shapes and colors, word clouds have several useful applications for social media and marketing as follows:

- Businesses could get to know their customers and how they view their products. Some organizations have used a very creative way of asking their fans or followers to post words about what that they think of their brand, taking all these words to a word cloud to understand what the most common impressions of their product brand are.

- Finding ways to know competitors by identifying a brand whose online presence is popular. Creating a word cloud from their content to better understand what words and themes hook the product target market.

In order to create a word cloud, one can write the Python code or use something that already exists. Andreas Mueller from NYU Center for Data Science created a word cloud in Python. This is pretty simple and easy to use. The `RemachineScript.ttf` font file can be downloaded from `http://www.fonts101.com/fonts/view/Script/63827/Remachine_Script`.

`STOPWORDS` consist of extremely common words, for example `a`, `an`, `the`, `is`, `was`, `at`, `in`, and many more. The following code creates a word cloud using a list of `STOPWORDS` in order to ignore them:

```
from wordcloud import WordCloud, STOPWORDS
import matplotlib.pyplot as plt
from os import path

d = path.dirname("__file__")
text = open(path.join(d, '/Users/MacBook/kirthi/results.txt')).read()

wordcloud = WordCloud(
    font_path='/Users/MacBook/kirthi/RemachineScript.ttf',
    stopwords=STOPWORDS,
    background_color='#222222',
    width=1000,
    height=800).generate(text)
```

In order to plot this, first set the figure size and use `imshow()` that will display the word cloud as an image.

```
# Open a plot of the generated image.
plt.figure(figsize=(13,13))

plt.imshow(wordcloud)
plt.axis("off")

plt.show()
```

To summarize, we will first extract the sentiments from the `TextBlob` example and assume that the extracted results are in `results.txt`. Then, we will use these words to visualize data as a word cloud with the `matplotlib` package.

The results of `wordcloud` are shown in the following image:

k-nearest neighbors

The **k-nearest neighbor** (**k-NN**) classification is one of the easiest classification methods to understand (particularly when there is little or no prior knowledge about the distribution of the data). The k-nearest neighbor classification has a way to store all the known cases and classify new cases based on a similarity measure (for example, the Euclidean distance function). The k-NN algorithm is popular in its statistical estimation and pattern recognition because of its simplicity.

For **1-nearest neighbor** (**1-NN**), the label of one particular point is set to be the nearest training point. When you extend this for a higher value of k, the label of a test point is the one that is measured by the k nearest training points. The k-NN algorithm is considered to be a lazy learning algorithm because the optimization is done locally, and the computations are delayed until classification.

There are advantages and disadvantages of this method. The advantages are high accuracy, insensitive to outliers, and no assumptions about data. The disadvantages of k-NN is that it is computationally expensive and requires a lot of memory.

One of the following distance metrics could be used:

$$Euclidean\ Distance\quad \sqrt{\sum_{i=1}^{k}(x_i - y_i)^2}$$

$$Manhattan\ Distance\quad \sum_{i=1}^{k}|x_i - y_i|$$

$$Minkowski\ Distance\quad \left(\sum_{i=1}^{k}(|x_i - y_i|)^q\right)^{\frac{1}{q}}$$

Let's consider an example where we are given a big basket of fruits with apples, bananas, and pears only. We will assume that the apples were red apples, not green. There is one characteristic that will distinguish these fruits from one another: color. Apples are red, bananas are yellow, and pears are green. These fruits can also be characterized by the weight of each. The following assumptions are made for the purpose of illustrating this example:

The shape characteristic is categorized as follows:

- For an apple, the shape value lies between 1 and 3, whereas the weight lies between 6 and 7 ounces
- For a pear, the shape value lies between 2 and 4, whereas the weight lies between 5 and 6 ounces
- For a banana, the shape value lies between 3 and 5, whereas the weight lies between 7 and 9 ounces

We have the data about the fruits in a basket as follows:

	Shape	Weight	Fruit
1	1.747993	6.244728	Apple
2	2.160436	6.548997	Apple
3	2.308360	6.568994	Apple
4	2.989498	6.116004	Apple
5	2.217408	6.298844	Apple
6	3.550124	5.148646	Banana
7	4.795393	5.729825	Banana
8	4.380994	5.491813	Banana
9	4.975395	5.243866	Banana
10	4.714245	5.061763	Banana
11	1.644232	6.710433	Apple
12	2.101244	8.531404	Pear
13	2.847359	8.541824	Pear
14	3.759746	8.609348	Pear
15	3.436196	7.667397	Pear
16	2.420651	7.471596	Pear
17	1.960733	6.678455	Apple
18	1.861635	6.320602	Apple

If we have an unlabeled fruit with a known weight and a color category, then applying the k-nearest neighbor method (with any distance formula) will most likely find the nearest *k* neighbors (if they are green, red, or yellow, the unlabeled fruit is most likely a pear, apple, or banana respectively). The following code demonstrates k-nearest neighbor algorithm using the shape and weight of fruits:

```
import csv
import matplotlib.patches as mpatches
import matplotlib.pyplot as plt

count=0
x=[]
y=[]
z=[]

with open('/Users/myhome/fruits_data.csv', 'r') as csvf:
    reader = csv.reader(csvf, delimiter=',')
    for row in reader:
        if count > 0:
            x.append(row[0])
```

```
        y.append(row[1])
        if ( row[2] == 'Apple' ): z.append('r')
        elif ( row[2] == 'Pear' ): z.append('g')
        else: z.append('y')
    count += 1

plt.figure(figsize=(11,11))

recs=[]
classes=['Apples', 'Pear', 'Bananas']
class_colours = ['r','g','y']
plt.title("Apples, Bananas and Pear by Weight and Shape", fontsize=18)

plt.xlabel("Shape category number", fontsize=14)
plt.ylabel("Weight in ounces", fontsize=14)

plt.scatter(x,y,s=600,c=z)
```

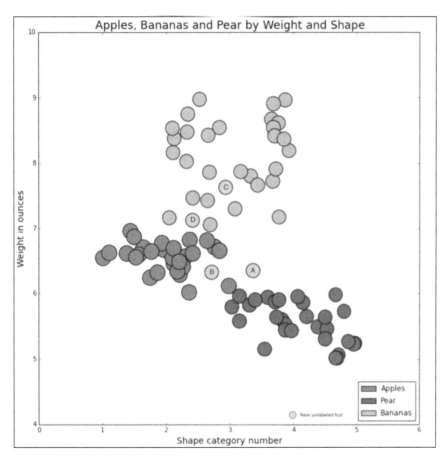

Let's pick four unlabeled fruits with their x and y values as *A(3.5,6.2)*, *B(2.75,6.2)*, *C(2.9, 7.6)*, and *D(2.4, 7.2)* with the following code:

```
from math import pow, sqrt
dist=[]
def determineFruit(xv, yv, threshold_radius):
  for i in range(1,len(x)):
    xdif=pow(float(x[i])-xv, 2)
    ydif=pow(float(y[i])-yv, 2)
    sqrtdist = sqrt(xdif+ydif))
    if ( xdif < threshold_radius and
         ydif < thresholdradius and sqrtdist < threshold_radius):
      dist.append(sqrtdist)
    else:
      dist.append(99)
  pear_count=0
  apple_count=0
  banana_count=0
  for i in range(1,len(dist)):
      if dist[i] < threshold_radius:
          if z[i] == 'g': pear_count += 1
          if z[i] == 'r': apple_count += 1
          if z[i] == 'y': banana_count += 1
  if ( apple_count >= pear_count and apple_count >= banana_count ):
    return "apple"
  elif ( pear_count >= apple_count and pear_count >= banana_count):
    return "pear"
  elif ( banana_count >= apple_count and banana_count >= pear_count):
    return "banana"

dist=[]
determine = determineFruit(3.5,6.2, 1)
print determine

'pear'
```

Logistic regression

As we have seen earlier, one problem with linear regression is that it tends to underfit the data. This gives us the lowest mean-squared error for unbiased estimators. With the underfit model, we will not get the best predictions. There are some ways to reduce this mean-squared error by adding some bias to our estimator.

Logistic regression is one of the ways to fit models for data that have true or false responses. Linear regression cannot predict all the probabilities directly, but logistic regression can. In addition, the predicted probabilities can be calibrated better when compared to the results from Naive Bayes.

For this discussion, by keeping our focus on the binary response, we can set the value of 1 to `true` and 0 to `false`. The logistic regression model assumes that the input variables can be scaled by the inverse log function; therefore, another way to take a look at this is that the log of the observed y value can be expressed as a linear combination of the n input variables of x, as shown in the following equation:

$$\log \frac{P(x)}{1 - P(x)} = \sum_{j=0}^{n} b_j x_j = z$$

$$\frac{P(x)}{1 - P(x)} = e^z$$

$$\Rightarrow P(x) = \frac{e^z}{1 + e^z} = \frac{1}{1 + e^{-z}}$$

As the inverse of a logarithmic function is an exponential function, the expression on the right-hand side appears to be a version of a sigmoid of the linear combination of the variables of x. This means that the denominator can never be 1 (unless z is 0). The value of $P(x)$ is therefore strictly greater than 0 and less than 1, as shown in the following code:

```
import matplotlib.pyplot as plt
import matplotlib
import random, math
import numpy as np
import scipy, scipy.stats
import pandas as pd

x = np.linspace(-10,10,100)
y1 = 1.0 / (1.0+np.exp(-x))
y2 = 1.0 / (1.0+np.exp(-x/2))
y3 = 1.0 / (1.0+np.exp(-x/10))

plt.title("Sigmoid Functions vs LineSpace")
plt.plot(x,y1,'r-',lw=2)
```

```
plt.plot(x,y2,'g-',lw=2)
plt.plot(x,y3,'b-',lw=2)
plt.xlabel("x")
plt.ylabel("y")
plt.show()
```

The following image shows a standard sigmoid function:

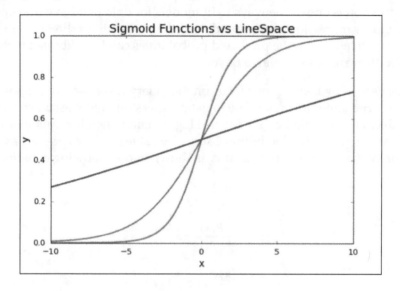

The following is an example showing probability of *happy* and *sad*.

$$P(happy) = \frac{e^z}{1+e^z}$$

$$P(sad) = 1 - P(happy) = \frac{1}{1+e^z}$$

Kaggle hosts all the machine learning competitions. It usually provides the training and test data. A while ago, predicting the survivors of the Titanic was contested on Kaggle based on the real data. The `titanic_train.csv` and `titanic_test.csv` files are for training and testing purposes respectively. Using the `linear_model` package from `scikit-learn`, which includes logistic regression, we can see that the following code is a modified version of the author's version who won the contest:

```
Import numpy as np
import pandas as pd
import sklearn.linear_model as lm
import sklearn.cross_validation as cv
import matplotlib.pyplot as plt
```

```
train = pd.read_csv('/Users/myhome/titanic_train.csv')
test = pd.read_csv('/Users/myhome/titanic_test.csv')
train[train.columns[[2,4,5,1]]].head()

data = train[['Sex', 'Age', 'Pclass', 'Survived']].copy()
data['Sex'] = data['Sex'] == 'female'
data = data.dropna()

data_np = data.astype(np.int32).values
X = data_np[:,:-1]
y = data_np[:,-1]

female = X[:,0] == 1
survived = y == 1

# This vector contains the age of the passengers.
age = X[:,1]
# We compute a few histograms.
bins_ = np.arange(0, 121, 5)
S = {'male': np.histogram(age[survived & ~female],
                          bins=bins_)[0],
     'female': np.histogram(age[survived & female],
                            bins=bins_)[0]}
D = {'male': np.histogram(age[~survived & ~female],
                          bins=bins_)[0],
     'female': np.histogram(age[~survived & female],
                            bins=bins_)[0]}
bins = bins_[:-1]
plt.figure(figsize=(15,8))
for i, sex, color in zip((0, 1),('male', 'female'), ('#3345d0',
'#cc3dc0')):
    plt.subplot(121 + i)
    plt.bar(bins, S[sex], bottom=D[sex], color=color,
            width=5, label='Survived')
    plt.bar(bins, D[sex], color='#aaaaff', width=5, label='Died',
alpha=0.4)
    plt.xlim(0, 80)
    plt.grid(None)

    plt.title(sex + " Survived")
    plt.xlabel("Age (years)")
    plt.legend()

(X_train, X_test, y_train, y_test) = cv.train_test_split(X, y, test_
```

```
    size=.05)
print X_train, y_train

# Logistic Regression from linear_model
logreg = lm.LogisticRegression();
logreg.fit(X_train, y_train)
y_predicted = logreg.predict(X_test)

plt.figure(figsize=(15,8));
plt.imshow(np.vstack((y_test, y_predicted)),
           interpolation='none', cmap='bone');
plt.xticks([]); plt.yticks([]);
plt.title(("Actual and predicted survival outcomes on the test set"))
```

The following is a linear regression plot showing male and female survivors of Titanic:

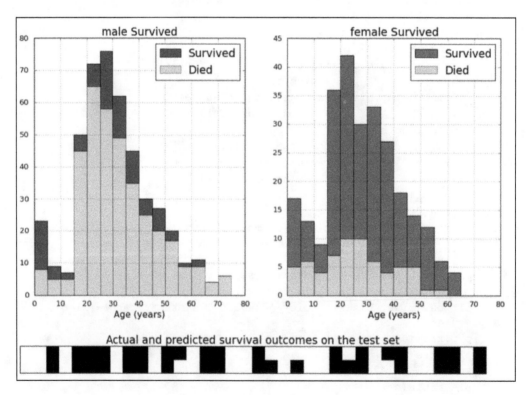

We have seen that `scikit-learn` has a good collection of functions for machine learning. They also come with a few standard datasets, for example, the iris dataset and the digits dataset for the classification and the Boston house prices the dataset for regression. Machine learning is about learning the properties of data and applying these properties to the new dataset.

Support vector machines

Support vector machines (**SVM**) are supervised learning methods that can be applied to regression or classification. These learning methods are an extension of nonlinear models, which empirically offers good performance and is successful in many applications, such as bioinformatics, text, image recognition, and so on. These methods are computationally inexpensive and easy to implement, but are prone to underfitting and may have low accuracy.

Let's understand the goal of SVM. The goal here is to map or find a pattern between x and y, where we want to perform the mapping from $X \rightarrow Y$ ($x \in X$ and $y \in Y$). Here, x can be an object, whereas y can be a label. Another simple example is that X is an n-dimensional real value space, whereas y is a set of -1, 1.

A classic example of SVM is that when two pictures of a tiger and a human being are given, X becomes the set of pixel images, whereas Y becomes the label that answers the question, that is, "is this a tiger or a human being?" when an unknown picture is given. Here is another example of the character recognition problem:

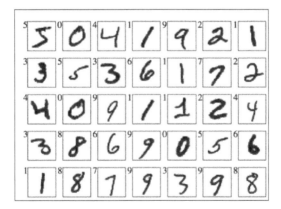

There are already many examples of SVM on the Internet, but here, we will show how you can use `scikit-learn` (`sklearn`) to apply the visualization methods on various machine learning algorithms that include SVM. In `sklearn`, among many other things, the `sklearn.svm` package includes the following SVR models:

```python
import numpy as np
from sklearn.svm import SVR
import matplotlib.pyplot as plt

X = np.sort(5 * np.random.rand(40, 1), axis=0)
y = (np.cos(X)+np.sin(X)).ravel()
y[::5] += 3 * (0.5 - np.random.rand(8))

svr_rbfmodel = SVR(kernel='rbf', C=1e3, gamma=0.1)
svr_linear = SVR(kernel='linear', C=1e3)
svr_polynom = SVR(kernel='poly', C=1e3, degree=2)
y_rbfmodel = svr_rbfmodel.fit(X, y).predict(X)
y_linear = svr_linear.fit(X, y).predict(X)
y_polynom = svr_polynom.fit(X, y).predict(X)

plt.figure(figsize=(11,11))
plt.scatter(X, y, c='k', label='data')
plt.hold('on')
plt.plot(X, y_rbfmodel, c='g', label='RBF model')
plt.plot(X, y_linear, c='r', label='Linear model')
plt.plot(X, y_polynom, c='b', label='Polynomial model')
plt.xlabel('data')
plt.ylabel('target')
plt.title('Support Vector Regression')
plt.legend()
plt.show()
```

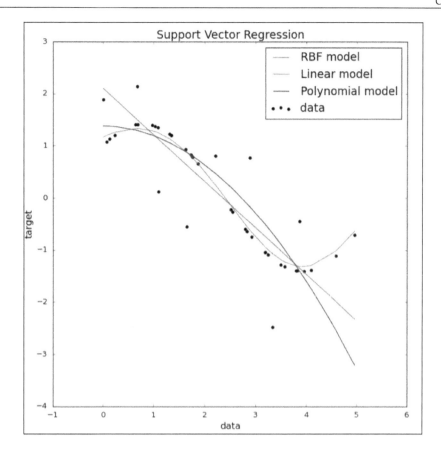

Principal component analysis

Principal component analysis (PCA) transforms the attributes of unlabeled data using a simple rearrangement and transformation with rotation. Looking at the data that does not have any significance, you can find ways to reduce dimensions this way. For instance, when a particular dataset looks similar to an ellipse when run at a particular angle to the axes, while in another transformed representation moves along the x axis and clearly has signs of no variation along the y axis, then it may be possible to ignore that.

k-means clustering is appropriate to cluster unlabeled data. Sometimes, one can use PCA to project data to a much lower dimension and then apply other methods, such as k-means, to a smaller and reduced data space.

However, it is very important to perform dimension reduction carefully because any dimension reduction may lead to the loss of information, and it is crucial that the algorithm preserves the useful part of the data while discarding the noise. Here, we will motivate PCA from at least two perspectives and explain why preserving maximal variability makes sense:

- Correlation and redundancy
- Visualization

Suppose that we did collect data about students on a campus that involves details about gender, height, weight, tv time, sports time, study time, GPA, and so on. While performing the survey about these students using these dimensions, we figured that the height and weight correlation yields an interesting theory (usually, the taller the student, the more weight due to the bone weight and vice versa). This may probably not be the case in a bigger set of population (more weight does not necessarily mean taller). The correlation can also be visualized as follows:

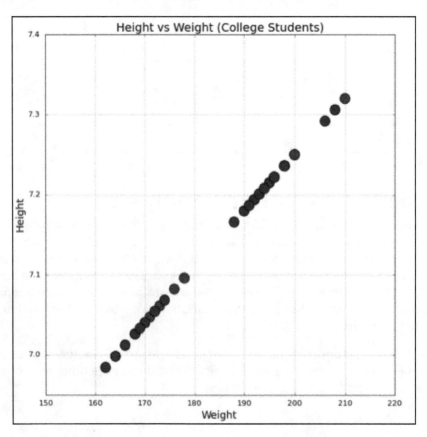

```python
import matplotlib.pyplot as plt
import csv

gender=[]
x=[]
y=[]
with open('/Users/kvenkatr/height_weight.csv', 'r') as csvf:
  reader = csv.reader(csvf, delimiter=',')
  count=0
  for row in reader:
    if count > 0:
        if row[0] == "f": gender.append(0)
        else:  gender.append(1)
        height = float(row[1])
        weight = float(row[2])
        x.append(height)
        y.append(weight)
    count += 1

plt.figure(figsize=(11,11))
plt.scatter(y,x,c=gender,s=300)
plt.grid(True)
plt.xlabel('Weight', fontsize=18)
plt.ylabel('Height', fontsize=18)
plt.title("Height vs Weight (College Students)", fontsize=20)
plt.legend()

plt.show()
```

Using `sklearn` again with the `preprocessing`, `datasets`, and `decomposition` packages, you can write a simple visualization code as follows:

```
from sklearn.datasets import load_iris
from sklearn.preprocessing import StandardScaler
import matplotlib.pyplot as plt

data = load_iris()
X = data.data

# convert features in column 1 from cm to inches
X[:,0] /= 2.54
# convert features in column 2 from cm to meters
X[:,1] /= 100
from sklearn.decomposition import PCA

def scikit_pca(X):

    # Standardize
    X_std = StandardScaler().fit_transform(X)

    # PCA
    sklearn_pca = PCA(n_components=2)
    X_transf = sklearn_pca.fit_transform(X_std)

    # Plot the data
    plt.figure(figsize=(11,11))
    plt.scatter(X_transf[:,0], X_transf[:,1], s=600, color='#8383c4',
alpha=0.56)
    plt.title('PCA via scikit-learn (using SVD)', fontsize=20)
    plt.xlabel('Petal Width', fontsize=15)
    plt.ylabel('Sepal Length', fontsize=15)
    plt.show()

scikit_pca(X)
```

This plot shows PCA using the `scikit-learn` package:

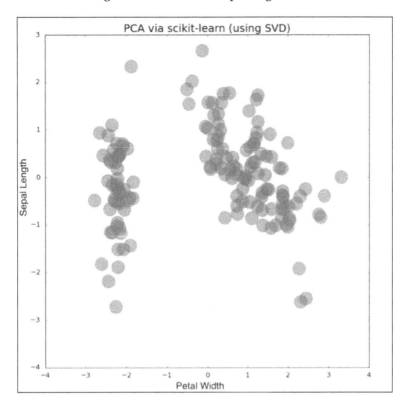

Installing scikit-learn

The following command will help the installation of the `scikit-learn` package:

```
$ conda install scikit-learn
Fetching package metadata: ....
Solving package specifications: .
Package plan for installation in environment /Users/myhomedir/anaconda:

The following packages will be downloaded:

    package                    |            build
    ---------------------------|-----------------
    nose-1.3.7                 |           py27_0          194 KB
    setuptools-18.0.1          |           py27_0          341 KB
```

```
pip-7.1.0                    |         py27_0        1.4 MB
scikit-learn-0.16.1          |      np19py27_0        3.3 MB
    ------------------------------------------------------------
                                       Total:         5.2 MB
```

The following packages will be UPDATED:

```
    nose:           1.3.4-py27_1      --> 1.3.7-py27_0
    pip:            7.0.3-py27_0      --> 7.1.0-py27_0
    scikit-learn:   0.15.2-np19py27_0 --> 0.16.1-np19py27_0
    setuptools:     17.1.1-py27_0     --> 18.0.1-py27_0
```

```
Proceed ([y]/n)? y
Fetching packages ...
```

For anaconda, as the CLI is all via conda, one can install it using conda. For other ways, by default, one would always attempt to use pip install. However, in any case, you should check the documentation for installation. As all the scikit-learn packages are pretty popular and have been around for a while, not much has changed. Now, in the following section, we will explore k-means clustering to conclude this chapter.

k-means clustering

k-means clustering originated from signal processing and is a popular method in data mining. The main intent of k-means clustering is to find some m points of a dataset that can best represent the center of some m-regions in the dataset.

k-means clustering is also known as partition clustering. This means that one needs to specify the number of clusters before any clustering process is started. You can define an objective function that uses the sum of Euclidean distance between a data point and its nearest cluster centroid. One can follow a systematic procedure to minimize this objective function iteratively by finding a brand new set of cluster centers that can lower the value of the objective function iteratively.

k-means clustering is a popular method in cluster analysis. It does not require any assumptions. This means that when a dataset is given and a predetermined number of clusters is labeled as k and when you apply the k-means algorithm, it minimizes the sum-squared error of the distance.

The algorithm is pretty simple to understand as follows:

- Given is a set of *n* points *(x,y)* and a set of *k* centroids
- For each *(x,y)*, find the centroid that is closest to that point (which determines the cluster this *(x,y)* belong to
- In each cluster, find the median and set this as the centroid of that cluster and repeat this process

Let's take a look at a simple example (this can be applied to a large collection of points) using k-means from the `sklearn.cluster` package. This example shows that with minimal code, you can accomplish k-means clustering using the `scikit-learn` library:

```
import matplotlib.pyplot as plt

from sklearn.cluster import KMeans

import csv

x=[]
y=[]

with open('/Users/myhomedir/cluster_input.csv', 'r') as csvf:
  reader = csv.reader(csvf, delimiter=',')
    for row in reader:
       x.append(float(row[0]))
       y.append(float(row[1]))

data=[]
for i in range(0,120):
  data.append([x[i],y[i]])

plt.figure(figsize=(10,10))

plt.xlim(0,12)
plt.ylim(0,12)

plt.xlabel("X values",fontsize=14)
plt.ylabel("Y values", fontsize=14)

plt.title("Before Clustering ", fontsize=20)

plt.plot(x, y, 'k.', color='#0080ff', markersize=35, alpha=0.6)

kmeans = KMeans(init='k-means++', n_clusters=3, n_init=10)
kmeans.fit(data)
```

```
plt.figure(figsize=(10,10))

plt.xlabel("X values",fontsize=14)
plt.ylabel("Y values", fontsize=14)

plt.title("After K-Means Clustering (from scikit-learn)", fontsize=20)

plt.plot(x, y, 'k.', color='#ffaaaa', markersize=45, alpha=0.6)

# Plot the centroids as a blue X
centroids = kmeans.cluster_centers_

plt.scatter(centroids[:, 0], centroids[:, 1], marker='x', s=200,
    linewidths=3, color='b', zorder=10)

plt.show()
```

Plotting the data before clustering looks like this:

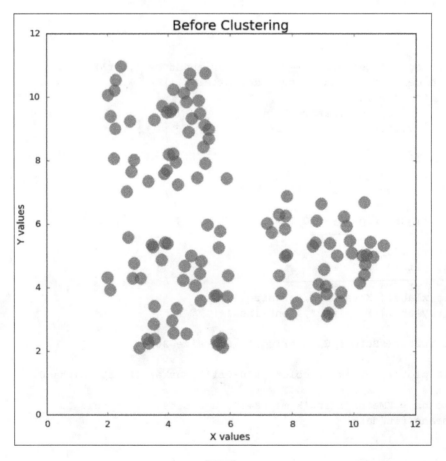

In this example, if we set *k*=5 for five clusters, then this cluster remains the same, but the other two clusters get split into two to obtain five clusters, as shown in the following diagram:

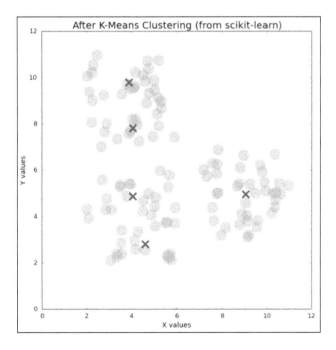

Summary

This chapter illustrates popular machine learning algorithms with examples. A brief introduction to linear and logistic regression was discussed. Using the college acceptance criteria for linear regression and the Titanic survivors for logistic regression, this chapter also illustrated how you can use the `statsmodels.formula.api`, `pandas`, and `sklearn.linear_model` packages for these regression methods. In both these examples, `matplotlib` has been used for visualization methods.

You learned about decision trees. Using the sports example (golf and tennis), we looked at the decision tree using the `sklearn` and `pydot` packages. Further, we discussed Bayes theorem and the Naïve Bayes classifier. Using the `TextBlob` package and the movie reviews data from the `nltk` corpora, we looked at the example of a word cloud visually using the `wordcloud` package.

You learned about the k-nearest neighbors algorithm. Here, we looked at an example that classified fruits based on their weight and shape, visually separating them by their color.

We also looked at the illustration of SVM in its simplest form with an example of how to generate data from the `sklearn.svm` package and plotted the results using the `matplotlib` library. You learned about PCA, how to determine the redundancy, and eliminate some of the variables. We used the iris example with the `sklearn.preprocesing` library to see how to visualize results. Finally, we looked at k-means clustering with an example of random points using `sklearn.cluster` as it is the simplest way you can achieve clustering (with minimal code). In the next chapter, we will discuss various examples of bioinformatics, genetics, and network.

7
Bioinformatics, Genetics, and Network Models

Scientific applications have multiple black boxes, and what goes inside these boxes is complex and often thought of as magical. However, they all follow a systematic set of protocols. These protocols are well known in the research community. For instance, network models are widely used to represent complex structured data, such as protein networks, molecular genetics, and chemical structures. Another interesting field in the research community is bioinformatics. This is a growing field that has lately generated a considerable amount of breakthrough in research.

In the field of biology, there are many different complex structures, such as DNA sequences, protein structures, and so on. In order to compare, let's take a look at some of the unknown elements within these structures. It is helpful to have a model that will visually display them. Similarly, in any application of the graph theory or networks, it is essentially beneficial to be able to visualize the complex graph structure.

Later in this chapter, we will discuss some interesting examples, such as social networks, directed graph examples in real life, data structures appropriate for these problems, and network analysis. For the purposes of demonstrating examples, here we will use specific libraries, such as metaseq, NetworkX, matplotlib, Biopython, and ETE toolkit, covering the following topics:

- Directed graphs and multigraphs
- The clustering coefficient of graphs
- Analysis of social networks
- The planar graph test and the directed acyclic graph test
- Maximum flow and minimum cut
- A genetic programming example
- Stochastic block models and random graphs

Directed graphs and multigraphs

First, we will review directed graphs and multigraphs. Later, we will figure out the options in Python to generate them. Also, we will take a look at an example where you may require directed graphs. Before we conceptually describe graphs and directed graphs, let's take a look at the different ways to understand when you can use graphs and directed graphs.

Computers that are connected to each other within a university campus area can be considered a connected graph, where each computer in this connection is viewed as a node or a vertex. The connected path is an edge, and in some cases, if there is only a one-way connection, then it is a directed graph. For instance, a very restricted federal network will not allow any connection from outside to go in, but will probably not restrict the other way around. The following are simple graphs showing distances between places:

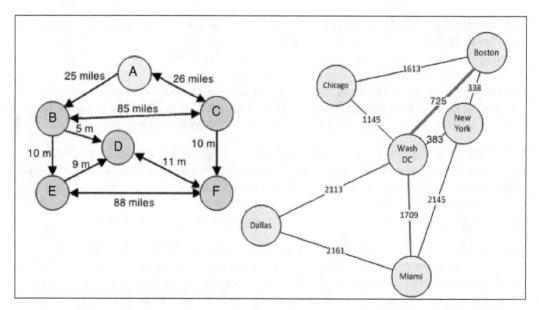

In the preceding examples, the graph with city labels **A** through **F** is a directed graph, and the other one on the right-hand side is an undirected graph. In the directed graph, if the arrow points both ways, there is a way to go both ways, whereas in the undirected graph, both ways are assumed. If we were to represent these graphs using some data structure, what would that be? Also, if we were to plot these kinds of graphs, which libraries do we use and how do we accomplish it?

Storing graph data

Graph data is usually represented as an adjacency matrix, unless it is sparse. An adjacency matrix is a matrix that has V_2 rows, assuming that the graph has a V vertex or a node. For example, for the two graphs shown in the preceding figure, the adjacency matrix looks similar to the following tables:

	A	B	C	D	E	F
A	0	25	26			
B		0	85	5	10	
C	26	85	0			10
D				0		11
E				9	0	88
F				11	88	0

	Chicago	Boston	New York	Wash DC	Miami	Dallas
Chicago	0	1613		1145		
Boston	1613	0	338	725		
New York		338	0	383	2145	
Wash DC	1145	725	383	0	1709	2113
Miami			2145	1709	0	2161
Dallas				2113	2161	0

For undirected graphs, by symmetry, it is enough to use half the storage (no need to store all the information from A to B and B to A). The blank entries show that there is not enough data about the distance. If the matrix is sparse, where most of the entries are not filled, then you can store it as a list of lists. Fortunately, there are convenient methods in `scipy` to deal with sparse matrices. The following code is only for the first graph shown in the preceding figure:

```
import scipy.sparse as sparse

matrixA = sparse.lil_matrix((6,6))

matrixA = sparse.lil_matrix( [[0,25,26,0,0,0], [0,0,85,5,10,0],
    [26,85,0,0,0,10], [0,0,0,0,0,11],[0,0,0,9,0,88],[0,0,0,11,88,0]])
print matrixA
(0, 1)   25
(0, 2)   26
```

```
(1, 2)    85
(1, 3)    5
(1, 4)    10
(2, 0)    26
(2, 1)    85
(2, 5)    10
(3, 5)    11
(4, 3)    9
(4, 5)    88
(5, 3)    11
(5, 4)    88
```

Displaying graphs

The preceding example only shows how to represent the graph using the `scipy` library (the `scipy.sparse` package in particular). However, in the following section, we will see how to display these graphs. Although there are numerous Python packages that you can choose from to display graphs, the top three popular choices among these are `NetworkX`, `igraph` (from `igraph.org`), and `graph-tool`. Let's take a look at an example of graph display using these three packages.

igraph

Originally, `igraph` was intended for R users, but later, the Python version was added. For smaller graphs, you can add the vertices and edges and display them very easily, but in most cases, graphs are not small; therefore, `igraph` offers functions that reads the data of a graph from files conveniently and displays it.

Currently, `igraph` offers several formats, such as `dimacs`, `dl`, `edgelist`, `graml`, `graphdb`, `gml`, `lgl`, `ncol`, and `pajek`. GraphML is an XML-based file format and can be used for large graphs, and the NCOL graph format is suited for large graphs with a weighted edge list. The LGL graph format can also be used for a large graph layout with weighted edges. Most others use a simple textual format. Only the DL file format is fully supported by `igraph`, and for all others, `igraph` only supports partial file formats.

Similar to many other Python packages, the good part about `igraph` is that it offers very convenient ways to configure and display graphs and stores them in the SVG format so that they can be embedded in an HTML file.

Let's take a look at one example that involves the `pajek` format (for more details on pajek, you can refer to `http://vlado.fmf.uni-lj.si/pub/networks/pajek/`). There are many other parameters. A few among these are `labelcolor`, `vertexsize`, and `radius` for some vertex shapes. We will see two examples here. The first example has assigned labels and edges for a small graph, whereas the second example reads the data of a graph from a file and displays it. The following example shows a labeled graph using the `igraph` package:

```
from igraph import *

vertices = ["A", "B", "C", "D", "E", "F", "G", "H", "I", "J"]

edges = [(0,1),(1,2),(2,3),(3,4),(4,5),(5,6),(6,7),(7,1),
         (1,8),  (8,2),(2,4),(4,9),(9,5),(5,7),(7,0)]

graphStyle = { 'vertex_size': 20}
g = Graph(vertex_attrs={"label": vertices}, edges=edges,
directed=True)
g.write_svg("simple_star.svg", width=500, height=300, **graphStyle)
```

There are 10 vertices in the star graph that forms five triangles and a pentagon. Also, there are 15 edges because the five triangles complete the set of edges. It is a very simple graph, where each edge is defined by the associated vertex numbers that starts from zero. The following labeled graph plot is the result of the preceding Python example:

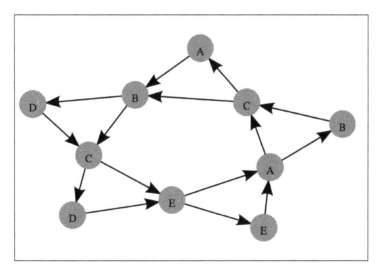

This second example illustrates not only how to read the graph data from a file, but also how to save the plot in the SVG format so that you can embed the SVG data in HTML:

```
from igraph import read

g=read("ragusa.net",format="pajek")

g.vs["color"]="#3d679d"
g.es["color"]="red"

graphStyle={ 'vertex_size': 12, 'margin': 6}
#graphStyle["layout"]=g.layout("fr")   # optional

g.write_svg("ragusa_graph.svg", width=600, height=600,**graphStyle)
```

The pajek format file is read using the read function from igraph. When you set up the edge and the vertex color, you can generate the SVG format of the graph. There are several different layouts that igraph offers that you can experiment with. The following plot shows a graph that was created using the igraph package by reading the graph data from a file:

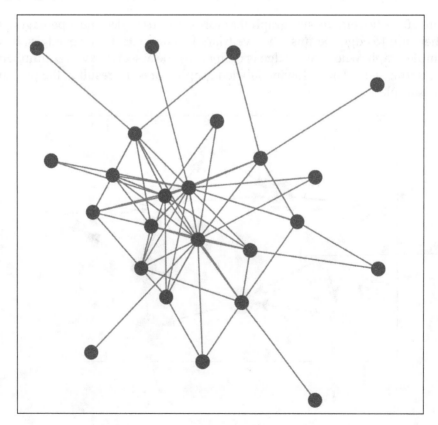

The graph data in the `pajek` format was obtained from the `pajek` networks website (`http://vlado.fmf.uni-lj.si/pub/networks/pajek/data/gphs.htm`) from a file named `Rgausa16.net`. Once a data file from here is downloaded, you can use it in a similar way and display the graph, as shown in the preceding image. If we use the `tinamatr.net` data and set the circular layout, then the graph would appear in a circular layout, as shown in the following code:

```
graphStyle["layout"]=g.layout("circle")
```

NetworkX

One of the reasons this Python package is called `NetworkX` is because it is a library for network and graph analysis. From finding the shortest path from a source node or vertex to the destination node or vertex, finding the degree distribution to figure the nodes that are similar to the junction, and finding the clustering coefficient of a graph, there are several ways to perform a graph analysis.

The study of graphs has been around for a while and is applicable in neurobiology, chemistry, social network analysis, page ranks, and many more such interesting areas today. Social networks are assortative truly in the sense of joining similar affiliated members, and biological networks are the opposite. In other words, the friendship between Facebook users or the academicians (who are coauthors) can be visualized easily via graphs. Python packages offer users many options. Often, users choose several of these to combine the best of their individual functionalities.

`NetworkX` offers graph building and analysis capabilities. You can read and write network data in standard and nonstandard data formats, generate graph networks, analyze their structure, and build several models. The following Python code shows how one can create a directed graph by just using `matplotlib`:

```python
import matplotlib.pyplot as plt
import pylab
from pylab import rcParams

import networkx as nx
import numpy as np

# set the graph display size as 10 by 10 inches
rcParams['figure.figsize'] = 10, 10

G = nx.DiGraph()

# Add the edges and weights
G.add_edges_from([('K', 'I'),('R','T'),('V','T')], weight=3)
G.add_edges_from([('T','K'),('T','H'),('I','T'),('T','H')], weight=4)
G.add_edges_from([('I','R'),('H','N')], weight=5)
G.add_edges_from([('R','N')], weight=6)
```

```
# these values to determine node colors
val_map = {'K': 1.5, 'I': 0.9, 'R': 0.6, 'T': 0.2}
values = [val_map.get(node, 1.0) for node in G.nodes()]

edge_labels=dict([((u,v,),d['weight'])
                 for u,v,d in G.edges(data=True)])

#set edge colors
red_edges = [('R','T'),('T','K')]
edge_colors = ['green' if not edge in red_edges else 'red' for edge in
G.edges()]

pos=nx.spring_layout(G)

nx.draw_networkx_edges(G,pos,width=2.0,alpha=0.65)
nx.draw_networkx_edge_labels(G,pos,edge_labels=edge_labels)

nx.draw(G,pos, node_color = values, node_size=1500,
  edge_color=edge_colors, edge_cmap=plt.cm.Reds)

pylab.show()
```

The following diagram illustrates how you can use `NetworkX` to configure the edge weights and the visual aesthetics of a graph. Among several approaches of displaying a directed graph, `NetworkX` took a different approach by showing a thick bar at the end, rather than using an arrow symbol that determines the direction of a graph.

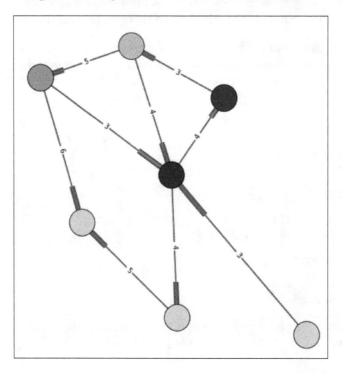

When there is a scientific study that involves a collection of elements that represent things or people, the association between them is better represented in the form of graphs, where these elements are vertices or nodes. In most of these cases, the centrality visually identifies nodes that are significantly important. Python packages (such as `NetworkX`) have many useful functions for graph analysis that includes finding cliques in the graph. For smaller graphs, it is easier to visually inspect intricate details, but for larger graphs, one would want to recognize a pattern of behavior, such as isolated cluster groups.

Typically, the labels for nodes and edges depend on what you are trying to display as a graph. For instance, protein interaction can be displayed as a graph. A more complex example will be a sequence space graph, where a graph node represents a protein sequence, whereas an edge represents a single DNA mutation. It would be easier for scientists to zoom into these images to see patterns, as shown in the following image. This example does not use Python and uses interactive programming to zoom and view the intricate details.

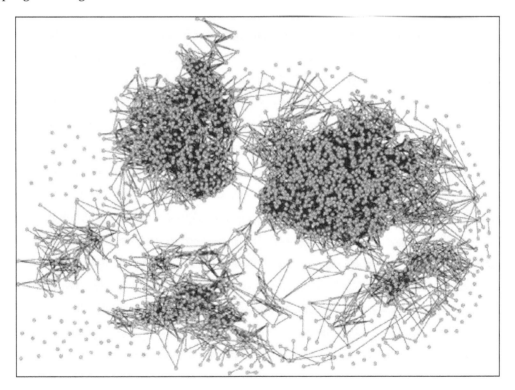

 The preceding image has been taken from
`http://publications.csail.mit.edu/`.

Sometimes, you would want to highlight different routes on a map. For instance, if a road map is being displayed and you have to display the routes that the Olympic cycling team is going to follow this year on this map, you can do something similar to the following code:

```
import networkx as nx
from pylab import rcParams

# set the graph display size as 10 by 10 inches
rcParams['figure.figsize'] = 10, 10

def genRouteEdges(r):
    return [(r[n],r[n+1]) for n in range(len(r)-1)]

G=nx.Graph(name="python")
graph_routes = [[11,3,4,1,2], [5,6,3,0,1], [2,0,1,3,11,5]]
edges = []
for r in graph_routes:
    route_edges = genRouteEdges(r)
    G.add_nodes_from(r)
    G.add_edges_from(route_edges)
    edges.append(route_edges)

print("Graph has %d nodes with %d edges" %(G.number_of_nodes(),
G.number_of_edges()))

pos = nx.spring_layout(G)
nx.draw_networkx_nodes(G,pos=pos)
nx.draw_networkx_labels(G,pos=pos)

colors = ['#00bb00', '#4e86cc', 'y']
linewidths = [22,14,10]

for ctr, edgelist in enumerate(edges):
    nx.draw_networkx_edges(G,pos=pos,edgelist=edgelist,
        edge_color = colors[ctr], width=linewidths[ctr])
```

Using convenient methods from NetworkX for a specific route, you can easily highlight the routes with different colors and line widths, as shown in the following image:

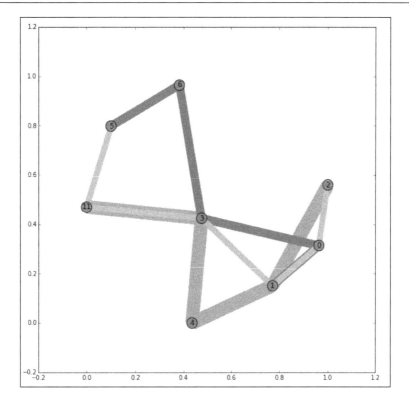

As shown in the preceding image, by controlling the highlights of routes, you can recognize different routes on a map.

Additionally, from the shortest path to degree distribution to clustering coefficients, NetworkX offers a variety of ways to perform a graph analysis. One simple way to see the shortest path is shown in the following code:

```
import networkx as nx

g = nx.Graph()
g.add_edge('m','i',weight=0.1)
g.add_edge('i','a',weight=1.5)
g.add_edge('m','a',weight=1.0)
g.add_edge('a','e',weight=0.75)
g.add_edge('e','h',weight=1.5)
g.add_edge('a','h',weight=2.2)

print nx.shortest_path(g,'i','h')
nx.draw(g)

#printed shortest path as result
['i', 'a', 'h']
```

One more example using `NetworkX` (particularly reading the data in the GML format) is the "coappearance of characters in the *Les Miserables* novel", which we downloaded from the datasets available from `gephi.org` at `https://gephi.org/datasets/lesmiserables.gml.zip`.

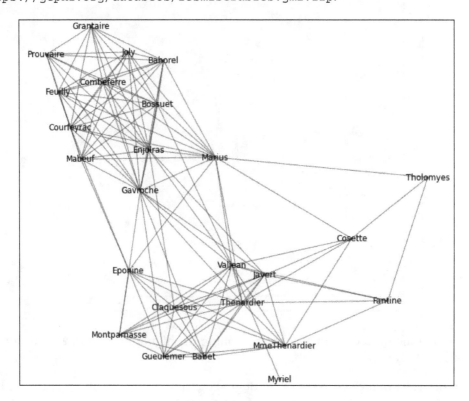

The preceding plot is the result of the program that reads the association of characters from *Les Miserables* and creates a network diagram, as shown in the following code:

```
import networkx as nx
from pylab import rcParams
rcParams['figure.figsize'] = 12, 12

G = nx.read_gml('/Users/kvenkatr/Downloads/lesmiserables.gml',
relabel=True)
G8= G.copy()
dn = nx.degree(G8)
for n in G8.nodes():
  if dn[n] <= 8:
    G8.remove_node(n)
pos= nx.spring_layout(G8)
```

```
nx.draw(G8, node_size=10, edge_color='b', alpha=0.45, font_size=9,
pos=pos)
labels = nx.draw_networkx_labels(G8, pos=pos)
```

Graph-tool

Among the three packages, igraph, networkx, and graph-tool, the graph-tool package is the hardest to install, especially on a Mac OS. Graph-tool has many convenient functions and is also considered very efficient in terms of centrality-related algorithms. This includes k-core, PageRank, minimum spanning tree, and the single source shortest path. The comparison table is available at https://graph-tool.skewed.de/performance. The module that includes centrality-related algorithms as mentioned earlier is graph_tool.centrality.

```
import graph_tool.all as gtool

gr = gtool.collection.data["polblogs"]
gr = gtool.GraphView(gr, vfill=gtool.label_largest_component(gr))

cness = gtool.closeness(gr)

gtool.graph_draw(gr, pos=gr.vp["pos"], vertex_fill_color=cness,
                vertex_size=gtool.prop_to_size(cness, mi=5, ma=15),
                vorder=cness, vcmap=matplotlib.cm.gist_heat,
                output="political_closeness.pdf")
```

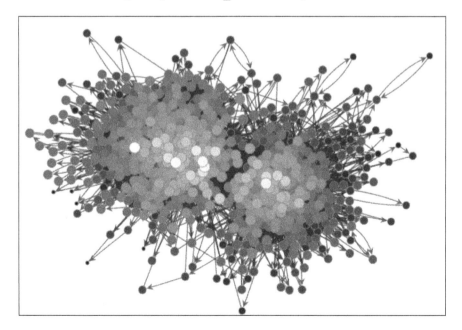

The prefix centra in the "centrality" word truly means that some entity (in this context, this would be a node or vertex) is central. Also, many other entities are connected to the central entity. So, we can ask a reasonable question, that is, what are the characteristics that makes a vertex important? In the `graph_tool` centrality module, there are nine centrality-related algorithms that are offered, and *PageRank* is one among these, in addition to *closeness*.

PageRank

The `graph_tool.centrality .pagerank()` function generates the PageRank of the *v* vertex. Most people who know Google's PageRank understand how the measure works. In a nutshell, it is a way to measure how important web page *A* is (in terms of how many outside web sites *B* are depending on web page *A* and also on how many web pages *A* depends on – in graph theory they are called in-degree and out-degree). In addition to these, Google applies many other external factors to rank a web page. In the preceding example, if we replace the line that finds closeness by PageRank as follows:

```
pagerank = gtool.pagerank(gr)
```

This should generate a graph with the emphasis on PageRank. In addition to the centrality measure, there is one other factor called the clustering coefficient of a graph.

The clustering coefficient of graphs

The clustering coefficient of a node or a vertex in a graph depends on how close the neighbors are so that they form a clique (or a small complete graph), as shown in the following diagram:

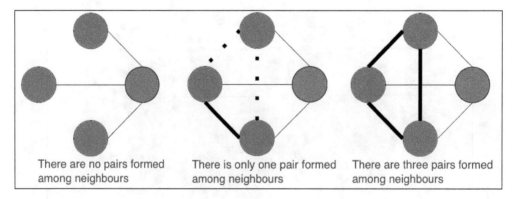

| There are no pairs formed among neighbours | There is only one pair formed among neighbours | There are three pairs formed among neighbours |

There is a well known formula to cluster coefficients, which looks pretty heavy with mathematical symbols. However, to put it in simple words, take a look at the following equation:

$$C_i = \frac{2 \times (links\ to\ the\ node\ i)}{n_b (n_b - 1)}$$

where n _ b is the number of neighbors to node i

This involves keeping track of the links at every vertex and calculating the clustering index at every vertex, where the neighbor of a node in the most obvious sense is a node that is only one link away from that node. Clustering index calculation is shown here:

$$C_i = \frac{2 \times (links\ to\ the\ node\ i)}{n_b (n_b - 1)}$$

where n _ b is the number of neighbors to node i

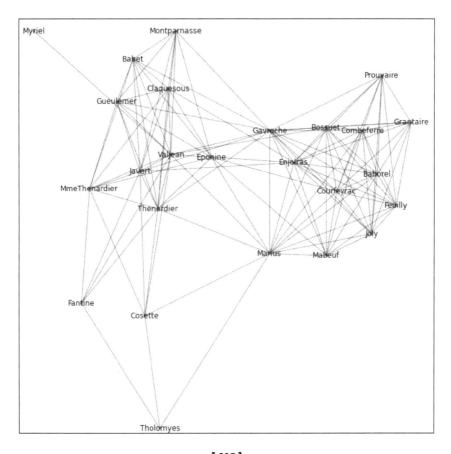

The following code illustrates how you can show the characters of the *Les Miserables* novel and how each character is associated or connected to other characters:

```python
import networkx as nx
from pylab import rcParams
rcParams['figure.figsize'] = 12, 12

G = nx.read_gml('/Users/kvenkatr/Downloads/lesmiserables.gml',
relabel=True)
G8= G.copy()

dn = nx.degree(G8)

for n in G8.nodes():
  if dn[n] <= 8:
    G8.remove_node(n)

pos= nx.spring_layout(G8)
nx.draw(G8, node_size=10, edge_color='b', alpha=0.45, font_size=9,
pos=pos)
labels = nx.draw_networkx_labels(G8, pos=pos)

def valuegetter(*values):
    if len(values) == 1:
        item = values[0]
        def g(obj):
            return obj[item]
    else:
        def g(obj):
            return tuple(obj[item] for item in values)
    return g

def clustering_coefficient(G,vertex):
    neighbors = G[vertex].keys()
    if len(neighbors) == 1: return -1.0
    links = 0
    for node in neighbors:
        for u in neighbors:
            if u in G[node]: links += 1
    ccoeff=2.0*links/(len(neighbors)*(len(neighbors)-1))
    return links, len(neighbors),ccoeff

def calculate_centrality(G):
    degc = nx.degree_centrality(G)
    nx.set_node_attributes(G, 'degree_cent', degc)
```

```
    degc_sorted = sorted(degc.items(), key=valuegetter(1),
reverse=True)
    for key, value in degc_sorted[0:10]:
        print "Degree Centrality:", key, value
    return G, degc


print "Valjean", clustering_coefficient(G8,"Valjean")
print "Marius", clustering_coefficient(G8,"Marius")
print "Gavroche", clustering_coefficient(G8,"Gavroche")
print "Babet", clustering_coefficient(G8,"Babet")
print "Eponine", clustering_coefficient(G8,"Eponine")
print "Courfeyrac", clustering_coefficient(G8,"Courfeyrac")
print "Comeferre", clustering_coefficient(G8,"Combeferre")
calculate_centrality(G8)
```

There are two results of the preceding code; the first part is the textual output that
gets printed, whereas the second part is the network diagram that gets plotted, as
shown in the following code and diagram:

```
#Text Results printed
Valjean (82, 14, 0.9010989010989011)
Marius (94, 14, 1.032967032967033)
Gavroche (142, 17, 1.0441176470588236)
Babet (60, 9, 1.6666666666666667)
Eponine (36, 9, 1.0)
Courfeyrac (106, 12, 1.606060606060606)
Comeferre (102, 11, 1.8545454545454545)

Degree Centrality: Gavroche 0.708333333333
Degree Centrality: Valjean 0.583333333333
Degree Centrality: Enjolras 0.583333333333
Degree Centrality: Marius 0.583333333333
Degree Centrality: Courfeyrac 0.5
Degree Centrality: Bossuet 0.5
Degree Centrality: Thenardier 0.5
Degree Centrality: Joly 0.458333333333
Degree Centrality: Javert 0.458333333333
Degree Centrality: Feuilly 0.458333333333
```

The graph results are shown here below.

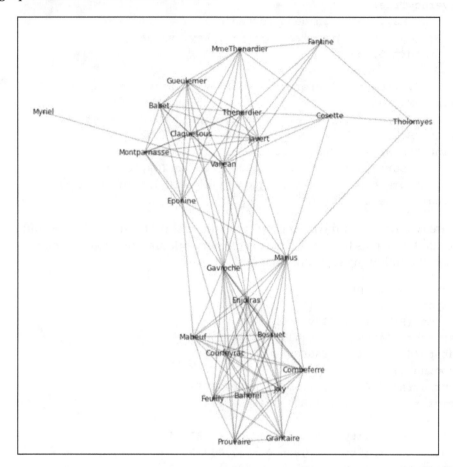

Clearly among all, so far we have found that *Comeferre* happens to have a larger clustering coefficient (0.927). Often, when we plot a large graph in two dimensions, it is not easy to visually see the clustering coefficient.

Analysis of social networks

Accessing data from social networks, such as LinkedIn, Facebook, or Twitter, used to be much simpler and easier several years ago. Now, most of the APIs have restrictions. Also, the accessing methods are a little bit more involved. First, one has to get authentication (which used to be the case even earlier) and then use methods that access either friends or connections. We have only chosen Twitter for demonstrating the analysis of social network data here, but you can also find other social media data in a similar way.

In order to access Twitter data, as we noticed from the previous chapters (when we discussed word clouds), you have to get authentication keys to access their APIs. There are four keys: CONSUMER_KEY, CONSUMER_SECRET, ACCESS_TOKEN_KEYS, and ACCESS_TOKEN_SECRET. Once these credentials are verified via Python successfully, you can call GetFriends() and GetFollowers() to get the list of friends and followers. There are many packages available in Python to access Twitter data. So, it is very confusing which ones to use. We have used tweepy in past examples. Here, in the following code, we will use Python-Twitter because it has convenient modules to get data, summarize it, store it in cPickle, and then visualize it.

```python
import cPickle
import os
import twitter  # https://github.com/ianozsvald/python-twitter

# Usage:
# $ # setup CONSUMER_KEY, CONSUMER_SECRET, ACCESS_TOKEN_KEY, ACCESS_
TOKEN_SECRET
# as environment variables
# $ python get_data.py  # downloads friend and follower data to ./data

# Errors seen at runtime:
# raise URLError(err)
# urllib2.URLError: <urlopen error [Errno 104] Connection reset by
peer>

DATA_DIR = "data"  # storage directory for friend/follower data

# list of screen names that we'll want to analyze
screen_names = [ 'KirthiRaman', 'Lebron' ]

def get_filenames(screen_name):
    """Build the friends and followers filenames"""
    return os.path.join(DATA_DIR, "%s.friends.pickle" % (screen_
name)), os.path.join(DATA_DIR, "%s.followers.pickle" % (screen_name))

if __name__ == "__main__":

    # deliberately stripped my keys
    t = twitter.Api(consumer_key='k7atkBNgoGrioMS...',
                consumer_secret='eBOx1ikHMkFc...',
                access_token_key='8959...',
                access_token_secret='O7it0...');

    print t.VerifyCredentials()

    for screen_name in screen_names:
```

```
fr_filename, fo_filename = get_filenames(screen_name)
print "Checking for:", fr_filename, fo_filename
if not os.path.exists(fr_filename):
    print "Getting friends for", screen_name
    fr = t.GetFriends(screen_name=screen_name)
    cPickle.dump(fr, open(fr_filename, "w"), protocol=2)
if not os.path.exists(fo_filename):
    print "Getting followers for", screen_name
    fo = t.GetFollowers(screen_name=screen_name)
    cPickle.dump(fo, open(fo_filename, "w"), protocol=2)
```

The friends and followers information is dumped in cPickle. By running the following commands (as explained in `https://github.com/ianozsvald/python-twitter`), you can run the following code:

```
python get_data.py
python summarise_data.py
python draw_network.py
```

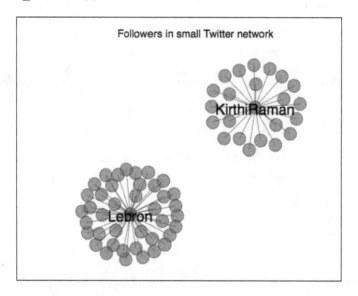

The planar graph test

Planar graphs are graphs that can be drawn on a plane without any intersecting edges. In order to draw them, you have to start from a vertex, draw from edge to edge, and keep track of the faces as the drawing continues. According to Kuratowski, a graph is planar if it does not contain a subgraph that is part of the complete graph on five vertices.

The following is a simple example of a planar graph:

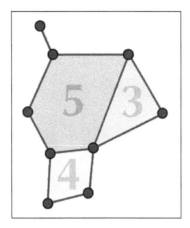

Euler's formula connects a number of vertices, edges, and faces. According to Euler's formula, if a finite and connected planar graph is drawn in the plane without any intersecting edge, and if *v* represents the number of vertices, *e* represents the number of edges, and *f* represents the number of faces, then $v - e + f = 2$.

Besides `Mayavi`, `NetworkX`, and `planarity`, you can use the `gamera` package to create and display graphs. However, `gamera` is only available on Windows. We have a simple example here that uses `planarity` and `NetworkX`:

```
import planarity
import networkx as nx

# complete graph of 8 nodes, K8
G8=nx.complete_graph(8)

# K8 is not planar
print(planarity.is_planar(G8))

# Will display false because G8 is not planar subgraph
K=planarity.kuratowski_subgraph(G8)

# Will display the edges
print(K.edges())

#Will display the graph
nx.draw(G8)

False
[(0, 4), (0, 5), (0, 7), (2, 4), (2, 5), (2, 7), (3, 5), (3, 6), (3,
7), (4, 6)]
```

This example illustrates that the following complete graph of eight nodes is not planar:

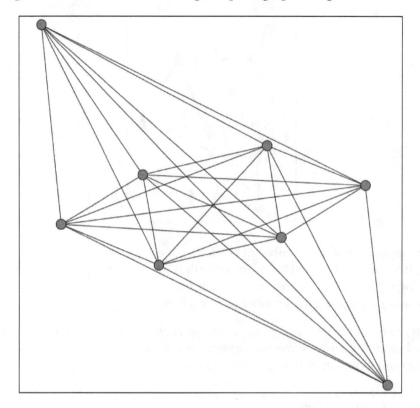

The preceding diagram shows that a planar graph with only eight nodes could look messy, so a graph with more nodes will look more complex.

The directed acyclic graph test

Let's take a look at what a directed acyclic graph (*DAG*) is first. A directed acyclic graph is a graph that is directed, which means that the edges from a given vertex *A* to *B* will be directed in a particular direction (*A->B or B->A*) and is acyclic. Acyclic graphs are those graphs that are not cyclic, which also means that there is no cycle (they don't go around in cycle).

What is a good example of a DAG? A tree or even a trie. We all know what they are because it was discussed in one of the previous chapters of this book. A good example of using trie is to store the words of dictionaries and have a spell check algorithm. We will not go further into details about this, but in the context of visualization and to check whether a graph is acyclic or not, we will determine the Python packages that offer methods to test whether a graph is acyclic or not.

NetworkX has a convenient function called `is_directed_acyclic_graph` (Graph). Here is an example of a graph that is acyclic; using this function, we will test to see whether it returns true:

```
import matplotlib.pyplot as plt
import pylab
from pylab import rcParams

import networkx as nx
import numpy as np

# set the graph display size as 10 by 10 inches
rcParams['figure.figsize'] = 10, 10


G = nx.DiGraph()

# Add the edges and weights
G.add_edges_from([('K', 'I'),('R','T'),('V','T')], weight=3)
G.add_edges_from([('T','K'),('T','H'),('T','H')], weight=4)
# these values to determine node colors
val_map = {'K': 1.5, 'I': 0.9, 'R': 0.6, 'T': 0.2}
values = [val_map.get(node, 1.0) for node in G.nodes()]

edge_labels=dict([((u,v,),d['weight'])
                  for u,v,d in G.edges(data=True)])

#set edge colors
red_edges = [('R','T'),('T','K')]
edge_colors = ['green' if not edge in red_edges else 'red' for edge in
G.edges()]

pos=nx.spring_layout(G)

nx.draw_networkx_edges(G,pos,width=2.0,alpha=0.65)
nx.draw_networkx_edge_labels(G,pos,edge_labels=edge_labels)

nx.draw(G,pos, node_color = values, node_size=1500,
  edge_color=edge_colors, edge_cmap=plt.cm.Reds)

pylab.show()
nx.is_directed_acyclic_graph(G)

True
```

The acyclic graph from this example is displayed in the following diagram:

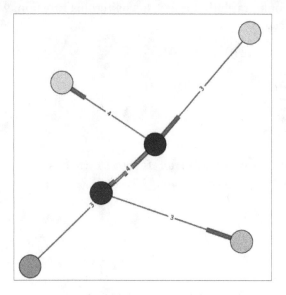

Maximum flow and minimum cut

A flow network is a directed graph from a source to a destination with capacities assigned along each edge. Just as we can model a street map as a directed graph in order to find the shortest path from one place to another, we can also interpret a directed graph as a "flow network". Some examples of flow networks are liquid flowing through pipes, current passing through electrical networks, and data transferring through communication networks. The following is an example graph flow diagram:

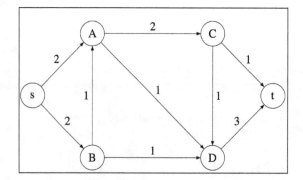

The edges of the G graph are expected to have a capacity that indicates how much flow the edge can support. If this capacity is not present, then it is assumed to have infinite capacity. The maximum flow of the flow network G here is 4.

In the `NetworkX` package, the `maximum_flow_value(Graph, from, to)` function evaluates the maximum flow of a graph, as shown in the following code:

```
import networkx as nx
G = nx.DiGraph()
G.add_edge('p','y', capacity=5.0)
G.add_edge('p','s', capacity=4.0)
G.add_edge('y','t', capacity=3.0)
G.add_edge('s','h', capacity=5.0)
G.add_edge('s','o', capacity=4.0)

flow_value = nx.maximum_flow_value(G, 'p', 'o')

print "Flow value", flow_value
nx.draw(G, node_color='#a0cbe2')

Flow value 4.0
```

The graph from the preceding code is being tested for `maximum_flow_value`, and the display of this graph is shown in the following diagram:

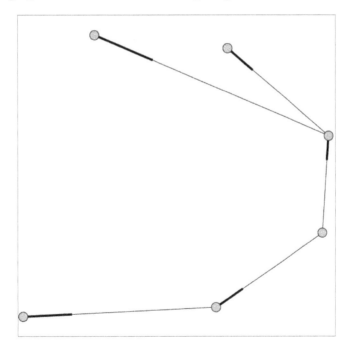

A genetic programming example

CnvKit is also available, but it is a CLI and not easy to use. In addition to this, PyCogent, which was developed by researchers at NCBI from the National Institutes of Health (NIH), is a useful tool. However, they are not easy to use. We will use a package called Bio (https://github.com/biopython/biopython/tree/master/Bio) and libraries from *Python programming for biology*.

In general, every experiment, research project, or study has *sequence* as the key object that is used in bioinformatics. As a mathematician, my visual thought of a sequence relates to a string with certain patterns (such as ATAGCATATGCT). To begin with, here is a simple example that shows a sequence, GC ratio, and codons:

```
from Bio.Seq import Seq
from Bio.Alphabet import IUPAC
from Bio.SeqUtils import GC

def DNACodons(seq):
    end = len(seq) - (len(seq) % 3) - 1
    codons = [seq[i:i+3] for i in range(0, end, 3)]
    return codons DNACodons(my_seq)
my_seq = Seq('GGTCGATGGGCCTAGCAGCATATCTGAGC', IUPAC.unambiguous_dna)
print "GC Result==>", GC(my_seq)

DNACodons(my_seq)
[Seq('GGT', IUPACUnambiguousDNA()),
 Seq('CGA', IUPACUnambiguousDNA()),
 Seq('TGG', IUPACUnambiguousDNA()),
 Seq('GCC', IUPACUnambiguousDNA()),
 Seq('TAG', IUPACUnambiguousDNA()),
 Seq('CAG', IUPACUnambiguousDNA()),
 Seq('CAT', IUPACUnambiguousDNA()),
 Seq('ATC', IUPACUnambiguousDNA()),
 Seq('TGA', IUPACUnambiguousDNA())]

GC Result==> 58.6206896552
```

Let's consider two molecular structures, collect certain atoms, and try to plot their positions with their *Phi* and *Psi* angles. The allowed molecular structures are DNA, RNA, and protein. Using the `Modelling` and `Maths` modules from the `PythonForBiology` library, we will attempt to plot these structures side by side:

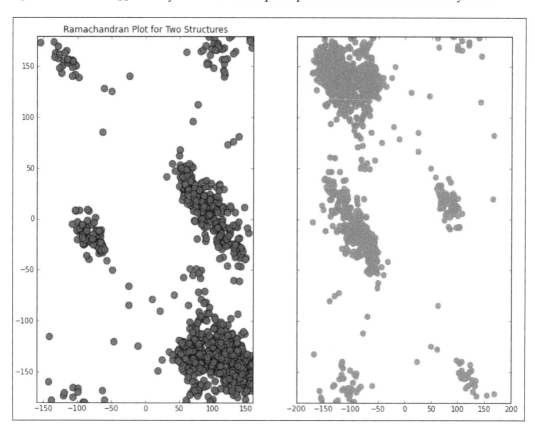

The two plots uses data from two files: `testTransform.pdb` and `1A12.pub`. This contains the **regulator of chromosome condensation (RCC1)** of humans, as shown in the following code:

```
# bio_1.py
#
import matplotlib.pyplot as plt
from phipsi import getPhiPsi
from Modelling import getStructuresFromFile

def genPhiPsi(fileName):
    struc = getStructuresFromFile(fileName)[0]
```

```
      phiList = []
      psiList = []
      for chain in struc.chains:
        for residue in chain.residues[1:-1]:
          phi, psi = getPhiPsi(residue)
          phiList.append(phi)
          psiList.append(psi)

      return phiList, psiList

  if __name__ == '__main__':

    phiList = []
    psiList = []
    phiList, psiList = genPhiPsi('examples/testTransform.pdb')

    phiList2 = []
    psiList2 = []
    phiList2, psiList2 = genPhiPsi('examples/1A12.pdb')

    plt.figure(figsize=(12,9))
    f, (ax1, ax2) = plt.subplots(1, 2, sharey=True, figsize=(12,9))

    ax1.scatter(phiList, psiList, s=90, alpha=0.65)
    ax1.axis([-160,160,-180,180])
    ax1.set_title('Ramachandran Plot for Two Structures')
    ax2.scatter(phiList2, psiList2, s=60, alpha=0.65, color='r')
    plt.show()
```

The library used in this example will be available with the code examples in a file called PythonForBiology.zip. You can extract it and run this code via a command line, assuming that you have numpy and matplotlib installed.

Stochastic block models

In the previous chapters, we have already discussed stochastic models using the Monte Carlo simulation. So far, we have been discussing graphs and networks, so purely from that context, a community structure can also be viewed as a graph. In such graphs, nodes often cluster together as densely connected subgraphs. In general, the probability of an edge between two such nodes is a function of the cluster to which the node belongs.

A popular choice for such a network partition is the stochastic block model. A simple definition of a stochastic block model is characterized by a scalar *n*. This represents the number of groups or the number of clusters and a matrix that shows the nodes and their connections. For a more rigorous mathematical definition, you can refer to a statistics book.

Among a few Python packages that support stochastic models, PyMC is one that offers **Markov Chain Monte Carlo** (**MCMC**) and three building blocks for probability models, such as stochastic, deterministic, and potential. In addition to PyMC, there is another interesting package called **StochPy** for Stochastic Modeling. The SSA module in particular offers convenient methods (http://stochpy.sourceforge.net/examples.html). The first example uses pymc with a normal distribution to display a composite plot and another with an MCMC model, as shown in the following code:

```
import pymc as mc

from pylab import rcParams

# set the graph display size as 10 by 10 inches
rcParams['figure.figsize'] = 12, 12
z = -1.

#instead of 0 and 1, some unknown mu and std goes here:
X = mc.Normal( "x", 0, 1, value = -3. )

#Here below, one can place unknowns here in place of 1, 0.4
@mc.potential
def Y(x=X, z=z):
  return mc.lognormal_like( z-x, 1, 0.4,  )

mcmc = mc.MCMC( [X] )
mcmc.sample(10000,500)
mc.Matplot.plot(mcmc)
```

The example shown here is to illustrate how you can display a complex model in very few lines of code:

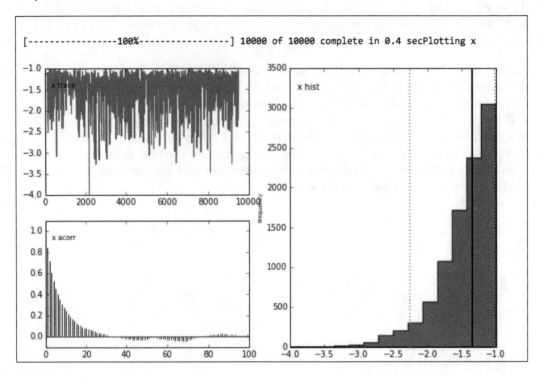

There are examples in PyMC for `disaster_model`, and with MCMC and 50,000 simple iterations, the model display appears as follows:

```python
from pymc.examples import disaster_model
from pymc import MCMC

from pylab import hist, show, rcParams

rcParams['figure.figsize'] = 10, 10

M = MCMC(disaster_model)
M.sample(iter=65536, burn=8000, thin=16)

hist(M.trace('late_mean')[:], color='#b02a2a')

show()
```

If we were to show the histogram plot of mean values from the model, this is one option of using PyMC:

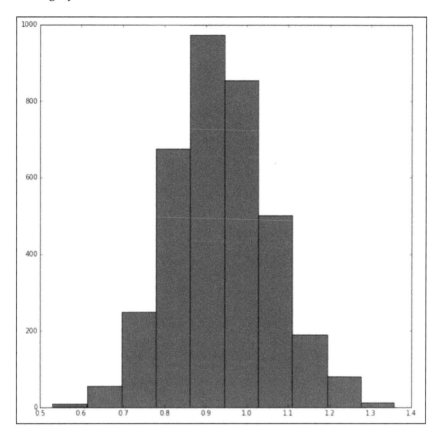

The following code uses the `stochpy` timeseries trajectory data for simulation:

```
import stochpy as stp
smod = stp.SSA()

from pylab import rcParams
# set the graph display size as 10 by 10 inches
rcParams['figure.figsize'] = 12, 12

smod.Model('dsmts-003-04.xml.psc')
smod.DoStochSim(end=35,mode='time',trajectories=2000)
smod.GetRegularGrid()
smod.PlotAverageSpeciesTimeSeries()
```

StochPy has several convenient methods to simulate stochastic models and display the results, as shown in the following image:

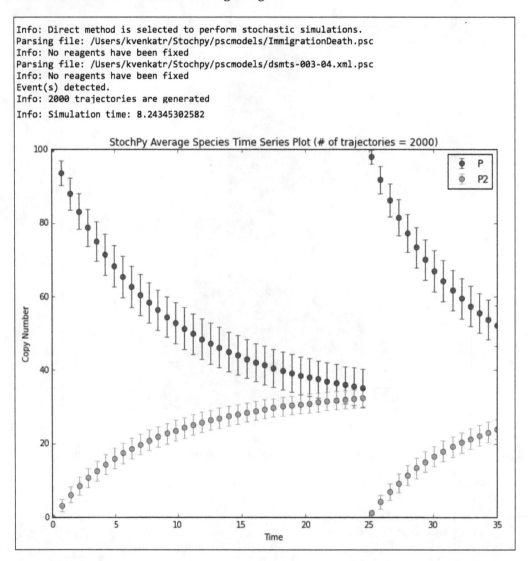

```
Info: Direct method is selected to perform stochastic simulations.
Parsing file: /Users/kvenkatr/Stochpy/pscmodels/ImmigrationDeath.psc
Info: No reagents have been fixed
Parsing file: /Users/kvenkatr/Stochpy/pscmodels/dsmts-003-04.xml.psc
Info: No reagents have been fixed
Event(s) detected.
Info: 2000 trajectories are generated
Info: Simulation time: 8.24345302582
```

Summary

This chapter illustrates the examples of networks and bioinformatics and the choice of Python packages to be able to plot the results. We looked at a brief introduction to graphs and multigraphs and used the sparse matrix and distance graphs to illustrate how you can store and display graphs with several different packages, such as NetworkX, igraph (from igraph.org), and graph-tool.

The clustering coefficient and centrality of graphs demonstrates how you can compute clustering coefficients so that they are able to know how significant a node or vertex is in the graph. We also looked at the analysis of social network data with an illustration of Twitter friends and followers visually, using the Python-Twitter package and the NetworkX library.

You also learned about genetic programming samples with a demonstration of how you can see codons in a DNA sequence and how to compute GC ratio with the bio package. In addition to this, we demonstrated how to display the structures of DNA, RNA, or protein.

The planar graph test, the acyclic graph test, and maximum flow using the NetworkX package, along with a very few lines of code of how to test all of these was discussed. In addition, you can plot stochastic block models with several choices, such as PyMC or StochPy. In the next chapter, we will conclude with advanced visualization methods that you can choose from.

8
Advanced Visualization

Visualization methods have transformed from the traditional bar and pie graphs several decades ago to much more creative forms lately. Designing visualization is not as straightforward as picking one from the many choices that a particular tool offers. The right visualization conveys the right message, and the wrong visualization may distort, confuse, or convey the wrong message.

Computers and storage devices within them are useful in not only storing large chunks of data using data structures, but also to use the power of computing via algorithms. According to Michael Bostock, the creator of D3.js and a leading visualization expert, we should visualize the algorithm and not just the data that feeds into it. An algorithm is the core engine behind any process or computational model; therefore, this algorithm has become an important use case for visualization.

Visualizing algorithms has only been recognized in the recent past few years, and one interesting place to explore this concept is `visualgo.net`, where they have some advanced algorithms to teach data structures and algorithms. Visualgo contains algorithms that can be found in Dr. Steven Halim's book titled *Competitive Programming*. Another similar interesting visualization methods have been made available by Prof. David Galles from the University of San Francisco (`https://www.cs.usfca.edu/~galles/visualization/`). There are other such contributions to teach algorithms and data.

We discussed many different areas, including numerical computing, financial models, statistical and machine learning, and network models. Later in this chapter, we will discuss some new and creative ideas about visualization and some simulation and signal processing examples. In addition, we will cover the following topics:

- Computer simulation, signal processing, and animation examples
- Some interesting visualization methods using HTML5
- How is Julia different from Python? — advantages and disadvantages
- Why is D3.js the most popular visualization tool when compared with Python
- Tools to create dashboards

Computer simulation

A computer simulation is a discipline that gained popularity for more than several decades. It is a computer program that attempts to simulate an abstract model. The models of computer simulation can assist in the creation of complex systems as a way to understand and evaluate hidden or unknown scenarios. Some notable examples of computer simulation modeling are weather forecasting and aircraft simulators used for training pilots.

Computer simulations have become a very productive part of mathematical modeling of systems in diverse fields, such as physics, chemistry, biology, economics, engineering, psychology, and social science.

Here are the benefits of simulation models:

- Gaining a better understanding of an algorithm or process that is being studied
- Identifying the problem areas in the processes and algorithm
- Evaluating the impact of changes in anything that relates to the algorithmic model

The types of simulation models are as follows:

- **Discrete models**: In this, changes to the system occur only at specific times
- **Continuous models**: In this, the state of the system changes continuously over a period of time
- **Mixed models**: This contains both discrete and continuous elements

In order to conduct a simulation, it is common to use random probabilistic inputs because it is unlikely that you would have real data before any such simulation experiment is performed. It is therefore common that simulation experiments involve random numbers whether it is done for a deterministic model or not.

To begin with, let's consider several options to generate random numbers in Python and illustrate one or more examples in simulation.

Python's random package

Python provides a package called `random` that has several convenient functions that can be used for the following:

- To generate random real numbers between 0.0 and 1.0, or between specific start and end values
- To generate random integers between specific ranges of numbers
- To get a list of random values from a list of numbers or letters

```
import random

print random.random() # between 0.0 and 1.0
print random.uniform(2.54, 12.2) # between 2.54 and 12.2
print random.randint(5,10)   # random integer between 5 and 10

print random.randrange(25)   # random number between 0 and 25
#   random numbers from the range of 5 to 500 with step 5
print random.randrange(5,500,5)

# three random number from the list
print random.sample([13,15,29,31,43,46,66,89,90,94], 3)
# Random choice from a list
random.choice([1, 2, 3, 5, 9])
```

SciPy's random functions

NumPy and SciPy are Python modules that consist of mathematical and numerical routines. The **Numeric Python (NumPy)** package provides basic routines to manipulate large arrays and matrices of numeric data. The `scipy` package extends NumPy with algorithms and mathematical techniques.

NumPy has a built-in pseudorandom number generator. The numbers are pseudorandom, which means that they are generated deterministically from a single seed number. Using the same seed number, you can generate the same set of random numbers, as shown in the following code:

```
Import numpy as np
np.random.seed(65536)
```

A different random sequence can be generated by not providing the seed value. NumPy automatically selects a random seed (based on the time) that is different every time a program is run with the following code:

```
np.random.seed()
```

An array of five random numbers in the interval [0.0, 1.0] can be generated as follows:

```
import numpy as np
np.random.rand(5)
#generates the following
array([ 0.2611664,  0.7176011,  0.1489994,  0.3872102,  0.4273531])
```

The rand function can be used to generate random two-dimensional arrays as well, as shown in the following code:

```
np.random.rand(2,4)
array([
[0.83239852, 0.51848638, 0.01260612, 0.71026089],
[0.20578852, 0.02212809, 0.68800472, 0.57239013]])
```

To generate random integers, you can use randint (min, max), where min and max define the range of numbers, in which the random integer has to be drawn, as shown in the following code:

```
np.random.randint(4,18)
```

Use the following code to draw the discrete Poisson distribution with $\lambda = 8.0$:

```
np.random.poisson(8.0)
```

To draw from a continuous normal (Gaussian) distribution with the mean as $\mu = 1.25$ and the standard deviation as $\sigma = 3.0$, use the following code:

```
np.random.normal(2.5, 3.0)

#for mean 0 and variance 1
np.random.mormal()
```

Simulation examples

In the first example, we will select geometric Brownian motion, which is also known as exponential Brownian motion, to model the stock price behavior with the **Stochastic Differential Equation (SDE)**:

$$dS_t = \mu \, S_t \, dt + \sigma \, S_t \, dW_t$$

In the preceding equation, *Wt* is Brownian motion, μ the percentage drift, and σ is the percentage volatility. The following code shows Brownian motion plot:

```
from numpy.random import standard_normal
from numpy import zeros, sqrt
import matplotlib.pyplot as plt

S_init = 20.222
T =1
tstep =0.0002
sigma = 0.4
mu = 1
NumSimulation=6

colors = [ (214,27,31), (148,103,189), (229,109,0), (41,127,214),
(227,119,194),(44,160,44),(227,119,194), (72,17,121), (196,156,148)]

# Scale the RGB values to the [0, 1] range.

for i in range(len(colors)):
    r, g, b = colors[i]
    colors[i] = (r / 255., g / 255., b / 255.)

plt.figure(figsize=(12,12))

Steps=round(T/tstep); #Steps in years
S = zeros([NumSimulation, Steps], dtype=float)
x = range(0, int(Steps), 1)

for j in range(0, NumSimulation, 1):

    S[j,0]= S_init
    for i in x[:-1]:
        S[j,i+1]=S[j,i]+S[j,i]*(mu-0.5*pow(sigma,2))*tstep+ \
            sigma*S[j,i]*sqrt(tstep)*standard_normal()
```

```
        plt.plot(x, S[j], linewidth=2., color=colors[j])

    plt.title('%d Simulation using %d Steps, \n$\sigma$=%.6f $\mu$=%.6f
    $S_0$=%.6f ' % (int(NumSimulation), int(Steps), sigma, mu, S_init),
            fontsize=18)
    plt.xlabel('steps', fontsize=16)
    plt.grid(True)
    plt.ylabel('stock price', fontsize=16)
    plt.ylim(0,90)

    plt.show()
```

The following plot shows the results of six simulations using Brownian motion:

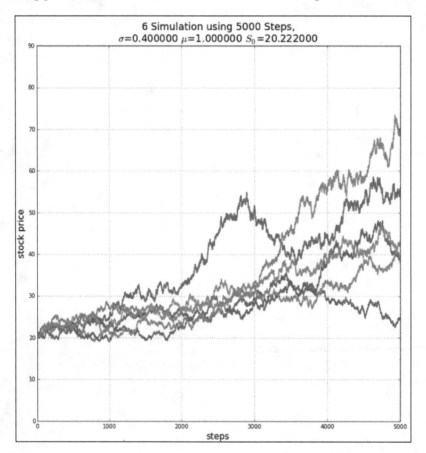

Another simulation example here demonstrates how you can apply the Hodrick–Prescott filter to get a smoothed curve representation of the stock price data that falls under the class of time series data:

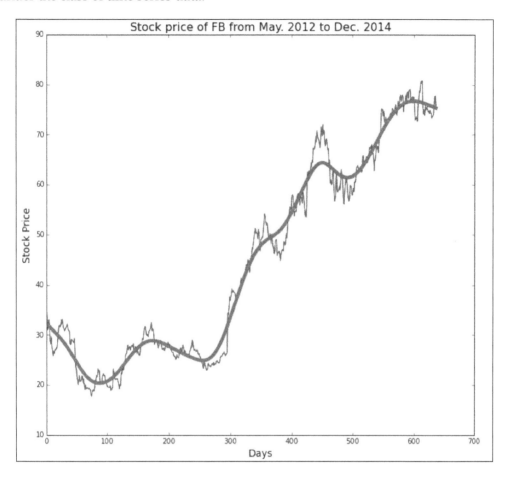

Here, we will use the finance subpackage in `matplotlib` to generate the stock price data for a range of dates with the start date as May 2012 and the end date as Dec 2014. Using the `hold` method of `matplotlib`, you can show the smoothed curve together with the stock price plot, as shown in the following code:

```
from matplotlib import finance
import matplotlib.pyplot as plt

import statsmodels.api as sm

titleStr='Stock price of FB from May. 2012 to Dec. 2014'
```

```
plt.figure(figsize=(11,10))

dt1 = datetime.datetime(2012, 05, 01)
dt2 = datetime.datetime(2014, 12, 01)
sp=finance.quotes_historical_yahoo('FB',dt1,dt2,asobject=None)

plt.title(titleStr, fontsize=16)
plt.xlabel("Days", fontsize=14)
plt.ylabel("Stock Price", fontsize=14)

xfilter = sm.tsa.filters.hpfilter(sp[:,2], lamb=100000)[1]

plt.plot(sp[:,2])
plt.hold(True)
plt.plot(xfilter,linewidth=5.)
```

In addition to these examples, you can simulate a queue system or any process that is event-based. For instance, you can simulate a neural network, and one such package that helps to model one quickly is available at `http://briansimulator.org`. Take a look at their demo programs for more details.

Signal processing

There are many examples in signal processing that you could think of, but we will choose one specific example that involves convolution. A convolution of two signals is a way to combine them to produce a filtered third signal. In a real-life situation, signal convolutions are applied to smoothen images. To a great extent, convolution is also applied to calculate signal interference. For more details, you can refer to a book on microwave measurements, but we will attempt to show you some simple examples.

Let's consider three simple examples here. The first example illustrates the convoluted signal of a digital signal and simulates the analog signal using hamming, as shown in the following code:

```
import matplotlib.pyplot as plt
from numpy import concatenate, zeros, ones, hamming, convolve

digital = concatenate ( (zeros(20), ones(25), zeros(20)))
norm_hamming = hamming(80)/sum(hamming(80))
res = convolve(digital, norm_hamming)
plt.figure(figsize=(10,10))
plt.ylim(0, 0.6)
plt.plot(res, color='r', linewidth=2)
```

```
plt.hold(True)
plt.plot(data, color='b', linewidth=3)
plt.hold(True)
plt.plot(norm_hamming, color='g', linewidth=4)
plt.show()
```

In this example, we will use concatenate and zeros and ones from numpy to produce digital signals, hamming to produce analog signals, and convolve to apply convolutions.

If we plot all the three signals, that is, digital signals, analog hammings, and convolved result signals (res), the resulting signal will be shifted as expected, as shown in the following graph:

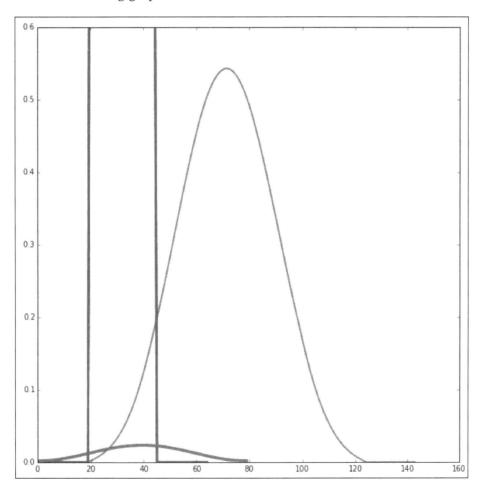

In another example, we will use a random signal, that is, `random_data` and apply **fast Fourier transform (FFT)** as follows:

```python
import matplotlib.pyplot as plt
from scipy import randn
from numpy import fft

plt.figure(figsize=(10,10))
random_data = randn(500)
res = fft.fft(random_data)
plt.plot(res, color='b')
plt.hold(True)
plt.plot(random_data, color='r')
plt.show()
```

Using `randn` from `scipy` to generate random signal data and `fft` from `numpy` that performs fast Fourier transform, the result that comes out of the transform is plotted in blue and the original random signal is plotted in red using `matplotlib`, as shown in the following image:

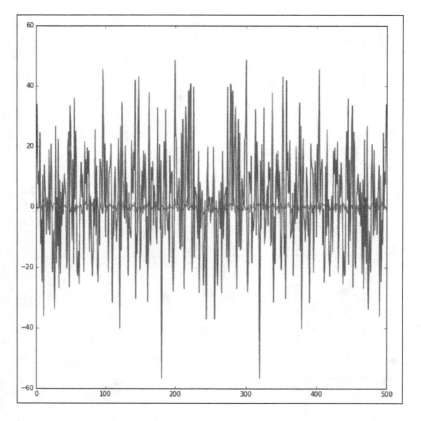

In the third example, a simple illustration of how to create an inverted image using the `scipy` package is shown. Before we get to the actual Python code and the results, let's try to analyze how an inverted image will help in visualizing data.

It is debated that in certain cases, inverted colors create less strain on our vision and is comfortable to look at. Surprisingly, if we place the original image and the inverted image side by side, inverted images will help in visualizing certain areas that may otherwise be difficult in the original image, if not for all images at least in certain cases. The following code shows how you can convert an image to an inverted image using `scipy.misc.pilutil.Image()`:

```
import scipy.misc as scm
from scipy.misc.pilutil import Image

# open original image
orig_image = Image.open('/Users/kvenkatr/Desktop/filter.jpg')

# extract image data into array
image1 = scm.fromimage(orig_image)
# invert array values
inv_image = 255 - image1

# using inverted array values, convert image
inverted_image = scm.toimage(inv_image)

#save inverted image
inverted_image.save('/Users/kvenkatr/Desktop/filter_invert.jpg').
```

The inverted image result is shown along with the original image here:

Similarly, other filtering mechanisms can be applied to any image using some of the following functions:

```
convolve()           Multidimensional convolution.
correlate()          Multi-dimensional correlation.
gaussian_filter()    Multidimensional Gaussian filter
```

A full list of functions is shown at http://tinyurl.com/3xubv9p.

Animation

You can accomplish animation in Python using matplotlib, but the results are saved in a file in the MP4 format that can be used to be replayed later. The basic setup for the animation is as follows:

```
import numpy as np
import matplotlib.pyplot as plt
from matplotlib import animation

# Set up the figure, axis, and the plot element to be animated
fig = plt.figure()
ax = plt.axes(xlim=(0, 3.2), ylim=(-2.14, 2.14))
line, = ax.plot([], [], lw=2)
```

Make sure that the animation package is imported from matplotlib, sets the axes, and prepares the necessary plotting variables (this is just an empty line) as follows:

```
# initialization function: plot the background of each frame
def init():
    line.set_data([], [])
    return line,
```

The initialization of plotting needs to be performed before starting any animation because it creates a base frame, as shown in the following code:

```
# animation function.  This is called sequentially
def animate(i):
    x = np.linspace(0, 2, 1000)
    xval = 2 * np.pi * (x - 0.01 * i)
    y = np.cos(xval) # Here we are trying to animate cos function
    line.set_data(x, y)
    return line,
```

Here is the animate function that takes the frame number as the input, defines the changed x and y values, and sets the plotting variables:

```
anim = animation.FuncAnimation(fig, animate, init_func=init,\
        frames=200, interval=20, blit=True)
anim.save('basic_animation.mp4', fps=30)
plt.show()
```

The actual animation object is created via `FuncAnimation` and passes the `init()` and `animate()` functions, along with the number of frames, **frames per second (fps)**, and time interval parameters. The `blit=True` parameter tells you that only the changed part of the display needs to be redrawn (otherwise, one may see flickers).

Before you attempt to perform an animation, you have to make sure that `mencoder` or `ffmpeg` is installed; otherwise, running this program without `ffmpeg` or `mencoder` will result in the following error: `ValueError: Cannot save animation: no writers are available. Please install mencoder or ffmpeg to save animations.`. The following image shows an animation of trigonometric curves, such as sin or cos:

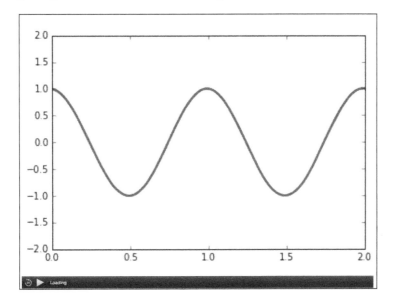

You can embed this MP4 file in an HTML for display and press the play button in the bottom-left corner to see the animation.

There is an interesting demonstration of a double pendulum animation by Jake Vanderplas at
`https://jakevdp.github.io/blog/2012/08/18/matplotlib-animation-tutorial/`
and a dynamic image animation at
`http://matplotlib.org/examples/animation/dynamic_image2.html`.

In this book, so far we have discussed visualization methods that involve how to plot in Python or create external formats (such as MP4). One of the reasons why JavaScript-based visualization methods are popular is because you can present them on the Web and also associate some event-driven animation to them. **Support Vector Graphics (SVG)** is gaining popularity for many reasons, and one among them is the *ability to scale to any size without losing details.*

Visualization methods using HTML5

A simple illustration of SVG to display circles using feGaussianBlur is shown in the following code:

```
<svg width="230" height="120" xmlns="http://www.w3.org/2000/svg"
xmlns:xlink="http://www.w3.org/1999/xlink">
    <filter id="blurMe">
        <feGaussianBlur in="SourceGraphic" stdDeviation="5" />
    </filter>

    <circle cx="60"  cy="80" r="60" fill="#E90000" />
    <circle cx="190" cy="80" r="60" fill="#E90000"
      filter="url(#blurMe)" />
    <circle cx="360"  cy="80" r="60" fill="#4E9B01" />
    <circle cx="490" cy="80" r="60" fill="#4E9B01"
      filter="url(#blurMe)" />
    <circle cx="660"  cy="80" r="60" fill="#0080FF" />
    <circle cx="790" cy="80" r="60" fill="#0080FF"
      filter="url(#blurMe)" />
</svg>
```

The first two circles are drawn with the radius as 60 and are filled with the same color, but the second circle uses the blurring filter. Similarly, adjacent circles in green and blue also follow the same behavior (for a colored effect, refer to http://knapdata.com/dash/html/svg_circle.html), as shown in the following image:

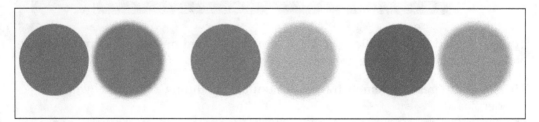

How can we use this blurring concept when the data presentation needs parts-of-whole in visualization, but does not combine to become a whole. What does this mean? Let's consider two examples. In the first example, we'll consider a class of students enrolled in foreign languages (in some cases, more than one language). If we were to represent the distribution as follows, how would we do it?

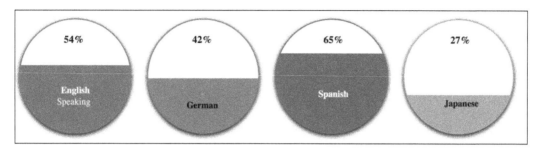

You can generate the SVG format via the Python program, as show in the following code:

```
import os
display_prog = 'more' # Command to execute to display images.
svcount=1

class Scene:
    def __init__(self,name="svg",height=400,width=1200):
        self.name = name
        self.items = []
        self.height = height
        self.width = width
        return

    def add(self,item): self.items.append(item)

    def strarray(self):
        var = [ "<html>\n<body>\n<svg height=\"%d\" width=\"%d\" >\n"
% (self.height,self.width),
                "    <g id=\"setttings\">\n",
                "      <filter id=\"dropshadow\" height=\"160%\">\n",
                "        <feGaussianBlur in=\"SourceAlpha\"
stdDeviation=\"5\"></feGaussianBlur>\n",
                "          <feOffset dx=\"0\" dy=\"3\"
result=\"offsetblur\"></feOffset>\n",
                "          <feMerge>\n",
                "            <feMergeNode></feMergeNode>\n",
```

```
                "                 <feMergeNode in=\"SourceGraphic\"></
feMergeNode>\n",
                "          </feMerg>\n",
                "     </filter>\n"]
        for item in self.items: var += item.strarray()
        var += [" </g>\n</svg>\n</body>\n</html>"]
        return var


    def write_svg(self,filename=None):
        if filename:
            self.svgname = filename
        else:
            self.svgname = self.name + ".html"
        file = open(self.svgname,'w')
        file.writelines(self.strarray())
        file.close()
        return


    def display(self,prog=display_prog):
        os.system("%s %s" % (prog,self.svgname))
        return


def colorstr(rgb): return "#%x%x%x" % (rgb[0]/16,rgb[1]/16,rgb[2]/16)


class Text:
    def __init__(self, x,y,txt, color, isItbig, isBold):
        self.x = x
        self.y = y
        self.txt = txt
        self.color = color
        self.isItbig = isItbig
        self.isBold = isBold
    def strarray(self):
        if ( self.isItbig == True ):
          if ( self.isBold == True ):
            retval = [" <text y=\"%d\" x=\"%d\" style=\"font-
size:18px;font-weight:bold;fill:%s\">%s</text>\n" %(self.y, self.x,
self.color,self.txt) ]
          else:
            retval = [" <text y=\"%d\" x=\"%d\" style=\"font-
size:18px;fill:%s\">%s</text>\n" %(self.y, self.x, self.color,self.
txt) ]
        else:
          if ( self.isBold == True ):
```

```
            retval = [" <text y=\"%d\" x=\"%d\" style=\"fill:%s;font-
weight:bold;\">%s</text>\n" %(self.y, self.x, self.color,self.txt) ]
        else:
            retval = [" <text y=\"%d\" x=\"%d\" style=\"fill:%s\">%s</
text>\n" %(self.y, self.x, self.color,self.txt) ]
    return retval

class Circle:
    def __init__(self,center,radius,color, perc):
        self.center = center #xy tuple
        self.radius = radius #xy tuple
        self.color = color   #rgb tuple in range(0,256)
        self.perc = perc
        return

    def strarray(self):
        global svcount
        diam = self.radius+self.radius
        fillamt = self.center[1]-self.radius - 6 + (100.0 - self.
perc)*1.9
        xpos = self.center[0] - self.radius
        retval = ["  <circle cx=\"%d\" cy=\"%d\" r=\"%d\"\n" %\
                (self.center[0],self.center[1],self.radius),
                "    style=\"stroke: %s;stroke-width:2;fill:white;filt
er:url(#dropshadow)\"  />\n" % colorstr(self.color),
                "  <circle clip-path=\"url(#dataseg-%d)\" fill=\"%s\"
cx=\"%d\" cy=\"%d\" r=\"%d\"\n" %\
                (svcount, colorstr(self.color),self.center[0],self.
center[1],self.radius),
                "    style=\"stroke:rgb(0,0,0);stroke-width:0;z-
index:10000;\"  />\n",
                "<clipPath id=\"dataseg-%d\"> <rect height=\"%d\"
width=\"%d\" y=\"%d\" x=\"%d\"></rect>" %(svcount,diam,
diam,fillamt,xpos),
                "</clipPath>\n"
                ]
        svcount += 1
        return retval

def languageDistribution():
    scene = Scene('test')
    scene.add(Circle((140,146),100,(0,128,0),54))
    scene.add(Circle((370,146),100,(232,33,50),42))
    scene.add(Circle((600,146),100,(32,119,180),65))
```

```
        scene.add(Circle((830,146),100,(255,128,0),27))
        scene.add(Text(120,176,"English", "white", False, True))
        scene.add(Text(120,196,"Speaking", "#e2e2e2", False, False))
        scene.add(Text(340,202,"German", "black", False, True))
        scene.add(Text(576,182,"Spanish", "white", False, True))
        scene.add(Text(804,198,"Japanese", "black", False, True))

        scene.add(Text(120,88,"54%", "black", True, True))
        scene.add(Text(350,88,"42%", "black", True, True))
        scene.add(Text(585,88,"65%", "black", True, True))
        scene.add(Text(815,88,"27%", "black", True, True))

        scene.write_svg()
        scene.display()
        return

    if __name__ == '__main__': languageDistribution()
```

The preceding example gives an idea to create custom svg methods for visualization. There are many other svg writers in Python today, but none of them have demonstrated the methods to display the one that we have shown here. There are also many different ways to create custom visualization methods in other languages, such as Julia. This has been around for almost three years now and is considered suitable for numerical and scientific computing.

How is Julia different from Python?

Julia is a dynamic programming language. However, it is comparable to C in terms of performance because Julia is a low-level virtual machine-based just-in-time compiler (JIT compiler). As we all know, in Python, in order to combine C and Python, you may have to use Cython.

Some notable advantages of Julia are as follows:

- Performance comparable to C
- The built-in package manager
- Has lisp-like macros
- Can call Python functions using the PyCall package
- Can call C functions directly
- Designed for distributed computing
- User-defined types are as fast as built-ins

The only disadvantage is that you have to learn a new language, although there are some similarities with C and Python.

D3.js (where D3 in short means DDD, which stands for **document-driven data**) is one among the competing frameworks in Python for visualization.

D3.js for visualization

D3.js is a JavaScript library for presenting data on the Web and helps in displaying data, using HTML, SVG, and CSS.

D3.js attaches data to **Document Object Model (DOM)** elements; therefore, you can use CSS3, HTML, and SVG to showcase their data. Furthermore, as JavaScript has event listeners, you can make the data interactive.

Mike Bostock created D3.js during his PhD work at the Stanford Visualization Group. First, Mike worked with the Stanford Visualization Group to produce Protivis, which then eventually became D3. Mike Bostock, Vadim Ogievetsky, and Jeffrey Heer produced a paper titled *D3: Data-Driven Documents*, which can be accessed at http://vis.stanford.edu/papers/d3.

In practice, the underlying principle of D3.js is to use the CSS style selector to select from DOM nodes and then use the jQuery style to manipulate them. Here is an example:

```
d3.selectAll("p")                 // select all <p> elements
  .style("color", "#FF8000")      // set style "color" to value "#FF8000"
  .attr("class", "tin")           // set attribute "class" to value "tin"
  .attr("x", 20);                 // set attribute "x" to 20px
```

One of the many advantages of D3 is that by simply accessing a mechanism of DOM, you can create a stunning representation of data. Another advantage is that by fully using the power of JavaScript combined with the power of computing today, you can easily add the navigational behavior quickly. There is a large collection of such visualizations available at `http://bost.ocks.org/mike/`. One example of D3 visualization plot is shown here:

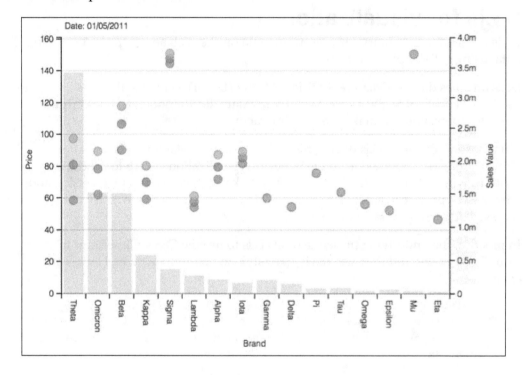

There are many visualization examples that you can produce, and among the examples in the gallery (`http://christopheviau.com/d3list/gallery.html#visualizationType=lollipop`), my favorite is the one that tells the story about different aggregations using multiple series and multiple axes, which can be viewed at `http://tinyurl.com/p988v2u` (also shown in the preceding image).

Dashboards

Python has many advantages compared to D3. When you combine these two, you can use the best of both. For instance, Python offers some very good options of packages for numerical and scientific computing. For this reason, it has been very popular to academia.

There are very few interesting data visualization and collaboration tools that have emerged lately, and one such tool is Plotly (`https://plot.ly`). The Python dashboard collection can be accessed at `https://plot.ly/python/dashboard/`. As this is fairly new, we have not had a chance to explore further to see what one can do. Splunk offers an SDK to create Python-based dashboards at `http://dev.splunk.com/view/SP-CAAADSR`, and Pyxley is a collection of packages that combine the power of Python and JavaScript to create web-based dashboards. One of the examples from Splunk Dashboard is shown here:

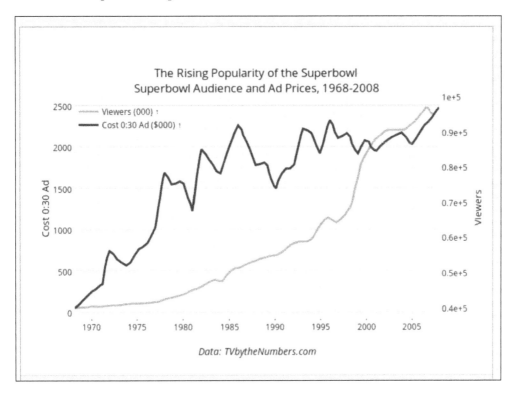

One of the examples of Plotly is shown in the preceding image. It demonstrates how you can generate a visualization that looks pretty, is easy to understand, and is navigable at `http://tinyurl.com/pwmg5zr`.

Summary

This chapter illustrates additional topics that were not covered in the previous chapters, such as signal processing and animation using Python. In addition, we also compared Python with D3.js and Julia and determined their strengths. Several examples of signal processing were discussed. We also looked at the convolution of analog and digital signal spectrums using `numpy` and `matplotlib`.

We also looked at an example of animation and demonstrated how you can generate the MP4 format animation via Python. We also compared Julia with Python and listed a few advantages of Julia over Python and compared them to see the differences.

Further, we showcased the strengths of D3.js, highlighting the difference between this JavaScript-based visualization tool and Python. Finally, we discussed the options available for dashboards and listed a few options to create Python-based dashboards.

Go Forth and Explore Visualization

Python has been around since 1991 and has gained popularity among the community of scientists and engineers. Among many libraries, `numpy`, `scipy`, and `matplotlib` have been widely used in scientific computing. Sage covers the areas of algebra, combinatorics, numerical mathematics, number theory, and calculus using an easy browser interface via IPython. Another popular package called `pandas` can be used to store and process complex datasets.

There are multiple tools to run and edit Python programs, and one among them is Anaconda from Continuum. One of the advantages of Anaconda is that it does not cost anything and comes inbuilt with most necessary packages. The underlying command-line tool for managing environments and Python packages is `conda`, and the editor is Spyder.

In the past, installing Spyder was complicated because it involved downloading and installing it in a multistep process. Installation in the recent versions has been very straightforward, and one can download and install all the components together automatically in one step.

An overview of conda

Conda is a command line-tool that is responsible for managing environments and Python packages, rather than using `pip`. There are ways to query and search the packages, create new environments if necessary, and install and update Python packages into the existing conda environments. This command-line tool also keeps track of dependencies between packages and platform specifics, helping you to create working environments from different combinations of packages. To check the version of `conda` that is running, you can enter `conda --version` in Python and it will show, for example, `conda 3.18.2` as the version.

A conda environment is a filesystem directory that contains a specific collection of `conda` packages. To begin using an environment, simply set the PATH variable to point it to its bin directory.

Here is an example of the package installation from the command line using `conda`:

```
$ conda install scipy

Fetching package metadata: ....
Solving package specifications: .
Package plan for installation in environment /Users/MacBook/anaconda:

The following packages will be downloaded:

    package                 |         build
    ------------------------|-----------------
    flask-0.10.1            |         py27_1        129 KB
    itsdangerous-0.23       |         py27_0         16 KB
    jinja2-2.7.1            |         py27_0        307 KB
    markupsafe-0.18         |         py27_0         19 KB
    werkzeug-0.9.3          |         py27_0        385 KB

The following packages will be linked:

    package                 |           build
    ------------------------|-----------------
    flask-0.10.1            |         py27_1
```

```
itsdangerous-0.23      |      py27_0

jinja2-2.7.1           |      py27_0

markupsafe-0.18        |      py27_0

python-2.7.5           |      2

readline-6.2           |      1

sqlite-3.7.13          |      1

tk-8.5.13              |      1

werkzeug-0.9.3         |      py27_0

zlib-1.2.7             |      1


Proceed ([y]/n)?
```

Any dependencies on the package that we are installing will be recognized, downloaded, and linked automatically.

Here is an example of package update from the command line using conda:

```
$ conda update matplotlib

Fetching package metadata: ....

Solving package specifications: .

Package plan for installation in environment /Users/MacBook/anaconda:


The following packages will be downloaded:


    package                   |            build

    --------------------------|-----------------

    freetype-2.5.2            |                0        691 KB

    conda-env-2.1.4           |           py27_0         15 KB

    numpy-1.9.2               |           py27_0        2.9 MB

    pyparsing-2.0.3           |           py27_0         63 KB

    pytz-2015.2               |           py27_0        175 KB

    setuptools-15.0           |           py27_0        436 KB

    conda-3.10.1              |           py27_0        164 KB

    python-dateutil-2.4.2     |           py27_0        219 KB

    matplotlib-1.4.3          |        np19py27_1       40.9 MB
```

```
-------------------------------------------------------------
                                  Total:          45.5 MB
```

The following NEW packages will be INSTALLED:

```
    python-dateutil: 2.4.2-py27_0
```

The following packages will be UPDATED:

```
    conda:              3.10.0-py27_0      --> 3.10.1-py27_0
    conda-env:          2.1.3-py27_0       --> 2.1.4-py27_0
    freetype:     2.4.10-1           --> 2.5.2-0
    matplotlib:       1.4.2-np19py27_0 --> 1.4.3-np19py27_1
    numpy:              1.9.1-py27_0       --> 1.9.2-py27_0
    pyparsing:          2.0.1-py27_0       --> 2.0.3-py27_0
    pytz:             2014.9-py27_0        --> 2015.2-py27_0
    setuptools:       14.3-py27_0          --> 15.0-py27_0
```

Proceed ([y]/n)?

In some cases, there are more steps involved in installing a package via conda. For instance, to install wordcloud, you will have to perform the steps given in this code:

```
#step-1 command
conda install wordcloud


Fetching package metadata: ....
Error: No packages found in current osx-64 channels matching: wordcloud


You can search for this package on Binstar with
# This only means one has to search the source location
binstar search -t conda wordcloud


Run 'binstar show <USER/PACKAGE>' to get more details:
Packages:

                        Name | Access        | Package Types   |
```

```
         ----------------------- | ------------ | --------------- |
             derickl/wordcloud | public       | conda           |
Found 1 packages


# step-2 command
binstar show derickl/wordcloud


Using binstar api site https://api.binstar.org
Name:    wordcloud
Summary:
Access:  public
Package Types:  conda
Versions:
   + 1.0


To install this package with conda run:
conda install --channel https://conda.binstar.org/derickl wordcloud


# step-3 command
conda install --channel https://conda.binstar.org/derickl wordcloud


Fetching package metadata: ......
Solving package specifications: .
Package plan for installation in environment /Users/MacBook/anaconda:


The following packages will be downloaded:

    package                    |              build
    ---------------------------|----------------
    cython-0.22                |             py27_0       2.2 MB
    django-1.8                 |             py27_0       3.2 MB
    pillow-2.8.1               |             py27_1       454 KB
    image-1.3.4                |             py27_0        24 KB
    setuptools-15.1            |             py27_1       435 KB
    wordcloud-1.0              |         np19py27_1        58 KB
```

```
    conda-3.11.0                  |        py27_0            167 KB
    --------------------------------------------------------------
                                           Total:           6.5 MB
```

```
The following NEW packages will be INSTALLED:
    django:     1.8-py27_0
    image:      1.3.4-py27_0
    pillow:     2.8.1-py27_1
    wordcloud:  1.0-np19py27_1
```

```
The following packages will be UPDATED:
    conda:      3.10.1-py27_0 --> 3.11.0-py27_0
    cython:     0.21-py27_0   --> 0.22-py27_0
    setuptools: 15.0-py27_0   --> 15.1-py27_1
```

```
Finally, the following packages will be downgraded:

    libtiff:    4.0.3-0       --> 4.0.2-1
```

```
Proceed ([y]/n)? y
```

Anaconda is a free Python distribution for scientific computing. This distribution comes with Python 2.x or Python 3.x and 100+ cross-platform tested and optimized Python packages. Anaconda can also create custom environments that mix and match different Python versions.

Packages installed with Anaconda

The following command will display a list of all the packages in the Anaconda environment:

```
conda list
```

The featured packages in Anaconda are Astropy, Cython, h5py, IPython, LLVM, LLVMpy, matplotlib, Mayavi, NetworkX, NLTK, Numexpr, Numba, numpy, pandas, Pytables, scikit-image, scikit-learn, scipy, Spyder, Qt/PySide, and VTK.

In order to check the packages that are installed with Anaconda, navigate to the command line and enter the `conda list` command to quickly display a list of all the packages installed in the default environment. Alternatively, you can also check Continuum Analytics for details on the list of packages available in the current and latest release.

In addition, you can always install a package with the usual means, for example, using the `pip install` command or from the source using a `setup.py` file. Although `conda` is the preferred packaging tool, there is nothing special about Anaconda that prevents the usage of standard Python packaging tools.

> IPython is not required, but it is highly recommended. IPython should be installed after Python, GNU Readline, and PyReadline are installed. Anaconda and Canopy does these things by default. There are Python packages that are used in all the examples in this book for a good reason. In the following section, we have updated the list.

Packages websites

Here is a list of Python packages that we have mentioned in this book with their respective websites, where you can find the most up-to-date information:

- **IPython**: This is a rich architecture for interactive computing (http://ipython.org)
- **NumPy**: This is used for high performance and vectorized computations on multidimensional arrays (http://www.numpy.org)
- **SciPy**: This is used for advanced numerical algorithms (http://www.scipy.org)
- **matplotlib**: This is used to plot and perform an interactive visualization (http://matplotlib.org)
- **matplotlib-basemap**: This is a mapping toolbox for matplotlib (http://matplotlib.org/basemap/)
- **Seaborn**: This is used to represent statistical data visualization for matplotlib (http://stanford.edu/~mwaskom/software/seaborn)
- **Scikit**: This is used for machine learning purposes in Python (http://scikit-learn.org/stable)
- **NetworkX**: This is used to handle graphs (http://networkx.lanl.gov)
- **Pandas**: This is used to deal with any kind of tabular data (http://pandas.pydata.org)

- **Python Imaging Library (PIL)**: This is used for image processing algorithms (http://www.pythonware.com/products/pil)

- **PySide**: This acts as a wrapper around Qt for **graphical user interfaces (GUIs)** (http://qt-project.org/wiki/PySide)

- **PyQt**: This is similar to PySide, but with a different license (http://www.riverbankcomputing.co.uk/software/pyqt/intro)

- **Cython**: This is used to leverage C code in Python (http://cython.org)

About matplotlib

The matplotlib package comes with many convenient methods to create visualization charts and graphs. Only a handful of these have been explored in this book. You will have to explore matplotlib further from the following sources:

- http://www.labri.fr/perso/nrougier/teaching/matplotlib/

- http://matplotlib.org/Matplotlib.pdf

One should also refer to other packages listed in the previous section, which are libraries that make plotting more attractive.

Index

Symbols

1-nearest neighbor (1-NN) 261

A

anaconda
  packages, installed 342, 343
Anaconda distribution of Spyder from
        Continuum Analytics 95
Anaconda from Continuum Analytics 104
analytics 5
animation 326-328
Anscombe's quartet
  URL 16
array indexing
  about 140
  logical indexing 142
  numerical indexing 141
Artificial Intelligence (AI) 225
author-driven narratives 70-72

B

balloon layout 89
bar graphs 26, 27
Bayesian linear regression 228-230
Bayes theorem 251, 252
Bio package
  URL 306
Bokeh 117, 118
box-and-whisker plot 78, 79
box plot 30, 31, 78
bubble charts 33-35

C

Canopy Express 102
Canopy from Enthought 95, 100, 101
circular layout 87, 88
classification methods 238, 239
clustering 8
cognitive context
  URL 2
command-line interface (CLI) 91
Comma Separated Value (CSV) 43
computer simulation
  about 316, 317
  animation 326-328
  benefits 316
  dashboards 334, 335
  examples 319-322
  Julia 332-334
  Python, random package 317
  SciPy's random 317, 318
  signal, processing 322-326
  types 316
  visualization methods, HTML5
        used 328-332
conda 106-109, 338-342
correlation coefficients 77
Cython 344
  URL 192

D

D3.js
  for visualization 333-335
dashboards 334
data 2

data analysis 5
data analytics 5
data collection 7
data preprocessing 7, 8
data processing 8
datasets
  getting 9
data source
  URL 19, 175
data structures
  dictionaries 146-148
  queues 146
  sets 145
  stacks 143
  tries 153, 154
  tuples 144
data transformation
  about 5, 6
  data collection 6
  data, organizing 8
  data preprocessing 7, 8
  data processing 8
  datasets, getting 9
data visualization
  about 17
  before computers 12, 13
  developments 14
  history 11
  URL 12
decision tree
  about 246
  example 246-248
deterministic model
  about 180
  gross return 180-190
dictionaries
  about 146-148
  for matrix representation 148
  memoization 152
  sparse matrices 149
diffusion-based simulation 218, 219
directed acyclic graph test 302-304
directed graphs 282
Disco
  URL 138
Document Object Model (DOM)
    elements 333

E

Ebola example
  about 43-49
  URL 44
economic model 179
event listeners 85, 86

F

fast Fourier transform (FFT) 324
financial model 179
flow network
  maximum flow 304, 305
font file
  URL 163
frames per second (fps) 327

G

Gapminder 63, 64
genetic programming
  example 306-308
geometric Brownian simulation 214-218
Gestalt perception
  principles 73-75
good visualization 18-20
graph data
  storing 283
graphical user interfaces (GUIs) 344
graphs
  clustering coefficient 294-298
  displaying 284
  igraph 284-287
  NetworkX 287-292
graph-tool
  about 293, 294
  PageRank 294
  URL 293

H

histogram 78
Humanitarian Data Exchange (HDX) 43
human perception
  URL 15

I

IDE tools
  about 92
  interactive tools, types 92
  Python 3.x versus Python 2.7 92
igraph 284-287
information
  about 3
  transforming, to insight 10, 11
  transforming, to knowledge 9, 10
information visualization 72
integrated development environment
    (IDE) 83, 91
Interactive Editor for Python (IEP) 95-99
interactive tools
  about 92
  IPython 93, 94
  Plotly 94, 95
Interactive visualization packages 116, 117
IPython
  about 93, 94, 343
  URL 84

J

JIT (just-in-time) compilation 138
Julia 332, 333

K

Kernel Density Estimation (KDE) 36-39
k-means clustering 276-279
k-nearest neighbor (k-NN) 226, 227, 261-264

L

layouts
  balloon layout 89
  circular layout 87, 88
  radial layout 88
linear models 228
linear regression 239-245
logical indexing 142
logistic regression 265-269

M

machine learning 225, 226, 237
matplotlib
  about 343, 344
  sources 344
matplotlib-basemap 343
Mayavi 110
MKL functions 136, 137
Monte Carlo simulation
  about 191
  implied volatilities 207-211
  in basketball 196-202
  inventory problem 192-196
  URL 192
  volatility plot 202-206
Moving Average Convergence/Divergence
    (MACD)
  URL 168
multigraphs 282

N

Naïve Bayes classifier
  about 252, 253
  TextBlob, installing 254
  TextBlob used 254-258
natural language processing (NLP)
    tasks 254
NetworkX 110, 343 287
New York Stock Exchange (NYSE) 164
numerical indexing 141
Numerical Python Package (NumPy)
  about 122, 343
  interpolation, example 125
  linear algebra, summary 128
  reshape manipulation 124
  shape manipulation 124
  universal functions 122, 123
  vectorizing functions 126-128

P

pajek format
  URL 285
pajek networks
  URL 287

Pandas 343
perception and presentation methods
  about 72, 73
  Gestalt principles 73-75
pie charts 26-29
planar graph test 300-302
Plotly 110 94, 95
plots
  animated and interactive plots, creating
    231-236
portfolio valuation 211-213
positive sentiments
  viewing, word clouds used 259
Principal component analysis (PCA)
  about 271-274
  scikit-learn, installing 276
Probability Density Function (PDF) 36
PyCharm 95-97
PyDev 95-98
pygooglechart 110
PyQt 344
PySide 344
Python
  about 91, 337
  IDE tools 92
  packages 343
  performance 137
Python 3.x
  versus Python 2.7 92
Python IDE, types
  about 95
  Anaconda from Continuum Analytics 104,
    105
  Canopy, from Enthought 100-103
  Interactive Editor for Python (IEP) 98, 99
  PyCharm 96, 97
  PyDev 97, 98
Python Imaging Library (PIL) 344

Q

queues 146

R

radial layout 88
reader-driven narratives
  about 62
  example narratives 69
  Gapminder 63, 64
  union address, state 64
  USA, mortality rate 65-68
Relative Strength Indicator (RSI)
  URL 168

S

Scalar selection 138
scatter plots
  about 31-33
  URL 32
Schelling Segregation Model (SSM) 221
Scientific PYthon Development
    EnviRonment (Spyder) 104
Scientific Python Package (SciPy)
  about 122-132, 343
  linear equations, example 133
  packages 129
  vectorized numerical derivative 134
scientific visualization 72
Scikit 343
scikit-learn
  installing 276
  package, URL 245
Seaborn 343
sets 145
signal processing 322
slicing
  about 139, 140
  flat used 140
social networks
  analysis 298-300
sparse matrices
  visualize sparseness 150, 151
sports example
  about 49, 50, 51
  results, visually representing 52-61
  URL 49
Spyder
  about 105
  components 105, 106
square map plot 112, 114
SSA module
  URL 309
stacks 143

statistical learning 225, 226
Stochastic block models 308-311
Stochastic Differential Equation (SDE) 319
stochastic model
  about 191
  diffusion-based simulation 218, 219
  geometric Brownian simulation 214-218
  Monte Carlo simulation 191
  portfolio valuation 211-213
  simulation model 214
stock price
  URL 164
stories
  author-driven narratives 62, 70, 71
  creating, with data 62
  reader-driven narratives 62
Support vector machines (SVM) 269
surface-3D plot 110-112
sypder-app 84

T

tab completion
  URL 84
TextBlob
  URL 164, 252
threshold model 221
tries 153, 154
tuples 144, 145
Twitter text 161-164

V

Veusz 110
VisPy
  about 117-119
  URL 119
visualization
  about 16, 17
  benefits 15
  example 173-176
  information visualization 72
  matplotlib used 155
  planning, need for 42
  plots 21-25
  scientific visualization 72
  URL 15, 25

visualization, best practices
  about 75
  comparison and ranking 76
  correlation 76, 77
  distribution 78, 79
  location-specific or geodata 80
  part to whole 81
  trends over time 82
visualization, interactive
  about 85
  event listeners 85, 86
  layouts 86
visualization plots, with Anaconda
  about 109, 110
  square map plot 112, 114
  surface-3D plot 110-112
visualization tools, in Python
  about 82
  Anaconda, from Continuum Analytics 84
  Canopy, from Enthought 83
  development tools 83
VSTOXX data
  URL 204, 211

W

Wakari 117
web feeds 159
word clouds
  about 156
  data, obtaining 164-172
  input for 159
  installing 156
  stock price chart, plotting 164
  Twitter text 161-164
  used, for viewing positive sentiments 259
  web feeds 159
World Health Organization (WHO) 43

Thank you for buying
Mastering Python Data Visualization

About Packt Publishing

Packt, pronounced 'packed', published its first book, *Mastering phpMyAdmin for Effective MySQL Management*, in April 2004, and subsequently continued to specialize in publishing highly focused books on specific technologies and solutions.

Our books and publications share the experiences of your fellow IT professionals in adapting and customizing today's systems, applications, and frameworks. Our solution-based books give you the knowledge and power to customize the software and technologies you're using to get the job done. Packt books are more specific and less general than the IT books you have seen in the past. Our unique business model allows us to bring you more focused information, giving you more of what you need to know, and less of what you don't.

Packt is a modern yet unique publishing company that focuses on producing quality, cutting-edge books for communities of developers, administrators, and newbies alike. For more information, please visit our website at www.packtpub.com.

About Packt Open Source

In 2010, Packt launched two new brands, Packt Open Source and Packt Enterprise, in order to continue its focus on specialization. This book is part of the Packt Open Source brand, home to books published on software built around open source licenses, and offering information to anybody from advanced developers to budding web designers. The Open Source brand also runs Packt's Open Source Royalty Scheme, by which Packt gives a royalty to each open source project about whose software a book is sold.

Writing for Packt

We welcome all inquiries from people who are interested in authoring. Book proposals should be sent to author@packtpub.com. If your book idea is still at an early stage and you would like to discuss it first before writing a formal book proposal, then please contact us; one of our commissioning editors will get in touch with you.

We're not just looking for published authors; if you have strong technical skills but no writing experience, our experienced editors can help you develop a writing career, or simply get some additional reward for your expertise.

Learning Python Data Visualization

ISBN: 978-1-78355-333-4   Paperback: 212 pages

Master how to build dynamic HTML5-ready SVG charts using Python and the pygal library

1. A practical guide that helps you break into the world of data visualization with Python.

2. Understand the fundamentals of building charts in Python.

3. Packed with easy-to-understand tutorials for developers who are new to Python or charting in Python.

Python Data Visualization Cookbook

ISBN: 978-1-78216-336-7   Paperback: 280 pages

Over 60 recipes that will enable you to learn how to create attractive visualizations using Python's most popular libraries

1. Learn how to set up an optimal Python environment for data visualization.

2. Understand the topics such as importing data for visualization and formatting data for visualization.

3. Understand the underlying data and how to use the right visualizations.

Please check **www.PacktPub.com** for information on our titles

Learning IPython for Interactive Computing and Data Visualization

ISBN: 978-1-78216-993-2   Paperback: 138 pages

Learn IPython for interactive Python programming, high-performance numerical computing, and data visualization

1. A practical step-by-step tutorial which will help you to replace the Python console with the powerful IPython command-line interface.

2. Use the IPython notebook to modernize the way you interact with Python.

3. Perform highly efficient computations with NumPy and Pandas.

4. Optimize your code using parallel computing and Cython.

Practical Data Science Cookbook

ISBN: 978-1-78398-024-6   Paperback: 396 pages

89 hands-on recipes to help you complete real-world data science projects in R and Python

1. Learn about the data science pipeline and use it to acquire, clean, analyze, and visualize data.

2. Understand critical concepts in data science in the context of multiple projects.

3. Expand your numerical programming skills through step-by-step code examples and learn more about the robust features of R and Python.

Please check **www.PacktPub.com** for information on our titles

Printed in the USA
CPSIA information can be obtained
at www.ICGtesting.com
LVHW071403160124
769002LV00014B/1195

9 781783 988327